Dear Oliver
Thank you very much, *you*
are a blessing. Enjoy the book
and keep sharing the story.
William Levi 2/19/06

W9-BBB-589

Endorsements

If you have ever wanted to know the heart of Sudan and the people who have been used of God to, "rebuild the wall," you must read *The Bible or the Axe*.

—Dr. Vic Eliason, Vice President
VCY America Radio Network

William Levi has written a gripping account of his suffering as a Sudanese under Islamic persecution. He accurately describes the spiritual and physical struggle.

—Tom White, The Voice of the Martyrs

Sudan's Christian and non-Muslim south has been victimized by a genocidal war waged under Khartoum's banner of Islamic jihad over the past twenty years. Over two million southern Sudanese have perished and five million more were driven from their homes, largely through the regime's bombing campaigns, slave raids and consequent famines. With a change in U.S. policy under the leadership of President George W. Bush, there is now hope for a just peace for the first time in a generation. It is important for the West to know the facts about Sudan, and understand it from a Christian perspective. William Levi is well positioned to tell this story. He is a Christian leader, native to Sudan, who also was an activist for policy change in Washington. He was an integral part of the religious coalition that helped awaken an indifferent United States and change the course of history for southern Sudan. Levi is one of the few people who stood with feet in both worlds—that of the besieged Sudanese and that of American policymakers. This book reflects Levi's unique witness to a pivotal moment in Christianity at the turn of the 21st century. It has been a privilege to know him and to work with him.

—Nina Shea
Director,
Freedom House's Center for Religious Freedom
Vice Chair, U.S. Commission on
International Religious Freedom

The Bible or the Axe is a deeply moving account of the Sudan crisis as seen through the eyes of William Ochan Levi. His personal spiritual journey is especially relatable to those who are searching for God's Plan in our society. I recommend it highly.

—Dr. Kevin J. McDermott,
Industrial Engineering Professor,
New Jersey Institute of Technology

William Ochan Levi's *The Bible or the Axe* is a powerful, heart-wrenching account of one of the greatest untold stories of modern times. The massive persecution of Christians in the Sudan, and as such, comprises not only a gripping adventure story, but also an important document and testimony for all believers.

—Rabbi and Senior Pastor Jonathan Cahn,
Beth Israel Messianic Congregation.

the Bible or the Axe

one man's dramatic escape from persecution in the Sudan

William O. Levi
as told by A.F. Chai

WINEPRESS **WP** PUBLISHING

Packaged by WinePress Publishing, PO Box 428, Enumclaw, WA 98022. The views expressed or implied in this work do not necessarily reflect those of WinePress Publishing. The author(s) is ultimately responsible for the design, content and editorial accuracy of this work.

Unless otherwise noted, all Scriptures are taken from the King James Version of the Bible.

Scripture references marked RSV are taken from the Revised Standard Version of the Bible. © 1946, 1952, 1971 by the Division of Christian Education of the National Council of the Churches of Christ in the U.S.A. Used by permission.

ISBN 1-57921-732-X
Library of Congress Catalog Card Number: 2003116099

Dedication

This book is dedicated to the memory of my beloved parents,
Ajjugo and Anna Levi; and my childhood spiritual mentors,
maternal grandparents, Reverend Andrew and Lydia Vuni Wale.

—William Levi

To the many around the world who suffer for their beliefs.

—A. F. Chai

Table of Contents

Acknowledgements

Thanks to A. F. Chai, who donated greater than 1,000 hours of "spare" time over a period of two and one-half years to bring my story to life. Without a ghostwriter to dig up facts, review endless piles of notes, and conduct interviews, this book could not have been completed. Thanks to Grace Fallon for transcribing five audiotapes of my testimony. Thanks to Monica Rizzo for entering my testimony into a computerized format.

I would like to thank my many friends and spiritual mentors who have encouraged me to move forward with this book, including Paul Liben, Michael Fallon, Scott Davis, Bruce Boucard, Pastor David Liebherr, Vic Eliason, Gary Selman, Bill Rizzo, and Rabbi Jonathan Cahn.

A special thanks to my brothers, Michael, Joseph, and Benjamin, and their families for assisting me with family history and photography. Thanks to my lovely sisters, Angela, Jemima, Rebecca,

Rose, and Merriam, as well as their families for gracing the family photo. I love you all.

Thanks to my good friend, Michael Longwa, and my cousin, Reverend John, for all of your faithfulness and encouragement. Thanks to all of the staff members of Operation Nehemiah and their families. This book is your story, too.

I am eternally grateful to the many individuals who have supported me over the years, many of whom are mentioned in this book. And of course, I cannot forget to mention the love, support, and prayers of my wife, Hannah, and her parents, Robert and Ruth Kirkman.

May the Lord continue to bless the anonymous brother who sponsored the publication of this book. Without his generosity and kindness, it would not have been possible to print this book. He has been used of God in this ministry.

Foreword

And they said to me, the remnant that are left of the captivity there in the province are in great affliction and reproach: the wall of Jerusalem is broken down, and the gates thereof are burned with fire.

—Nehemiah 1:3

It was hot and so very dry. The little girl kept on walking, then crawling knowing only that she must escape the horror that lay behind. Foot by agonizing foot she traveled, ever aware of the scorching sear of dry air entering her tiny lungs with each breath. No tears flowed from her large, dark eyes—there was not enough moisture for such a luxury. The tears flowed inside of her mind and caught at her throat like the talons of a great bird.

"Mama," she whispered, but that was all. There was no strength left to speak to the rocks and dirt and twisted brush. There were no words left to cry out to the God her family had once depended on. She wondered vaguely if God had died, too, along with her mama and papa and older brothers and sisters.

If only the pictures in her memory would stop playing over and over again. The day had begun like any other. It might not have been *this* day, because the sun had risen once or twice since then. In any case, it was *the* day. The day had begun like any other, with Mama singing softly and preparing the family's meager breakfast over a small, hot fire. Papa had gone out hunting with big brother, and big sister was playing with the baby. Life was not easy, but Mama and Papa believed that God would provide food for His children, and they were thankful for what they had.

Mama had looked at her that morning and smiled. "Are you awake, little sleepy girl?"

She had scooted over to the fire to give her mama a hug. Mama gave her a bite of breakfast, a special taste of food just for her. Mama would probably eat one less bite of breakfast to make up for it. She remembered that bite of porridge, and her stomach burned with hunger. She never got a chance to eat the rest of her breakfast.

Mama stopped singing, and the wooden spoon dropped into the pot. It was funny how she could picture that spoon falling into the porridge. It seemed to happen with such strange slowness. Then she heard the shouts. Papa and the other men were running back to the village, yelling for their families to run. Run and hide—but where?

Mama grabbed the baby and ran outside in time to see Papa's face just before he was cloven in two by the swords of the jihad soldiers. He fell slowly, like the spoon falling, as his own blood wet the dry earth. She heard her mama scream.

"Yeshua, save us!"

As her mother sunk to her knees, the baby clutched to her breast, she was surrounded by a fury of soldiers.

The little girl ran. She ran without stopping. She ran without feeling the sere sharpness of the thorny underbrush. She ran until her body could no longer go on, and then she collapsed into a stand of tall savanna grass. Through the musky scent of the sun-scorched grass, she smelled something else. Her village was burning.

The day had begun like any other. She hid in the grass until the noise of the jihad soldiers stopped. Then it was quiet. For a moment, she wondered if she was the only person from her village left alive. Then she remembered Papa's voice yelling, *run!*

She got back up and started running. She ran southeast, toward the mountains. Across the mountains somewhere was Kenya. If she kept on running, she would get there. The little girl was tiny, and it was difficult to tell how old she was. Perhaps she was six or seven, perhaps eight or nine. She kept on walking, then crawling. The bite of porridge she had eaten a lifetime ago had long since been used up in her struggle to survive. How could she go on?

Mama, she thought, because she really didn't have the strength to whisper anymore. She could barely feel the sharp talons of her tears as they gripped her heart. She could hardly feel anything. She dreamed that she was walking through Kenya.

Are Mama and Papa in Kenya? She was supposed to run there. Perhaps she was already there. Perhaps she could rest now.

As she sank to the ground, she did not escape the watchful eyes of the circling birds. They sharpened their talons with hungry beaks. Becoming increasingly bold, they began to drift slowly closer to the ground.

It was June of 1993. I stared at the photo in the newsmagazine, aware that my breath was coming in short, stabbing gasps. I saw a beautiful little child—alone and exhausted—haunted by vultures. Her journey was over.

I allowed the magazine to slip from my fingers as I trembled with sorrow for Africa's lost daughter.

"God," I said aloud, "how can this happen?"

I stood, agitated, and paced the floor, willing myself not to cry as floods of memories washed over my consciousness. As I passed a mirror that hung on the wall, I stopped and stared. The face staring back at me was a face I no longer knew. It was an African face, like that of the little girl in the magazine. It was a face that knew the terror of South Sudan; and yet it was a face framed by a neat haircut and clean-shaven. The young man I saw was dressed in clothing suited to a successful American engineering school graduate.

Why did God allow me to escape the horror?

I could not erase the image of the little girl from my mind. How I wished that I could hold her and save her from the death and sorrow that stalked her! Rage boiled inside of me like poison as I thought of the evil men who would reduce a child to carrion. Throbbing pain in my temples made me aware that I had been breathing through clenched teeth for some time.

What can I do?

Slowly, the questions that burned in my mind started making sense to me. Maybe God had spared my life for a reason. Perhaps God meant for me to do something to help the children of Sudan. But what did God want me to do? I already had big plans for my life.

My own life had been marred by the effects of war and persecution. I had endured much before I ultimately made my escape to the Land of the Free. I had struggled to earn my way through college and had recently been rewarded with an engineering degree and a bright future. It was finally my turn to live a life of happiness and success.

After all I have been through, don't I deserve it?

I had caught the American Dream, and I wanted to run with it. I wanted to have a rewarding career, a loving family, and a beautiful home. How often I had pictured myself driving home from church with wife and children in tow, laughing, and enjoying the richness of God's blessings here in the United States. Of course, I would still be a devout Christian, doing good and serving in the church. I would raise my children to be upstanding and pure, as well as smart and athletic. God would be proud of me, a nice American Christian man with a nice American Christian family. Yes, God would be proud. *Wouldn't He?*

"I was hungry, and you gave me no meat."

The little girl's emaciated frame returned to my mind.

"I was thirsty, and you gave me no drink."

Her eyes were glazed and sunken as she crawled across the parched wilderness.

"I was a stranger, and you took me not in."[1]

I never knew her, but she was most likely from a Christian family, and that made her a member of my own household. How could I live a life of comfort and safety in America without caring deeply for my wounded brothers and little sisters? How could I allow myself to be moved by her suffering and then do nothing, to return to my own pleasant reality?

I knew God was speaking to my heart, but I resisted. Deep in my soul, I wanted to be able to put the past behind me—and put my head in the sand. I wished I could forget about the evil and the pain and the persecution and the desperate neediness of millions of people. After all, I was only one man. Besides, God had provided me with a college degree and the means to live a life of material success. Didn't He intend for me to live for Him in a suburban neighborhood with the other engineers, doctors, lawyers, and businessmen?

"Lord," I prayed as earnestly as I knew how, "please show me what You want me to do. Whatever it is, I will do it."

A sense of peace came over me, and I knew that my heart and my will were heading in the right direction. I didn't realize how many struggles lay ahead, but I knew enough to figure that God's plan was not always going to be easy for me. I picked the newsmagazine up from where it had landed on the floor and determined that I would read it—no matter how painful it might be.

To accompany the photo essay, there was a story about what American journalists had termed "the lost boys," after the orphaned boys in the children's movie, *Peter Pan*. But this story was not from a Disney film, and there was no happy ending. Young children whose families had been slaughtered by jihad warriors wandered alone through Sudan's vast wilderness, facing unspeakable danger and hardship. Children who had seen fathers and mothers brutally murdered, sisters raped, and brothers burned alive ran until they could run no more. Some were eaten by jackals. Some died alone of starvation, leaving only bones picked clean by the buzzards. Miraculously, some made it out to tell their stories to the stunned journalists.

As I read their story, a new and uncomfortable sensation arose in my heart. It was a feeling I had felt before, when I received news of my own father's murder at the hands of these same Islamic extremists. Was it vengeance? Was it hatred? The taste of it was bitterness in my mouth. I had escaped from Sudan just before the persecution of Christians rose to a fever pitch. I had seen it coming, and so had my father. My father, a Messianic Jew, was a man I had admired and loved with all my heart. When I fled the country, I suspected I might never see him again. Unfortunately, my suspicions were correct.

It was November of 1987. One month prior, I had experienced a disturbing dream. I was living in Lyon, France at the time, and I attended a church run by an American missionary. I don't recall the details of the dream, but I remember a very vivid sense of urgency to pray for my family. I was so disquieted by this dream that I stood before the church to ask that they pray immediately, because my family was in grave danger. The church was faithful to intercede on their behalf.

Four weeks passed. I will never forget the letter that I received that November day. It was addressed from my cousin, Samuel, who had been living in Kenya for some time. The village of my family, Corom, had been burned to the ground by the jihad forces on October 21, 1987. The people were exterminated, and the homes destroyed.

Miraculously, my mother, brothers, and sisters all escaped. They were camped out near the Ugandan border. My cousin chose his next words carefully, because he knew the pain they would cause. My dear abba, my father, Ajjugo, had been killed.

The thin paper, *par avion*, fluttered to the floor of my apartment. It drifted down slowly, like a leaf in the desert. My heart could feel its brittle substance. Now, six years later, the feeling had returned.

"Vengeance is mine," saith the Lord, "I will repay."[2]

That verse came to mind pretty readily. *OK, God, go for it.* Go ahead and give those terrorists what they deserve. Why not send fire from heaven to consume them? That sounds pretty reasonable to me. And then send them directly to an eternity in hell. That would be pretty good, too. While you're at it, why not give everybody out there what they really deserve. After all, this world is full of sinners.

"There is none righteous, not even one . . ."[3] That was true enough, but some people were a lot less righteous than others. Well, all right, don't give *everybody* what they deserve—otherwise nobody escapes hell. But give the *jihad* extremists what they deserve.

"Love your enemies . . ."[4] *God, you know I'm just not ready for that one.* How can I love the people who killed my father and forced my mother into exile again? How can I love the people who were responsible for atrocities against peaceful families and helpless children? It isn't humanly possible!

"With God, all things are possible . . ."[5] What did it mean for me, a Christian, to love my enemies? That was going to be something I would have to wrestle with. I needed a handle on what that sort of love really meant. I knew that while we were yet sinners, and therefore enemies of God, Christ died for us. That is the ultimate example of unconditional agape love. The Islamic extremists had harmed me and harmed my people. They were my enemies. And yet, God commanded me to love them. I knew this could not be an emotional love, a love born of friendship and community. It would have to be a supernatural love, an *agape* love. It would have to be a decision that I would need to make each and every day. I could *decide* to love them by praying for them regularly. I could *decide* to love them by refusing to seek vengeance. I could *decide* to love them by sharing the gospel message with them. I would rejoice in their repentance and take no joy in their tragedy. God's love is real love, whether or not I "feel" it.

God, I prayed, *please give me Your heart of forgiveness. Make me an instrument of Your peace and healing.*

Again, I felt a sense of peace; I knew that God was working in my heart to bring me to the place He wanted me to be. The remnant of my people was in great affliction and reproach. The gates of *Corom* and of countless other villages in the South Sudan had been burned with fire. As in the days of Nehemiah, the walls of our protection were broken down.

"And it came to pass, when I heard these words, that I sat down and wept."[6]

This is my story.

Introduction

The History of Sudan—Ancient times to the Present

Thine eyes have seen my unformed substance; And in Thy book they were all written, The days that were ordained for me, When as yet there were not one of them.

—Psalm 139:16

I don't believe in accidents. Even in the most tragic moments of human history, I believe that God's hand has been at work in the lives of men and of nations. In that sense, I believe that all true stories are "His" story. In times of war and poverty, as well as in times of peace and prosperity, God always has a plan and a purpose for His children. There are moments, of course, when God's plan doesn't seem to make any sense. When the Lord Jesus was mocked, scourged, and crucified, it seemed as though Satan had won. Even Jesus' disciples couldn't understand God's purpose that awful day. But out of the tomb came victory that had been ordained before the foundations of the world! Thus, the darkest page in the book of history became the masterstroke of God's redemptive plan.

Similarly, recent acts of brutal persecution against Christ's Body, the Church, have been very difficult to understand. Even so, the suffering of the Church does not lead us to defeat; although on the surface things may look grim. We must not doubt that the battle belongs to the Lord. All of the evil this poor world can muster is nothing compared to God. He is able to take it, turn it upside-down and use it to further His kingdom. That is the hope that sustains me.

God has written the book of my days so that I might serve Him in such a time as this. There is no army that can snatch me from the grip of His care or alter one single day of His plan for my life. And so it is with gratitude that I am able to relate to you my story—just one tiny part of "His" story.

As both a Messianic Hebrew and a native of the war-torn nation of Sudan, I have been given the privilege of seeing God at work in the histories of both my people and my country.

Sudan, the land of my birth, has been home to my people and my tribe for thousands of years; it is a part of who I am. Emerging from the shadow of Egyptian antiquity, the great Nubian kingdoms of Sudan birthed an early Christian dynasty that lasted for nearly ten centuries. Through Roman persecution, Arab conquest, and British rule, Sudan has been "struck down, but not destroyed."[7] It is the land of a remnant preserved by God through the millennia.

The recent history of my people in Sudan has been incredibly painful. Intense religious persecution and bitter civil war have ended the lives of millions of people over the past twenty years.

Only the Holocaust of WWII has exceeded the scope of the genocide. Political analysts throw up their hands and declare that the
situation cannot be resolved. In the eyes of the world, Sudan has
reason only for despair. But God has a plan, and I am blessed to be
a part of His work in that part of the world. God has called me to
serve my persecuted Christian brothers and sisters in Sudan and
to reach out in love with the message of the gospel to those who
persecute. Even now, God is in control of history, as He has been
from the very beginning. And in the very beginning, according to
the Bible, God touched the heart of Africa.

Cush, son of Ham, made his home near the joining of the Blue
and the White Nile Rivers sometime after the great deluge—and
long before the written history of man was first set to stone or
papyrus. But Cush was not the first to settle there. The second
chapter of Genesis tells us that this land inhabited by Noah's grand-
son originally contained the western boundaries of Eden. If that is
the case, it is possible that Adam and Eve once walked in Africa.
Modern archeologists now have evidence suggesting that the first
human beings originated in Africa, lending scientific credence for
the first time to her Edenic origins. Certainly, in the days before
the biblical flood, people had settled near the fertile river valleys
of the Nile system. The Bible says that the River Pishon encom-
passed all the lands of "Havilah." Havilah is the name of one of the
sons of Cush, who probably settled near his family of origin. Plen-
tiful gold, bdellium, and onyx—minerals that have been found
along the banks of the river that the Romans later called the White
Nile—enriched this land. The River Gihon "compasseth the whole
land of Ethiopia," and most likely refers to the Blue Nile. Although

the names of Pishon and Gihon have been lost in antiquity, the biblical references strongly suggest that these Edenic rivers were indeed the same rivers that flow through present-day Sudan.

Fertile ground and abundant resources in the Nile River valleys would have encouraged antediluvian society to flourish in prehistoric times; and Cush's progeny filled the region after the flood. The land was, in a very real sense, a cradle of ancient civilization. Great societies of antiquity can trace their roots to the land of Africa. In the days before Nimrod became a mighty hunter, and before the great ziggurat at Babel thrust a defiant stairway to God's heaven, the land that is now Sudan was home to established civilizations. As Nimrod's clan migrated north to Assyria, his Cushite forbears remained and prospered in Africa.

The Hamites inhabited the region to the north of Cush known as Egypt. In the days of Egypt's Old Kingdom, from around 2755-2255 B.C, the Land of Cush was heavily influenced by her more powerful neighbor to the north. Cush provided Egypt with rich natural resources such as gold, ivory, and human slaves. By the year 1570 B.C, Cush was largely an Egyptian province.

Although this was a time of great wealth and culture, the Hamites and Cushites had all but forgotten the Creator God of their ancestor Noah. The pharaohs were revered as gods during their lives, and their days were spent preparing for the journey to an afterlife of their own creation. Fabulous tombs and mummified remains of these ancient pharaohs give us a good idea of the religion of that period. Idolatry ruled the lands that once cradled Eden; but God's eternal plan of redemption began to take shape in the second millennium before Christ.

Joseph and the sons of Shem were first cousins to Cush, now a dozen times removed through the lines of Arphaxad, Shelah, Eber, Peleg, Reu, Serug, Nahor, Terah, Abraham, Isaac, and Jacob. God's people—my fathers—were to become a great nation in the land of Egypt, and the worship of the One True God would ultimately spread down the Nile River valley into the land of Cush.

The "*apiru*," or Hebrew peoples, were Semitic tribes of "foreigners" who settled in northern Africa sometime around 1,500 B.C to escape famine. At first, the nomadic tribesmen were welcomed by the Egyptians, but as the Hebrews flourished, they became a threat to the rule of the pharaohs. The Egyptian rulers responded to this threat with oppression and slavery. But God intended all of this for good. The Hebrew peoples were eventually delivered from bondage, and the laws and practice of the worship of Yahweh were finally formalized and recorded. The stage was being set for the coming of the Messiah who would be for all people. Africa figured prominently in the history of Israel and in the life of Christ.

The Nile River valley was very important in the ancient world. It provided a waterway from the African interior to the Mediterranean Sea, providing contact with both Europe and Asia. The proximity of her settlements to the Red Sea and thus the Sinai Peninsula permitted regular interaction with the Middle East. Egypt, Greece, Rome, Syria, and Arabia traded influence, wealth, and warfare with the prosperous kingdom of Cush.

By the eighth century B.C, Cushite wealth and power was great enough to eclipse that of the Egyptian Pharaohs. In fact, the "Black Pharaohs" ruled both kingdoms for a time. These Cushite pharaohs arose from the kingdom of Napata, which had been established by

King Pianki. This same kingdom extended uninterrupted into the era of the kingdoms of Meroe and Makuria, and ultimately into the great Nubian Christian Kingdom.

The "Ethiopia" of Bible times extended from Aswan and the Nubian Desert in the north to the region of modern-day Khartoum, Sudan in the south; and of course, it extended eastward into the horn of Africa. Although the name of Cush is commonly associated with what is now modern-day Sudan, sometimes the term "Ethiopia" was used to refer to the entire area south of Egypt.

This cosmopolitan region was also home to Jews of the Diaspora and proselytes who embraced monotheism. The Hebrews gained their name in Africa and have been a continuous presence in that continent ever since. Waves of new Hebrew immigration occurred after the Assyrian conquest of Israel in the eighth century B.C and again after the fall of Jerusalem some two hundred years later. There is evidence that Judean priests migrated to the Aswan region of the Nile around the time of the destruction of Solomon's temple. Archeological evidence of an ancient Jewish presence in the region still exists in the region of the Aswan Dam. A replica of Solomon's temple existed across the river from Aswan on Elephantine Island from around the time of the Babylonian conquest until the year 410 B.C, when it was burned by local pagans. It has been alleged that the priests from that temple fled to Axum, Ethiopia, bearing the Ark of the Covenant with them. Axum would have provided a haven for the fleeing priests, because an even more ancient Hebrew group resided there in the horn of Africa. It is not clear where these Hebrews came from, but according to the legend of the *Kebra Nagast* (Glory of the Kings), the great King Solomon fathered Menelik I, the first king of Ethiopia, by the Queen of Sheba. It is possible that this line of royal descendants produced some of the earliest Ethiopian Jews. Certainly there were close ties between Ethiopia, Yemen, and Israel in those days. Worshippers from Africa and Arabia often traveled up to Jerusalem; and merchants as well as royal envoys provided a vital exchange of news and goods.

The Bible indicates that Christianity was originally received in the Land of Cush in the first century, AD. By this time, the Roman Empire exerted considerable control in the region. The Book of Acts describes a meeting between the apostle Philip and a royal eunuch who was returning home to Africa after a pilgrimage to the city of Jerusalem. The eunuch was reading a messianic prophecy from the book of Isaiah when Philip explained its meaning—and its fulfillment in the life of Jesus Christ, the Messiah. Immediately, the eunuch stopped his chariot and asked to be baptized in a nearby body of water.

"And when they came up out of the water, the Spirit of the Lord snatched Philip away; and the eunuch saw him no more, but went on his way rejoicing" (Acts 8:39 RSV).

It isn't clear whether the Ethiopian eunuch was a Jew by birth or a proselyte, but the Holy Spirit certainly chose him for a very unique encounter with God. He was an important man—in charge of the treasury of Queen Candace. The title of "Candace" was given to all the Queens of Ethiopia in those days. This eunuch would have been headed to the capitol city of the kingdom of Meroe, located on the Nile River just north of the confluence of the Blue and the White Niles, in the heart of present-day Sudan. No doubt this influential man brought the good news of the Messiah back to the courts of Queen Candace and to the synagogues of the region.

Originally, the message of the Messiah was taken only to Jewish groups, and they were the first Christians.

The first church, which is also referred to as the "Old Church," or "*Kanisa Ajuza,*" in Arabic, was born in Dunqulah, the capitol city of ancient Meroe. Tradition holds that many of these very early believers were converted based on the testimony of the Ethiopian eunuch. It is certain that they helped form the kernel that developed many years later into the Nubian Christian Kingdom.

The new faith called Christianity spread quickly throughout northern Africa in the first century AD. It was an African, Simon of Cyrene (modern-day Libya), who carried the cross of Christ. There is some speculation that he was an important early convert to Christianity. He may be the "Simon the Black" (Acts 13:1) who later laid hands on Paul and Barnabas to commission them to bring the gospel to the world. By the end of the second century A.D, the majority of northern Africa was Christian, producing such early church fathers as Origen, Tertullian, and Augustine. It was Tertullian who was credited with the famous quotation: "The blood of the martyrs is the seed of the church." He was well acquainted with martyrdom, because the Romans at the time were killing African Christians at an alarming rate. Despite persecution, the Church grew steadily over the next three hundred years.

Eventually, Nubian royalty declared Christianity the "state" religion. The Nubian Cushite kingdom was predominantly Christian from AD 350 until AD 1500, when Muslim conquerors established Islam as the official religion. The Cushite Christians, famous for their skills with the lance, had held off the Islamists since 649 AD, when the Arabs conquered Egypt. They formed an uneasy truce with the Arabs for several centuries, maintaining the peace with an annual tribute of slaves.

During the twelfth and thirteenth centuries, Arab invasions hammered away at Christian resistance. Great numbers of Nubians were killed or sold into slavery, and the remaining Christians hid in remote areas without any communication with other Christians or the world at large. African Hebrews were also increasingly isolated; some had retreated during Nubian Christian rule and more sought remote haven as the Muslims advanced. As the Nubians fled, Arab settlers claimed the land and converted church buildings into mosques. The remaining Nubians were absorbed into the new culture through intermarriage and conversion.

In 1315 AD, a Muslim prince, born of Nubian royal blood, claimed the throne in Dunqulah. This led to a splintering of Nubian leadership and spawned the "dark age" of professional slave trading in the region. The Arabs changed the name of the land of Cush to "Sudan," meaning "the land of the Blacks." Christians and Jews who refused to convert to Islam scattered into the African interior. They ended up in Southern Sudan and parts of the modern Ethiopia, Libya, and the horn of Africa, where they maintained their faith and their African heritage within tribal groups. Finally, in approximately AD 1500, all traces of the Nubian Christian kingdom vanished.

After the Muslim conquest of the Christian kingdom of Nubia, several Islamic dynasties arose and fell. In 1504 AD, the Black Sultanate (*As Saltana az Zarqa*) was founded by the Funj, a confederation of Islamic tribes. They controlled Al Jazirah and districts from the rainforests of the south to the third cataract in the north.

Later, Islamic tribes called the Fur controlled the area Darfur. The economy of the Funj and Fur sultanates depended on the slave trade. The Muslims, both Arab and African, from the sultanates raided the African tribal villages regularly, stealing their neighbors to sell as slaves.

During the period of the Funj, the Ottoman Turks wrested control of Egypt from the Mamluks. Soon after, Sudan also fell under the expanding Islamic domination of the Ottoman Turks. In 1820, Turko-Egyptian rule under a Turko-Albanian general named Mohammed Ali Pasha swept over Sudan, eliminating the loosely affiliated Afro-Islamic confederations of sultanates. At this point, even remote churches and synagogues operated underground, because by then, a strict Islamic orthodoxy held sway. The *Turkiyah* were greedy and ruthless, exacting exorbitant taxes, ransacking ancient pyramids, and pushing the slave trade into high gear.

Africans who were captured by Arab slave traders were sold to Europeans on the island of Zanzibar, off the coast of the modern country of Tanzania. These slaves were exported to Arabia, Europe, and the Americas for forced labor and other abuses.

By this time, slavery had become a destabilizing crisis in Africa. Finally, though, some anti-slavery voices were beginning to be heard in the western world. William Wilberforce, an influential British man in the House of Commons, was an important figure in the anti-slavery movement. He was a devout Christian, and he challenged the logic behind men selling men for profit. He concluded that slavery was an "evil adventure" that must be eliminated at all costs.

But money speaks louder than morality in our fallen world, and there was a great deal of resistance to the idea of freedom for the slaves. Eventually morality prevailed through the courts of law in Great Britain and through war in the United States. Slavery was officially abolished in the western world, but not in the Islamic world, and not in Sudan.

In 1869, a British explorer, Sir Samuel Baker, made the first attempt via Egypt, Sudan, and Uganda to explore the sources of the Nile. He reported to the British authorities about his findings, which led to British interest in colonizing the Nile Valley and in ending slavery there as well.

In 1881, on the island of Aba on the Nile River near the modern town of Gezira, a small Islamic group led by a Sudanese Muslim named Mohammed Ahmed Mahdi rose up. Mahdi claimed to be "the awaited guide" sent by Allah to prepare the people for the Second Coming of the Prophet Isa (Jesus). He was not only opposed to Christians and Jews, but also to Turkish Islamic rule and British colonialism. He believed in *jihad* and the expansion of Islam by force into Africa, not unlike the beliefs of the modern Al Qaeda terrorist groups. He said he was strictly following in the footsteps of Mohammed of Mecca, and he felt he had a mandate to kill anyone who stood in his way. The Mahdi authorized the burning of all books of pedigrees, law, and theology, because he felt that hindered the progress of his new order. Between 1881 and 1884, the Mahdists had successive victories over the Turks and Egyptians in Sudan.

The British general, Charles Gordon, returned to the Sudan in 1885 to discuss the British role in Egypt and Sudan and to help Egypt deal with the Mahdists. He had governed Egyptian Sudan between 1877 and 1880. General Gordon was something of a hero to the Sudanese, because of his efforts to end the slavery that persisted in that nation. While he was in Khartoum, the city fell under siege from the Mahdists. He requested troops from Great Britain, but the British did not want to get involved in the conflict. His superiors demanded that he return to Britain to save himself, but he refused. Gordon was a man of convictions and felt honor-bound to defend the Sudanese people.

Unfortunately, the Mahdi dervishes killed General Gordon before help arrived from a hesitant England. His death triggered a thirst for revenge among the common people of Great Britain. Thirteen years of war between Anglo-Egyptian forces and the Mahdist Islamic Movement of Sudan followed the fall of Khartoum. Mohammed Ahmed Mahdi died shortly after Gordon was killed and his successor, the Khalifa ruler of the Mahdists, died in battle in 1899. By that time, the majority of Sudanese people welcomed his death and the subsequent demise of the Mahdist movement. Almost half of the entire Sudanese population had died during the Mahdist regime due to persecution, war, famine, and diseases. The economy was in shambles, and most of the orthodox religious leaders of the various faiths had disappeared entirely.

A coalition of Egyptian and British forces took control of the Sudan in the 1800s. Great Britain was mainly concerned with the preservation of its interest in the Suez Canal, which linked the English to their most valued colony, India. The British immediately saw the problem of religious and ethnic conflict between the North and the South, and they set about to stop it. During colonial rule, the North and South were strictly separated, and Arabs were not allowed into the southern territories. Slave raiding was ended.

It was then that missionaries were sent into the South to establish schools, churches, and medical clinics.

When European missionaries finally penetrated what they had in ignorance called "the Dark Continent," they found the fragile remnants of ancient African Christians and tribal Jewry alive and well and living in the Sudan.

As the Europeans worked among previously isolated tribal groups, they found very pious people—even though the influence of orthodoxy had been gone for centuries. Literacy had faded, but oral tradition remained. Many of these people, descended from Christian or Hebrew families, were very receptive to the gospel. After all, both Christianity and Judaism had flourished in Africa hundreds of years before the message of the Church had ever reached the remote and somewhat barbaric peoples of places like Great Britain. The "new" message of the missionaries was already understood at some level by many of the Sudanese.

It may be due to the legacy of the slave trade that Westerners today are largely ignorant of the spiritual and cultural heritage of the African people. One widely propagated lie during the time of European slave trade was that Hamitic blacks of Africa were cursed by God and destined for slavery. If anyone at that time had bothered to read their Bible, they would have discovered that it was not Ham who had been cursed, but Canaan, one of his sons (Genesis 9:25). No Canaanites remain in modern times, so that curse cannot be applied to any living people group. Even so, the myth of the curse persisted—probably because some people wanted to believe it and so to justify their immoral actions.

My family came from an African Hebrew tribal group. We traced our ancestry to the priestly line of Levi, and we had survived for hundreds of years in isolation—with an amazingly well preserved system of Levitical law and traditions. Circumcision took place on the eighth day, marriage was in the Levitical tradition, and many of our words were Hebrew in origin.

Most of our history had been handed down through the years by oral tradition. From our tribe and from others like ours emerged a new and vibrant Messianic Jewish population that came to know Yeshua for the first time. But even though a tiny remnant of God's people had been preserved to greet the western missionaries, all was not well with the spiritual life of Africa. Violent Islamization and tribal witchcraft had taken a terrible toll. A great war was being waged in the invisible realm for the souls of the African people.

It was with this great sense of the history of my people—descended from the ancient Hebrews—and the Great Commission of my Lord Jesus Christ that I was raised. With humility and awe I trace the interwoven cords of God's purpose through the Scriptures. My land and my people are found in the Genesis account, and both find the beginning of grace in the book of Acts.

Perhaps I shouldn't be surprised that the enemy is waging one of his most bitter battles in my homeland, among my people. While there is indeed a terrible physical battle going on, the heart of the battle is supernatural—and it has been raging there in the cradle of Eden since the fall of Adam.

The serpent of old has been at work from Cain's fratricide to modern-day genocide, trying to stamp out the people of God's covenants. In doing so, he hopes to defeat the plan of Christ. But the outcome of the conflict has been predetermined, and I am determined to be on the Lord's side. That is God's purpose for me.

Note: This brief chapter only scratches the surface of Sudanese history, which dates from prehistoric times. Scriptural, scholarly, and legendary sources were used. Historical information taken from the sources below:

The Original African Heritage Study Bible (KJV), Cain Hope Felder, Ph.D. editor, Word Pub.

The Library of Congress Web Site: http://lcweb2. loc.gov, keyword: Sudan

ArabNet: http://www.arab.net, keyword: Sudan

Ancient History Sourcebook: http://www.fordham.edu, keywords: Kush and Meroe

The Penguin Atlas of Ancient History, Colin McEvedy

The Kebra Negast, trans. E. A. Wallis Budge

Jacob's Children in the Land of the Mahdi, Jews of the Sudan, by Eli S. Malka

Personal notes of William Levi

CHAPTER ONE

Exile

The year 1964 was a turbulent one. The eyes of the world were on Leonid Brezhnev as he assumed leadership of the Soviet Union and on Lyndon Johnson as he escalated US involvement in South Vietnam. While the newsmakers focused on the Cold War, the Beatles "invaded" the States on the Ed Sullivan Show. The western world, intent on other problems, was barely aware of the unrest that was sweeping over the African continent.

Colonial rule was ending for many African nations, and several African states gained their independence from European control. Rival factions seeking to gain power created tensions in many regions, sparking military confrontations and ethnic conflict. Corruption and violence were commonplace as each group promoted their own self-interest. Sudan, the largest country in Africa, had been "liberated" from Great Britain ten years prior and was still in political turmoil. The northern region of Sudan was predominantly Arab and Muslim, while the southern region was predominantly African and Christian. Under British rule, religious and ethnic differences had been controlled by carefully isolating the northern and southern regions from one another.

The English government, growing ever more sensitive to Arab criticism of their management of the "southern problem," made a disastrous decision as they withdrew their colonial administration. Even though they knew that northern and southern regions were fundamentally incompatible, they determined that the whole of Sudan should be governed as one country. Great Britain handed over the reigns of leadership to the northern Arabs, and, predictably, the new regime replaced several hundred British colonial officials with northern Muslims. Violence erupted as the Southerners rebelled, and the two regions of the new independent republic were immediately plunged into conflict. Islamists from the North, led by General Ibrahim Abboud, dismissed the fledgling parliament in a coup in 1958, declaring martial law. At the root of this coup was a reincarnation of the Mahdist philosophy of the past.

General Joseph Lagu from the South responded with the Anya Nya Movement, an attempt to free South Sudan from the Islamic extremists in the North. The term, "anya nya," in the Madi language means, "snake poison." Students of the American Revolution probably recall a similar motto, "Don't tread on me," illustrated with a coiled snake. The message, of course, is the same. People who are oppressed by a more powerful majority often seek to "strike back." But as is often the case, the freedom fighters were military underdogs. The Anya Nya fought a guerilla style of warfare, with weaponry furnished by the only major power sympathetic to their plight, the state of Israel.

The Muslim leader, General Abboud, immediately expelled all of the western missionaries, because his regime wished to stop the spread of Christianity. This action was a prelude to rising persecution of anyone who refused to convert to Islam. In 1964, there was an escalation in the civil war; and persecution of Christians and other non-Muslims rose and began to peak. It soon became clear that resistance would be met with extreme violence. The army launched a major offensive to subdue the rebels and developed a reputation for atrocities committed against civilians. My parents used to quote the Sadiq El-Mahdi, a later Prime Minister of Sudan, who best expressed the intent of the Northern extremists.

He said, "In Southern Sudan, we do not want people, just their land and resources. We will kill everything, from trees to flies. We want the land—not the people."

It was during this time of war that I was born. I came into the world beneath the spreading branches of a tree; only a midwife assisted my mother. I was the seventh among twelve siblings, five boys and seven girls. We lost one of the girls and two of the boys in infancy. Our home was in a small village called Moli in the equatorial district on the eastern bank of the Nile River. My parents, Ajjugo and Anna Levi, were Messianic Hebrews of the tribe of Levi, the son of Jacob to whom the hereditary priesthood was entrusted. On my birthday, years before in 1948, Israel had become a nation.

In the year following my birth, the situation in the Sudan became increasingly unstable. The war escalated and spread from the larger population centers out into the countryside, until even small villages were in disarray. No one was safe. Our future was uncertain. Churches were burned, schools were closed, crops were destroyed, and western missionaries were expelled. The conflict had touched our small town. The parents in our community feared for the safety of their families, and many people determined to escape from Southern Sudan across the border into Uganda. My parents decided in late 1965 that the time had come to leave their beloved homeland.

With heavy hearts, they set about the difficult task of moving to Uganda. The trip was dangerous and harsh. The country of Sudan is the largest in Africa. At nearly one million square miles, it is about the size of Western Europe. Unlike Europe, however, there was no infrastructure in place across the vast interior. There were no roads to travel and no means of transportation. Families, often with several small children, were forced to travel the African wilderness on foot for hundreds of miles, struggling to cross rapidly flowing rivers and taking care to avoid predators—both animal and human. Older children helped to carry younger ones over the treacherous terrain.

My parents trusted that the Lord Jesus would be with us, just as He had been with the Israelites as they wandered through the wilderness so long ago. Of course, I do not remember the trip to Uganda, but I do know that God was faithful to my family. We were able to settle temporarily in Atyak, in northern Uganda. Although we were finally safe from the war in Sudan, things were very difficult there. We did not speak the Ugandan language, and the culture and environment were strange to us.

The United Nations was involved in the refugee situation at the time, and refugee camps had been set up for the Sudanese people. My parents, however, were suspicious and did not wish to be detained in any sort of refugee camp. The civil war had stirred up the specter of slavery again, and my father did not want us to become victims. My family had firsthand knowledge of slave-raiding Arabs who kidnapped African children and sold them into bondage. Arab slavers had murdered my great-grandfather, and his wife, my great-grandmother, was taken as a slave. She was pregnant at the time with my grandfather, Karan Levi, and she was determined that her child would be free. She made a daring escape from her captors in time to deliver a healthy baby boy.

The British had outlawed the practice of slave raiding, but the Islamists imposed no such restrictions. The large groups of Africans that huddled helplessly in refugee camps provided irresistible targets for kidnapping, mass murder, and other abuses. My parents were afraid to live in such a vulnerable situation. Finally, they decided to settle in the small village of Abalo Kodi, in Atyak, Uganda. My father had an uncle who had moved to Abalo Kodi many years prior, and it was good to know someone in the new land.

My very first memories as a child are those of growing up as a refugee in Uganda. I didn't think of myself as a refugee, because my parents provided me with the stability of their love and worked hard to build a home for us without the help of the UN camps. I just knew that I was born in the Sudan and that our family would return there some day. As it turned out, that day was a very long time in coming. Our family would have to make the best of a bad situation for nearly ten years.

My parents were farmers, hard working and industrious. They felt the Lord would have them to raise their children and their crops in peace. But the land in the Abalo Kodi region was not fertile, and the population was too dense. The additional crowding brought about by the refugee crisis made this particular location untenable for any sort of long term living arrangement. There was simply no way to grow the food necessary to support a family. My parents were soon forced to make the difficult decision to move on, trusting God to provide a place for them. They knew that they would have to step out in faith, believing that God had a good and perfect plan for their family. With fervent prayer and careful inquiry, my father sought out a home for us in the Ugandan wilderness. He was well aware that the wrong choice could prove disastrous.

I remember how it came about that our family moved away from the safety of Abalo Kobi into the untamed Ugandan wilderness with nothing but strong faith and strong arms to sustain us.

"We have decided to leave Abalo Kobi, Uncle."

My father's face reflected his resolve to find a suitable home for his growing family. It would be difficult to leave our uncle, because he was the only family member we had in Uganda, but Father was determined to leave the comfort of familiarity, so that he could build a better life for us.

"Ajjugo, are you sure? You have nowhere to go, and you have said yourself that you would never bring your children to a refugee camp."

Uncle's voice was low as he discussed the options available for his nephew's young family. The two men bent toward each other, absorbed in their discussion.

Suddenly, the younger man brightened. "There is a region near Mount Ambuluwa, and the soil there is virgin, unspoiled . . ."

"Mount Ambuluwa?" Uncle exclaimed. He scratched his head, furrowing his weathered brow with concern. "That area is a wilderness! No one has settled there before; it is closed to us."

46

"Then I will open it." Father's voice was calm, but firm.

"Do you know what you would be getting yourself into?" The older man frowned more deeply as his mind silently listed all of the obstacles that his nephew and his family would face. "What if you can't get enough to eat?"

Father was not worried. "Within a few months, I will be getting all the crops I need from that soil. In the meantime, we can eat plenty of wild fruits. I will bring some provisions along to help us get through the first few weeks."

"Nobody lives for miles around! You will be all alone, you know." Uncle's eyes searched those of my father and found a confident resolve in his gaze.

"Alone?" Mother interjected, her voice gently chiding. She had been listening quietly but could no longer refrain from speaking out. "The children and I are more than fit to help." Mother was hardworking and tough. She was not afraid to go with my father, and her ability to rise to the task really was substantial.

"And God will continue to keep us in the palm of His hand," Father added.

Uncle finally smiled, and he chuckled softly. He could see that my parents were resolute in their decision, so there was no reason to argue further. He didn't have any doubts about his nephew's abilities. My father's name, Ajjugo, meant "pillar" in our tongue. His name seemed to be prophetic of his character. My father was strong, straight, and upright—literally a pillar in our home. Although he had no formal education, he was a master of cultivation, construction, and animal husbandry. He was also a strong spiritual leader, and his opinion was well respected in the community.

My mother, Anna, was his helpmate in everything, and she completed him in every way. She had an inner beauty that radiated through her life and in her actions. Mama was gracious, hospitable, and tough—she and my father made a great team. Mother was not afraid of settling in the Ugandan wilderness.

"When do we leave?" Mother asked.

God blessed me with two wonderful parents, and I loved them very much. I still cherish my first memories of my parents working together to open the wilderness, building a home and a productive farm with nothing but hard work and trust in the Lord. And it was so beautiful. It was as if God had recreated the Garden of Eden right there in Uganda. Every type of animal and plant flourished in the unspoiled jungle.

We built our home atop a hill beside a huge tamarind tree. This leafy giant grew to over fifty feet tall, and its pretty yellow flowers gave way in season to a wild edible fruit. I remember that its broad boughs provided a dense shade, suitable for family gatherings away from the hot equatorial sun. Tamarind fruit, called "iti" in the Madi tongue, changes from green to brown when it is ripe and the juicy flesh is both sugary and sour. I loved to peel away the fibrous brown pod and suck out the juice, spitting out the seeds as I ate. My mother knew that it was an excellent source of vitamins, and she used it to flavor porridge and also for medicinal purposes.

When work was done, I learned to climb in the sturdy limbs of our tamarind tree. My brothers and sisters could play hide-and-seek among the green branches. Sometimes we would even climb to the top to get a better view if we heard an airplane fly overhead.

Living next to that tree was like living next to a park—complete with a playground and a free picnic basket. I suppose it kept us younger children busy while Mother and Father set about the serious business of construction.

Building a home with no nails, materials, or power tools is a skill passed down from father to son. I remember watching my father select the proper trees to build our new home. The dense tropical forest was rich with trees, reeds, bamboo, and herbs to be used in the building process.

"How about this tree, Father?" I asked, pointing out a sturdy-looking trunk. Father smiled and reached out to strip away a portion of the bark. Every part of life was an opportunity to teach, and Father was preparing a lesson for me.

"Fine looking bark, isn't it?" he commented as he peeled away the loose outer layer. "People tend to judge by appearances, but God looks upon our hearts."

As the bark was loosened and fell away, I could see the telltale burrow marks of an insect infestation. The tree was rotten inside!

"When you build your house, son, be sure to use the type of wood that will stand the test of time. If you don't, it will collapse and you will be right back where you started."

I watched with fascination as Father selected and cut the finest wood and reeds from the richness of the forest. When the materials were assembled, the process of construction could begin.

With no nails, and limited tools available, wood was lashed together with rope that was knotted and wrapped in a special way. My elder brother, Michael (called Odu), and I were eager to learn how.

I tied and wrapped with great care, imitating my father's experienced style.

"Is this the right way?" I asked. I was anxious to be helpful, but another lesson was on its way.

Father scrutinized my rope work with care. Finally, he shook his head. "You must follow the method I teach you. If you do not, the house will collapse."

Patiently, he demonstrated the proper lashing technique again, until I was able to master it.

As the wooden frame progressed, we prepared an adhesive for the walls of the house, using mud and herbs to form a sticky plaster. Soon, a sturdy frame house was standing.

The last part of home building involved raising the roof. This was a crucial process for the integrity of the house, and we were careful to weave tight mats of bamboo to keep the weather out.

While our home was being built, my parents did not neglect the planting of food. When my father had mentioned that the land near Ambuluwa Mountain was rich and unspoiled, he was understating the truth. The land was so fertile that plants seemed to spring to life wherever seed touched earth. When we first moved into the wilderness, we had nothing but some provisions that we carried from Uncle's village. It wasn't long, though, before we were truly self-sufficient. I can't remember a time when we didn't have plenty of fresh, delicious food provided for us from God's bounty. We drank from streams quite naturally. There was no pollution. Birds and animals of all kinds, such as ostriches, giraffes, lions, leopards, elephants, crocodiles, hippos, buffalo, and many others inhabited the forest. The work was very hard, but the land rewarded our efforts lavishly.

We were a happy family. So, although we were refugees driven from our true homeland by war, we did not live as oppressed people. My parents protected us from that. We just knew that we were living in another land, and my parents would often talk about going home to South Sudan some day.

By the time we were settled in our wilderness home, all of our relatives were scattered through Uganda. My maternal grandfather, Rabbi Vuni, left with his remaining family to settle in Gulu. We were unable to maintain contact with them during this time of political chaos, but we did find out later that Grandfather built a church in Gulu and became a pastor there. He sent two of my uncles, Abednego and Niklaus, to study in a seminary in Nairobi, Kenya.

In the Ugandan wilderness, we knew nothing of going to church, but we came to realize that we were part of the Body of Christ. My parents taught us about God and told us stories from the Bible. Our home was always open for fellowship and prayer. The great tamarind tree became a sort of outdoor chapel where we all could gather to sing and worship together. We had no money, so we joyfully brought the first fruits of all our labor as an offering to the Lord. In keeping with our Hebrew heritage, we never failed to remember the traditional feasts and holidays that had become a part of the very fabric of our lives over the centuries. We were so thankful for God's provision of a refuge for our family.

Soon, several Christian friends of ours from South Sudan began to hear of the little village that my father had started, and they came with their whole families to join us. Little by little, our tamarind tree covered a congregation. Over time, the work of plowing fields and raising roofs became lighter with many hands to help. Eventually, we had a flourishing community with men to build silos, women to weed the gardens, and children to grow together. We called our new village Ambuluwa. Our home was no longer a wilderness.

CHAPTER TWO

Ambuluwa

As our little village grew, our family continued to grow and prosper. My parents adopted a boy about my age named Francis. His mother was a relative in my father's family, but the child's father, a Ugandan trader, abandoned them both. Francis needed a stable family, and our family always had room for one more child. My little sister, Rose, was born, and she became a wonderful playmate and friend.

My older sisters, in the Levite tradition, were given responsibilities as women in our household. To me, they were surrogate mothers. They had full maternal authority over me, and I was obliged to obey them in everything. They carried me around on their backs through the day as they completed the portion of work that was delegated to them. They cared for me and taught me, and I loved them very much.

My elder brother, Michael, was the oldest male child, and in our tradition, that meant that many hopes and expectations were invested in him. We called him by the name "Odu," which means, "give thanks to the Lord." When women marry, they leave the family to join the family of their new husbands, but when men marry, they remain a part of their family of origin. So it was that Odu was sent to school as soon as it was possible to send him. My father knew that education would be the key to the advancement of our people and our family in modem society, and he hoped that Odu would succeed in this endeavor as a representative of our family.

All the other families in the community respected my father, the founder of our village. He was elected to a position of leadership when the need arose. He served as a judge or counselor in the resolution of disputes as they arose among neighbors. Both of my parents together often advised other couples on issues related to family relationships. Their advice was respected because they lived godly lives on a daily basis. Their answers were thoughtful, fair, and based on biblical principles.

In Ambuluwa, we never heard of anyone committing a crime, murdering someone, or abusing drugs and alcohol. There was no need for a prison. Although wild animals of every kind surrounded us, there were no guns. We had spears, arrows, and axes, but these were for hunting or for cutting wood. If anyone heard of another person purchasing a gun, everyone considered that person to be in error. In our minds, there was no purpose for a gun except to kill.

Family structure was the core of our society. It was considered shameful to be unmarried and without children. Children were considered a blessing of tremendous value. Divorce and children born out of wedlock were considered to be a stain on the entire family and a force of destruction in the community. For this reason, sexual immorality was absolutely prohibited. If a single girl became pregnant, she and her boyfriend would be given the opportunity to marry. If the boy refused, he would be forced to pay a dowry price, and he would be publicly flogged. Then he would forever forfeit the child that he had fathered to the girl and her family. He would be considered notorious, not marriage material. That would be a great burden and shame to him. This situation did not arise very often, and most marriages were arranged. The parents of a girl would take notice of a young man if he was hard working and industrious and of good moral character. This would be the type of man they would like their daughter to marry.

In the Levitical tradition, the groom must pay a price for his bride. Then, he would return to his parents' home to prepare a place for her. The period of preparation could take anywhere from six months to a year. When the new home was prepared, the bride's parents would invite the groom and his whole family to a banquet. After the wedding feast, the groom would return during the night to claim his bride.

Some people who have a western worldview may feel that paying a price for a bride is like purchasing a slave. This is not true. The relationships in the family are strong and loving, not at all demeaning or cruel. Women are equal partners and helpers in the Levitical home. The ancient tradition also echoes a beautiful scriptural illustration of Christ and His Church. Our Savior paid a price for us, and even now He is preparing a place for us in heaven. When He returns, He will claim us and we will live with Him forever. What a happy day that will be! When I see all the pain and destruction in families today, it breaks my heart. I wish everyone could experience the love and security of a family like those in our village. God's ways are not out-of-date; they were designed for our own well being. So far, our "enlightened" society has not devised a superior plan.

When I was a child, we didn't have any modern conveniences. There was no electricity, no telephone, no refrigerator, no TV, no radio, no movies, games, or restaurants. Even so, we did not want for entertainment during the evening hours. At the equator, we had twelve hours of daylight and twelve hours of night. This did not vary through the year. With no electricity, we found an inventive way to spend the hours before bedtime. Our entire community would gather together around the "O."

The "O" was a great circle that formed around a blazing fire. The fire was a place for fun, fellowship, and wonderful songs and stories. Everyone was given the chance to join in. Nobody was allowed to interrupt the storyteller as he was telling his tale. It was a special time for everyone in the village, and it was a special job to be chosen to gather the firewood for the "O." I remember going with my big brother to prepare the wood for the "O."

"Check each piece carefully," Odu said as he picked up a big log and pulled off a strip of loose bark. A scorpion plopped to the ground and scuttled away.

"Ugh!" I had been bitten by scorpions before, and I didn't relish the memory of their painful sting. "Why don't we just leave the scorpions in the wood? We can just let them burn up."

"Don't be stupid, William," Odu replied, in the tone of voice used by big brothers everywhere. "The scorpions won't burn."

"Why not?"

"Well, the wood gets hot, and then the scorpions all crawl out to get away from the fire. In the dark, nobody can see the scorpions. That's how people sitting around the fire get stung!"

"Oh, I didn't think of that." I reached down to pick up a piece of wood and turned it over carefully. There were no scorpions on it.

"Same with snakes. Make sure there aren't any snakes in the woodpile. That means we have to check all the wood before we burn it."

"OK." It turned out that gathering wood for the fire was more work than I thought it would be. Slowly, Odu and I picked through the logs.

"Time to fetch some tinder," Odu called. "Come on into the woods and look for small, dry branches."

Odu and I hurried through the underbrush, gathering sticks. The sun was already low on the horizon, so I knew we needed to hurry. Wildlife became more active at dusk, so it was important to be out of the woods by nightfall.

Suddenly, my brother froze. "William!" he hissed. "Look at this!"

I followed his gaze to an area near some bushes, and to my horror I saw a python squeezing the life out of a dog. "Let's pull the snake off of him!" I whispered.

"Are you crazy? That python will constrict you if you try to grab him." Odu stood silent for a moment, frowning in concentration. "I know!" he said at last. "Come on, let's get our arrows."

My brother and I turned and ran back to the village. Odu grabbed his bow and arrow and we raced back to the forest. Could we get back in time to save the dog?

The dog was still alive when we returned. Odu nocked his arrow and drew his bow. The arrow flew true to the snake's head. As the python expired, his coils relaxed, and we were able to release the dog. The dog looked up at us with gratitude, but the animal was having difficulty drawing breath. The snake had crushed his ribs.

"It's too late." Odu stooped to stroke the dying dog's matted fur. "He can't breathe."

We stayed and watched as the dog died, feeling sad and help-less. Then we turned back to the village. It was nearly time sit around the "O," and we needed to complete the task of gathering firewood. The stories would help to cheer us up.

As the light of sunset slowly faded, the people of our village began to gather around the fire that was beginning to crackle and blaze brightly. Everyone was in a good mood, anticipating the fel-lowship to come. The hard work of the day was over, and relax-ation seemed to be a just reward for all who had completed their tasks. Sitting around the "O" was something special for everyone, and the grownups especially hated to miss a social gathering. There was a proverb in our village: *Don't believe everything you hear around the "O"!* Sometimes the rumors and gossip would fly. Of course, even as children we knew that some things were best not spoken of in public. Most of the time, people spoke of history, of legend, of politics, or just plain fiction. It was all in fun.

Many of the stories used animals as characters; and since we all knew it was only a tall tale, the storyteller could let his imagina-tion run wild. Sometimes the stories were hilarious and outrageous, and sometimes they were quite scary. Around the fire, we all felt safe. When the fables and folktales began to wind down, we often spoke of spiritual things. It was a time to pray and sing spiritual songs together. The fellowship was not to be missed. If the weather was rainy, the diehard "O" sitters would wait for the storm to end and then light the fire with the driest wood they could find. The only other option would be going to sleep, because there isn't a lot that can be accomplished in the dark.

Sometimes, on clear nights, the skies would literally light up with a vast expanse of sparkling stars. When the moon was full, the light would be eerily bright and beautiful, casting faint shadows through the trees and homes of our village. On those nights, we children would take glass bottles and hold them up to reflect the light of the moon. We became familiar with all the crags and craters on the face of the lesser light, and the constellations became like friends to us. The shrieks of nocturnal creatures, the rhythmic hum and chirp of insects and the soughing of the warm breeze through the branches was at once electrifying and soothing. Nighttime in Ambuluwa was so deep and so vast that it was natural to ask the Creator, "What is man, that Thou art mindful of him?"[8] I was just a small child looking up into a universe that was extravagantly beautiful and immense beyond anyone's comprehension. What a mystery to know that He who holds stars without number in the palm of His hand could care for a little one like me.

But for all its beauty, night also brought danger to the village. I remember one night when we had all been sitting around the "O" for some time. My paternal grandfather, Karan Levi, had been telling one of his funny stories, and he was tired out. He was a great storyteller and he had quite a sense of humor. He wanted to head back to his house to go to sleep a bit earlier than everyone else did. My grandfather was blind, and his once handsome face was scarred. His eyes had been put out during a beating that he had received as a young man—at the hands of some Muslims who hadn't approved of his religion and ethnicity. He wasn't bitter about it, but sometimes he could be a little hard for a little kid like me to live with. He needed to be led about whenever he wanted to go somewhere, and I was often the one who had to lead him. If I didn't come to him quickly enough, I might get in trouble.

"Eh, Dark-neck!" the old man called. "Take me home." Grandfather always called me "long-neck" or "dark-neck" as a sort of nickname.

"Aww, I wanted to hear another story!"

Even from across the bonfire, I could see my mother's withering gaze. She didn't need to say a word. I knew I would be in for it if I didn't get up right away. With a sigh, I got up and scampered over to Grandfather.

"C'mon, Francis, help me bring some firewood for Grandpa." I nudged my adopted brother, who got up to accompany me. We picked up some wood that was still warm from the fire to carry back for our grandparents.

"Here I am, Grandpa," I said, and I reached out to hold his hand. He stood and nodded goodnight to the rest of the villagers. He was a tall man, still straight and strong. It was a shame that he was unable to see.

Without electricity in our homes, those of us with sight had no advantage over the blind at nighttime. Away from the light of the fire and the glow of the stars, it was quite as black as pitch inside of my grandparents' house. I literally could not see my hand in front of my face. Francis and I helped our grandparents inside, and then I brought an armload of warm wood in for the hearth. Suddenly, I stopped still as death. I could feel the hairs on the back of my neck prickle with foreboding. I couldn't explain it, but I had the sensation that someone or something was watching me. Something was hovering nearby in the darkness—something bad.

At that moment, a horrible rushing sound came toward me. I dropped the glowing wood, scattering stinging embers at my feet. I heard myself scream, and I turned and ran. Francis was outside the door, and he heard my screams. We both ran back to the "O" as fast as we possibly could.

"Abba! Help!" I panted. I was trembling with shock and fear. "Something terrible is inside of Grandfather's house. You must help him."

I heard a few guffaws around the circle, and I realized that the adults thought that Francis and I were making up a good story.

"You are just saying that. Don't make up stories."

"No, I am serious. There is something there—it tried to attack me. I don't know what it is. Please, come and see what it is."

Francis, wide-eyed, nodded in agreement. Murmurs arose, and most of the grownups quickly got up to go to Grandfather's house. They brought torches to light the way.

When the flames illuminated Grandfather's small house, we discovered what it was that had nearly gotten a hold of me. It was a fifteen-foot python!

"Must have been looking for a warm spot," remarked Father.

"Wow, the kids were telling the truth. They could have been constricted to death."

In the darkness, the python could have killed either of my grandparents that night. Everyone knew that a large python was serious business, and the adults debated amongst themselves how best to destroy the snake. They consulted the man who was considered to be the most knowledgeable about snake killing.

"Well," he said slowly, "we have to go for the head, if we don't want anyone to get hurt." He directed a group of men to grab the head of the snake at his signal. "I'll cut off his head as quick as I can."

The men swiftly executed their plan, and the snake was dead. I couldn't help thinking about the dog I had seen dying in the coils of a python not long before. I shuddered with the knowledge that Grandfather and I had come so close to being python victims. God had protected us once again.

As a little child, I grew up depending completely on God to take care of me. Snakes, illness, and natural disasters were always a possibility in our lives, but we did not fear. Neither were we concerned about the provision of food, shelter, and clothing. We just trusted that God would provide these things for us. As we lived in harmony with God's natural creation, His provision was obvious to us all. My family and my village combined our Christian faith with our rich Hebrew heritage as we lived in the wilderness. Everything was under God's control. In retrospect, I can see all the benefits of this simple life. We were protected from crime, our families were happy, we were well fed, and even the darkness did not bring us any harm. Western countries would regard our little village of Ambuluwa as "backward" and "impoverished," but now that I have seen both ways of life, I wonder who it is that really lives in poverty. In Ambuluwa, we were rich in love and community and we were rich toward God. All in all, it was a pretty good way to grow up.

CHAPTER THREE
Little Shepherds

I n our tiny community of Ambuluwa, it took the efforts of all the little children to cause the village to thrive. Every person, no matter how small, had a duty to do their very best for the well being of their parents, brothers, sisters, and neighbors. Nobody was given a free ride—everybody had to do the share of work for which they are best suited. The task of shepherding generally fell to the youngest boys. Although the work was usually not physically strenuous, it could be very dangerous and it required a great deal of responsibility. I began shepherding at the age of five, just a skinny slip of a boy, weighing perhaps forty pounds. Even though caring for sheep is a humble task, I felt proud to be given such an important job.

I remember the day when my adopted brother, Francis (also called Iddo), and I were introduced to our special role. We were busy doing the work reserved for babies, frightening birds.

"Gimme that rock, Francis!" I yelled, wresting the small gray projectile from his hand.

I ran straight toward a tree with branches that dipped gracefully down over a patch of Mother's best maize. I had spotted a group of hungry birds swooping down from the sheltering boughs like kamikaze fighters, expert in the art of "seek and destroy." I was not eager to share my family's dinner with thieves. Running as fast as my small legs could carry me, I heaved the rock at the branches.

"Hey, you got 'em!" Francis scampered after me, waving his arms like windmills. "Shoo, birds, go away!"

The birds were spooked briefly, and they fluttered up to higher branches, eyeing us with cocked heads and beady eyes. I guess they were sizing us up, because it didn't take long for them to decide that we weren't too frightening. Certainly, we weren't enough of a threat to keep them at bay for more than a few seconds. It was just a minor inconvenience to the flock of feathered diners to see to human children leaping in the air and making silly human noises. They were confident that we would eventually tire of the activity, and they were right. Before long, we were out of breath and had to stop hopping. We looked around for a more promising activity.

"What's Abba doing over there?"

"Dunno."

"Let's go over and see."

Father was hard at work as usual, pounding stakes into the ground and wrapping them together into some sort of tightly woven structure. He straightened up for a moment when he saw us and waved us over.

"Francis, William. Come here."

We scampered over quickly curious about what Dad was building. A small enclosure was beginning to take shape. Maybe there was something interesting for us to do.

"What do you want, Abba?"

"Boys," Father said as he wiped sweat from his forehead with a dusty hand, "I have a job for you to do." We stood attentively, waiting for orders while our dad turned back to his work. A man as hardworking as Father knew how to talk and work at the same time when something important needed to be done.

"Hold this here while I drive it into the ground."

Father hit a tough wooden stake until it was buried deeply in the soil. The stakes formed slats that were placed closely together, forming a strong wall.

"What are we building?" Francis probed the weave of the fortification with his finger.

"This will be a new stable for the sheep and goats." Father grabbed another slat and nodded at Francis, who quickly held it upright in place. "That's what I wanted to talk to you boys about."

We waited as he pounded the wood deep into the soil.

"You know, now that Michael is away at school, I need someone to take care of the animals. William . . . Francis . . . it's time for you to learn how to be shepherds. The first thing you are going to learn is how to build a pen. You help me, and you will learn how to do it next time." As he spoke, he lashed the wood together tightly, forming a strong stockade.

"Why do you have to put them so close together? The sheep are way too big to fit between that!"

"Because," Father paused as he struggled to force another stake into the ground, expelling grunts of air as he exerted himself. "This pen isn't to keep the sheep in as much as it is to keep the hyenas out."

"Hyenas?" I had heard scary stories about these vicious carnivores, and it made me a little nervous to think about hyenas stalking my sheep.

"You have to be careful; those hyenas will rip a sheep open and eat it alive. They suck out the intestines and leave the carcass."

I didn't reply, because the mental image of a hyena ripping open the sheep, which I cared for almost as if they were pets, was unsettling. I looked over at Francis. He looked a little scared.

"You have to drive the stakes in deep, too, because those hyenas will dig a hole right under a shallow driven fence. And even though they only eat one sheep, they won't stop killing until they've killed several and left them there, dead."

"That doesn't make any sense," I replied. We hunted wild animals and slaughtered domestic animals, but we never killed for sport. We only killed what was absolutely necessary to kill, only for the purpose of feeding our family. The thought of a wild animal killing other animals for no reason was foreign to me.

"You're right. It doesn't make sense." Father stood up again, bending backwards a bit to stretch his sore muscles. "That's why it is your job to watch out for hyenas and other wild animals, to protect the sheep. You have to be especially careful when you drive the sheep near caves, because that's where all sorts of predators like to hang out, waiting for dinner. If you see one, stand up on a rock and shout to try to scare it away. Don't lead them near the bushes in the evenings, because a python might grab one. And make sure the sheep don't step on any of the poisonous snakes. You have to keep a sharp eye out for them."

"Don't worry; we will do a good job." We stood proudly, like soldiers being commissioned into honorable service. "We will do our best."

Now that I live in the United States, I realize that modern parents consider children to be fragile creatures, incapable of assuming responsibility or of facing danger. In retrospect, I'm sure my parents were concerned about my safety, but in our community we relied on God to protect us—and our way of life had flourished for as long as anyone could recall. Mom and Dad were diligent to instruct us about how to deal with any possible danger. For example, they told us how to survive in a stampede of wild buffalo by lying flat on the ground. They told us it would be a big mistake to keep on running, because the animals would sweep you up with their horns and you would be gored and trampled to death. My father also was careful to explain how to keep watch for poisonous snakes and constrictors. Although the constrictors were not poisonous, they had the ability to quickly ambush and crush a child or a sheep in tight, muscular coils. Since my father could not swim, he was particularly concerned about the rivers. He warned us that we could easily be swept away in the headwaters, fast flowing streams that fed water from the mountains down into the great Nile River. We listened carefully to his instruction and committed everything to memory.

When we began our shepherding duties, we soon discovered that working in the forest wasn't always difficult or scary. It was fun! The forest was a place filled with tempting activities for a small boy, and I admit that there were times when the sheep did not receive the attention that they deserved. I loved to climb trees and swing from vines in the thick jungle foliage. I was a great climber. Since I was so light, I could easily shinny up any tree, branches or not. We enjoyed making swing sets by tying bits of wood between vines and hanging them several feet from the jungle floor, almost like a trapeze. Of course, sometimes they would break and I suffered some terrible falls, but God protected me from serious injury. We also made seesaws from wood that we wedged into the crook of a tree. It was great fun to balance with Francis as we teetered up and down. There was a certain type of tree that produced giant fibrous pods that we used to cut off and hollow out into a sort of canoe that was big enough to sit in. Then we would carve out a u-shaped trail in a muddy riverbank and ride the canoe down the hill into the water! I don't think you could find a better ride in any amusement park. It was also fun to mix mud and herbs or bits of straw to fashion any toy that my mind could imagine. I made bicycles, airplanes, people, and animals out of mud.

While we were caring for the animals, we lived off the land. We never had to pack our lunch when we brought our herds out to graze. We made rubber slingshots out of an elastic resin and used them to shoot birds to eat. I was not that good at hunting, but some of the boys were very talented with spears, arrows, or slingshots. One boy even killed two birds with one stone! The forest held a vast bounty of tropical fruits, as well. They were fresh, sweet, and delicious as well as a good source of vitamins. We drank water from clear, clean streams and caught fresh fish. We never were hungry. There was even a special type of tree that was used for cleaning the teeth!

I have fond memories of days spent having fun in the jungle. Unfortunately, there were days when I had too much fun. On one of those days, while I was enjoying a homemade swing, my mind began to wander. As if on cue, my sheep and goats began to wander, too. I didn't even notice that the goats had wandered away, into a neighbor's field. That day, they enjoyed a choice meal of beans and cassava.

"William!" From the sound of my father's voice, I knew that I was in big trouble.

It was too late. I knew that he could see me swinging from the tree. There was nothing I could do but climb down and face my punishment.

"You let the sheep get into our neighbor's field. They have destroyed a large area of the crop. What do you have to say for yourself?"

I hung my head in shame. The crop was the life-blood of our village; we needed the harvest to survive. The value of produce was like currency to us, because we did not have money for trade. Crop damage was very serious business.

"I'm sorry." I couldn't bring myself to look up.

"You will have to be punished for this, and I must make restitution for the damage you caused. Our neighbor was furious when he saw what our sheep had done, and I can't say that I blame him."

I couldn't open my mouth to say anything in reply, because I was already crying. I didn't always respond well to discipline, but my parents believed that to spare the rod is to spoil the child. They always made it very clear that I was expected to obey. Obedience in the wilderness was not just a matter of being a good, well-behaved little boy. It was literally a matter of life and death. That is why God tells us in the Ten Commandments that we ought to honor our father and our mother that our days may be long in the land that the Lord has given us. I can think of several instances when my disobedience in failing to heed my parents' instructions almost led to my death. But God in His mercy spared my life each time. I learned from my mistakes, and most of the time I did what I was instructed to do.

Time passed quickly, and I began to understand more and more about the cycles of life and the seasons in the forest. I learned to live in harmony with the natural world around me, and I sensed God's design and purpose in everything. Even events that on the surface seemed disastrous were all a part of His plan for the renewal and sustenance of His earth.

Uganda lies on the Earth's equator and, consequently, has a very unique climate. There are exactly twelve hours of daylight every day and exactly twelve hours of night. The angle of the sun is always directly overhead. As a boy, I learned how to tell the time by looking at my shadow. At noontime, I would have almost no shadow at all, and the length of the shadow after that would tell me when it was time to go home. Every morning the cock would crow and that was my alarm clock. There are no seasons of summer and winter on the equator. We lived with the rainy season and the dry season. Rainy and dry weather both had the potential to produce hazardous conditions for shepherds, and I encountered some very frightening situations while on duty, tending the flock. I remember vividly a terrifying day in late June one year when I was six or seven, at the end of a long dry season.

"Ouch, I stepped on another thorn!" Francis bent over to pull a long spine from the leathery sole of his foot. He massaged it gingerly until a single drop of blood was expressed, then tossed the offending stem into the bushes.

"That's nothing," I replied, "I've been stepping on those things all day. You don't see me complaining about it."

"I hate the dry season. Do you think we're in for a big drought?"

"Naw, the grownups always talk about drought, but then the big rains come again, same as every year."

"Well, I hate the way everything gets so dry. The stickers always seem to hurt more when they get all dry and hard."

"I heard Grandpa say that it was just about time for the rains to come, and he's really smart. He's always right about that sort of thing."

"I sure hope so! The grass couldn't get much drier than this. Plus, it's so hot out here today."

"But the most important thing is to find a good spot for the animals to graze. Let's stop here."

We stopped in a clearing that had plenty of grass. The sheep and goats seemed content to munch on the stuff that by this time of year was the consistency of straw.

Francis and I found a shady spot and picked some fruit to eat. We were already feeling a little bit tired and hungry, although it was only midday. Perhaps we should have noticed the change in the way the birds chattered and screeched, but we didn't. We just sat and rested and enjoyed our fruit.

"William," Francis whispered. "What's bothering the animals? Do you think there is a predator nearby?" He pointed silently to one of the goats. The goat seemed anxious—he was pawing the ground and lifting his head up high, sniffing the air. The other animals had stopped grazing and appeared uneasy.

I stood immediately, my heart thudding with a sudden rush of adrenaline. Francis was right—the animals were acting strangely. The danger could be coming from any direction. I grabbed my spear and turned slowly, scanning the bushes and trees. Was something out there, stalking the sheep? I was afraid it might be a pack of wild dogs or hyenas.

Suddenly, the underbrush shook and several small animals virtually exploded into the clearing. They were all running away from something.

"Francis, what is going on? I don't like this at all!"

"Me neither! Let's get out of here!"

"I'm with you. Let's get the herd and get home now!"

Getting the herd together was easier said than done. The animals were spooked, and they weren't obeying our directions. Francis and I ran and shouted, gathering the sheep as well as we could. Wild animals continued to crash through the underbrush, oblivious to our presence. The air, which had only recently been hot and still, was now rushing past our ears with a great whooshing sound. A thunderous roar was approaching our little clearing with horrifying speed and intensity. There was no longer any doubt about the nature of the threat that the animals had sensed.

"Fire!" Francis looked at me, his eyes widened with terror.

"We have to get the animals out of here! Run!"

The animals needed no more prodding. They were panicked, running away from the raging flames that consumed more and more of the tinder-dry forest each instant. Cinders flew everywhere, igniting new patches of brown grass and parched underbrush. We no longer felt the pain of razor-sharp thorns as they tore at our legs and feet. Our eyes burned from desiccated air and smoke, and our lungs ached with each breath. We were all running for our lives.

"Over here! Boys, come this way!"

Soon we could hear the shouts of the men from the village. They had seen the smoke, and they knew that we would need help. There were shepherd boys from each family wandering as far as four to five miles from safety. Everyone from the village was there to help gather boys and sheep and to protect Ambuluwa itself. Finally we were safe behind a strip of scorched earth. The fire could only burn through once, so we were out of danger.

When the threat to the village had passed, I was surprised to see a group of men gather with spears and arrows to chase the forest fire. They seemed to be in high spirits. I was staying close to my mother, still shell-shocked from my encounter with one of the most powerful forces in nature. I didn't understand why some men wanted to go back toward the fire.

"Mama," I whispered, pulling on her dress, "why are they all going back to the fire?"

"All the animals of the forest will run out ahead of the fire," she replied. "It will be an easy hunt for them." She squeezed my shoulders in a gentle hug. "But you can stay here with me."

I was more than happy to oblige. To this day, the experience with the forest fire remains as one of my most frightening experiences ever.

Not long after the fire swept through the forest, the rainy season arrived right on schedule. Within days, fresh green shoots began to appear through the ashes in a vigorous burst of renewal. Grandfather explained to me that the destruction of the forest was not really destruction at all, but rather a new beginning. Just as God brings trials into the lives of His children to create change and growth, He brings the cycle of drought, fire, and rain to create fresh growth and new life on the earth.

I was back on the job caring for the sheep, enjoying the warm rain and new growth of the rainy times. Seasonal streams and rivers were full of crystal clear fresh water. Sometimes when the weather was hot, all of the shepherd boys would get together to play games in the streams. One game we used to play was called *lokile*. We divided into groups, and members of each team would dive under the water. We would seek out members of the opposing team and then resurface with arms swinging at full force. The object, of course, was to hit your opponent. We also swam with stones to hit together beneath the water's surface. The loud *thunk* of the rocks was transmitted through the water so that everyone could hear it. Even though we were warned not to swim in the headwaters, we decided to do it anyway because no one was there to stop us. Although we were disobedient, we did learn to swim well and that proved to be a useful skill to master.

One day, Francis and I were out as usual tending the flock. It was during the rainy season, and seasonal streams were already brimming with rainwater. The ground was moist, saturated with rain, and the air was thick with humidity. The smell of hot, damp livestock and warm mud mingled with the scents of trampled elephant grass and flowering trees. It seemed as if the only air that was moving at all was the slow lung-fuls that passed in and out through our nostrils.

"Sure is quiet today."

"Yeah, even the trees have stopped rustling. There's just no wind at all."

"And it's hot, too."

"At least we have some clouds overhead."

Indeed, clouds hung low and dark over the unusually silent woods. Quietly, they were building in volume as the hot, moist air rose from the jungle below. Shade by shade, the afternoon light was being eclipsed by darkness.

"The clouds are getting kind of black," I remarked.

"Another thunderstorm coming, probably," Francis agreed.

We worked together to gather the sheep. It was getting late in the afternoon, and we figured we ought to head back. If the storm was going to be severe, we knew it would be best to be back home. Before too long, we were herding the animals back toward Ambuluwa.

The storm came quite suddenly, as is often the case in the tropics. One moment the air was perfectly still, and the next moment sheets of rain were being driven horizontally across the savanna. Bits of twigs flew through the air, biting at our skin as we hunched over with our backs toward the wind. Trees thrashed violently back and forth, losing fruits and leaves in the process. The sheep were perfectly willing to head back to the security of their fold, and we were in a hurry to get them there.

"William, we have a problem!" I could barely hear Francis above the howling of the tropical storm. He had been leading the way, and now he was yelling something about trouble ahead.

"What trouble? Come closer, I can't hear you!"

Francis jogged up to me to bring me the bad news. A seasonal stream that we had waded across on the way to pasture was now a raging torrent.

"We'll have to swim across!" he shouted.

"Let's go! It's only going to get worse!"

I followed Francis up to the banks of the stream. The saturated ground had permitted no water to soak in, and the entire downpour was running into the now flooded headwaters. It was impossible to tell how deep the water ran, but it was clearly running rapid.

"How will we get the sheep to safety?" Francis shouted.

"We'll just have to swim across with them!" I replied.

"But we aren't supposed to swim in running water," he reminded me. "We could get swept away."

We knew we would have to take the chance. We had to get the animals home safely, so we would do what needed to be done. We had to do it quickly, because the water was continuing to rise, and a flood could come at any moment. Our swimming games saved us that day, because we had become very strong and careful swimmers. One by one, we brought the sheep across to safety. None of the animals were lost or injured. When we returned home, our father understood that even though we were taking chances, we needed to keep the sheep safe. Eventually, he agreed that it was good to know how to swim well.

Each time Francis and I encountered some new danger, we grew in our knowledge and in our confidence. Fires, floods, snakes, and predators were just part of growing up as a shepherd boy in Uganda. Although we gained confidence in our own abilities, we never got cocky or sure of ourselves. We were all too aware of the powerful and capricious forces of nature that we had to contend with. Only God could protect us from His creation, because He is the One that the wind and the waves and the beasts obey. Trusting in God to keep us in the palm of His hand sustained us when we were in situations that were beyond our control.

One day, Francis and I were out in the forest as usual, in a spot four or five miles from home. It was a typical day, hot and humid, and we had been hard at work caring for the animals. We did not realize that it was going to be a day that would require God's help and protection.

As we were playing that day, I was struck with a severe headache like a clap of thunder inside my skull. I fell to the ground.

"Francis," I groaned, "help me."

My brother came running and knelt by my head. I could feel the coolness of his hand pressed against my brow.

"What's wrong, William? Are you OK?"

"My head . . . it hurts so bad . . ."

"Don't move, just rest!"

"I feel like I need to vomit"

Francis looked on helplessly as I proceeded to be sick. I was unable to move or get up.

"Are you OK? Should I go get Abba?"

I managed to nod assent. Francis could run fast, but a few miles through the jungle would take him at least an hour. If my father did not know what to do, there would be no one to help me. There were no doctors or hospitals anywhere near our home. All I could do was lie and wait for help.

I don't really recall what happened next; all I can remember is a haze of pain. I suppose I must have been there a couple of hours when my family arrived to bring me home. Father and the other villagers prayed over me, asking God to heal me, then I was given some herbs to drink. Thank God, my symptoms resolved with no long lasting ill effects.

I have since come to learn that my severe headache, vomiting, and faintness could have been due to heat stroke, which sometimes happens to young people when they exert themselves in hot, humid weather. If this was the case, God certainly intervened on my behalf, because this illness can be very serious or even fatal. I just know that all of us, whether we live in a modern city or in a remote wilderness, need to depend on our Creator to sustain us. Surely the Good Shepherd knew best how to take care of me, the little shepherd. "I am the good shepherd; and I know My own, and My own know Me, even as the Father knows Me and I know the Father; and I lay down My life for the sheep" (John 10:14–15, RSV).

I learned so many things from my job tending the sheep. I learned the value of hard work, the importance of responsibility, and the necessity of obedience. I saw the beauty of God's natural world and I learned how to respect it and care for it. But most of all, I gained a deep understanding of my Savior's love for me. Even so, I was getting older, almost eight years old. I began to long for the chance to learn how to read and write. I wished that I could go to school.

CHAPTER FOUR

New Friends

I could hardly contain my excitement. *I was going to go to school!*
The Catholic Church had opened up an elementary school for
refugee children, and I had a chance to attend. I was bursting
with the kind of wild energy that eight-year-olds possess in abundance. My arms and legs seemed to take on a fidgety life of their
own as Mother and Father discussed my fate. I dared to hope—I
dared to feel *sure* that they would let me go.

The primary schools would no longer admit children once they
reached a certain age. At around eleven years old, any refugee child
who had not yet begun his schooling would have to abandon all
hope of an education. Older children without any literacy skills
simply remained at home in their family groups and learned the
trade of their fathers. I loved my parents and I loved farming the
rich earth, but I could not bear the thought of being left out of the
world of the future.

There was a problem that would have to be overcome and it
was quite pressing. If I were to attend school during the day, there

would be no one to take care of the flock. My parents were too busy farming to take on the extra job of herding the livestock. Neither one of them had ever had the opportunity to attend school, but they understood the importance of a good education, especially in a world that they saw changing before their very eyes in so many ways. Deep down, they knew that the way of life that they had enjoyed for so many generations was threatened, and they were determined to make sure that their children were all prepared for whatever the future would bring. But even so, there was a dilemma—who would shepherd the sheep? I tried not to listen as my parents debated the issue in hushed but urgent tones.

"Don't worry yourself, Ajjugo," my grandfather said loudly enough to be heard above the discussion that my parents were engaged in. "I will shepherd the sheep in William's place."

My parents exchanged glances and for a moment their deliberation was stilled.

"Father . . ." My father paused awkwardly as he struggled to frame his reply as gently as possible.

Grandfather waved his hands dismissively. "I know, I know—I'm a blind old man. But that doesn't mean I don't know a thing or two about shepherding. Maybe even more than you, son."

My father took the bait. "OK, I'm listening."

"We will drive stakes into the field, one for each sheep. I will tie each sheep to a tether, and they can graze as much as they want without wandering away. When they have eaten all the grass within their reach, we can place the stakes in fresh pasture."

Grandfather leaned toward me and his leathery hands traced the shape of my face and neck. He smiled fondly at me, causing the scars on his face to twist happily. "Little Long-neck here will finally be able to go to school. He's a good boy."

"Thank you, Grandpa!" I wrapped my small arms around his frame in a grateful hug. I knew that he was making a sacrifice for me, and I would not forget it.

Mother chuckled softly, and then I knew that the issue was settled. "So William," she teased, "you are a good boy, are you? Now you have to be a smart boy, too."

"Yes, Mama!" I exclaimed. "I *am* smart, you'll see!"

"Will you please stop jumping up and down?" Mother grabbed the edge of the table just in time to stop a bowl from tumbling over the side. "You'll upset the table!"

"I guess this means you'll be needing some supplies." Father's statement was meant to be taken as a nod of approval to Grandfather's plan. He leaned back and pressed his hands together, like he always did when he was thinking hard about something.

It was no small thing in those days to find school supplies. We couldn't just stop by the local discount mart and stock up on pencils, papers, and notebooks. And for the first time in my life, I was acutely aware that I had never owned a pair of shoes. The soles of my feet were tough and leathery as a buffalo hide from thorns, hot embers, and sharp stones that had etched their legacy into my unprotected skin. Shoes would be nice, but I knew I didn't really need them to make the trip to school. I would need a book bag and something to write with. That was the bare minimum.

I looked up, and I could tell that the wheels were still turning inside my dad's head. I wondered what he was planning. Soon, I had my answer.

The next day, I woke up to find that Father had loaded up a bundle of freshly harvested cotton and was filling some jars with water. He was getting ready to go somewhere.

"Come on, boys," he boomed, waving Francis and me over to his side. "We're going to get some school supplies!"

Francis and I glanced at each other. I wondered if my eyes were as big and round with excitement as his were. "Yes! We get to go, too!"

I had never been to a town before, and I had never seen a store. The thought of going on a trip to buy school supplies was as exotic to me as a trip to the moon. I was ready to go immediately, but Abba had other plans.

"Anna," he called to my mama, "bring out Michael and the girls."

Soon our whole family was gathered around the big bundles of cotton. My father held my mother's hand and bowed his head.

"Dear heavenly Father," he prayed, "we dedicate this, the first fruits of our cotton harvest, to you. As we send the boys to school, we pray that You will use this cotton to grow the children into educated men in Your service. Lord, we dedicate this cotton to You, and we dedicate these boys to You also. Amen."

I opened my eyes and scanned the faces of the members of my dear family. Everyone was looking at me, and I was filled with gratitude at the knowledge of their sacrifice on my behalf. It was sobering to think of myself as a grownup some day, serving God with education purchased with a load of cotton.

The ten-mile walk to a neighboring village seemed to take no time at all. The town was called Wili-Wili, and Sudanese refugees populated it. Some of the people who lived there had been merchants and craftsmen back in the old country, and they had set up a market with real shops and many wonderful products. I took in the sights with a sense of wonder. The first shop we entered was that of a tailor. Father approached the owner of the establishment with a sample of our fine cotton.

"Yes, it is a fine, healthy-looking cotton," the man remarked. He reached out to accept a piece from my father. He pulled at the strands carefully and smoothed them between his narrow fingers. "What do you need?"

Father pointed to some bolts of material that were stored against the wall. "We need short-sleeved shirts from the green cloth, and I'll take some of the khaki to make into backpacks."

The tailor smiled and nodded in the general direction of Francis and me. "Boys going to school?"

"Yes, sir!" my father replied with a broad grin. His muscular frame straightened with pride. "These boys are sharp."

"We need boys like that," the tailor replied. There was a serious note in his voice that let me know that his was more than a casual remark to humor little children. I remembered the prayer my father had offered that morning on our behalf, and for a moment I felt the gravity of the hope that was being invested in me. I knew deep down that the future of our people depended on little boys like me. I wasn't sure quite how, but I did know that God would have to play a big part in it. The problems our people faced were far too big even for grownups. Our problems were God-sized.

I wandered through the market place as my father bartered the load of cotton we had hauled from Ambuluwa. Stacks of pencils and piles of theme books, texts, and papers entranced me. There were even shelves stocked with real shoes! What a curiosity! Soon we had uniforms, backpacks, books, and pencils. We were ready for school.

The walk home was easy with no cotton to haul, and our new school supplies seemed weightless. I knew that I wouldn't be getting much sleep that night; my thoughts were racing far too rapidly.

I'll never forget the next morning and my first day at school. The hardest part of school was the daily commute. We had to walk several miles to the neighboring town of Nyigeri. It was a small town, but it was near the dirt road that led from Uganda to Sudan. Although no one had a car, the town of Nyigeri was accessible by virtue of that little road and that made it an important location.

School started at eight o'clock sharp. Of course, we didn't have any clocks, so we got up with the crowing of the cock just before dawn. We figured that six o'clock was about the time of sunrise, and we knew that it would take at least two hours to walk to school if we kept a brisk pace and the rivers were running low. There weren't any roads, but enough people traveled between villages to form a sort of a beaten track. The track passed over four rivers, and during rainy season these rivers became raging torrents, overflowing their banks and making the walk to school treacherous. Sometimes we would get drenched or lose our books in the water. In the dry season, the savanna grass was so tall that it became difficult to pass. The grass produced its seeds in season, which were small and sharp as needles.

My first day of school was in January of the year, and the trail was not too tough to travel then. It was great running to school with my big brother, Michael, also called Odu, who was going to be in the highest grade in the school, primary three. I was going to be starting primary one.

After our long trek through the forest, we finally reached our destination. "Francis, look!" I pointed to two large mud buildings with roofs of thatch. "There it is!"

Francis bent over, grasping his knees as he tried to catch his breath. "Good! I'm ready to sit down!"

Odu laughed and clapped Francis on the back so that he nearly lost his balance. "You aren't gonna sit down yet!" he chuckled. "What's the matter, all tired out?"

I didn't understand what Odu was getting at until I noticed one of the teachers gathering all of the children together. "Time for calisthenics," he called cheerfully.

"What's calis . . . calisthenics?" I whispered.

I didn't have to wait long to find out. The teacher blew his whistle, and all of us had to run laps around the compound. After several laps, we did some stretching and strengthening exercises. There would definitely be no fidgeting during class. We were beat!

Before class, we had prayers. Catholics ran the school, and I understood the prayers. I also enjoyed the Bible lessons we learned in religion class. I was interested in learning more.

We also had lessons in health and hygiene, English, and of course, reading and writing. Most of the teaching was done in our tribal language, Mali. I loved learning the alphabet.

We learned many songs in school, and I remember one song in particular helped motivate us all to study. Our headmaster required us to sing this song. It was a Mali language song, but its meaning was something like this:

I want to know the alphabet, so that when I grow up
And I have an education; I will know how to read and how to write.
I can go into foreign countries.
I can speak other languages. I can speak in English.
I will speak correctly so people can understand me.
And when I come back to my country, I will develop my country.
I will also raise the people's standard of living.

Our headmaster was a mentor to us, and he was trying to prepare us mentally for the long struggle to reclaim our own country. He considered us to be a precious resource for the future. He taught us to respect our parents and our teachers as well. Our teachers were all refugees, just like us, and we loved them for what they were doing for us. We all held steadfastly to the things that gave us hope—God, family, and education.

After the morning lesson, it was time to break for recess. We all rushed outside, excited to be able to play with kids our own age. One boy in my class wasn't from my village, but I had seen him before. His name was Michael Longwa. He was a relative of my mother's family, and his mom was a widow. His dad, mom's cousin, had been a chaplain in the Anya-Nya army. Jihad forces had killed him while little Michael was still too young to remember.

"Hi, William. Hi, Francis!" He ambled over to us with a sneaky look on his face. "Want to play some soccer?"

Michael Longwa was about my size, but he had a reputation for being tough. I hoped that his invitation to play soccer wasn't an invitation to get flattened.

"Sure!" Francis answered without hesitation. "Let's set up some goals."

As Francis and some other boys gathered long sticks to use as goal posts, Michael approached me and produced his soccer ball. It was nothing but a ball of old clothes tied together with strings, but Michael tossed it like it was regulation.

"Betcha can't beat me," Michael teased coolly.

"Sure I can! Give it here . . ." I reached out to grab the ball, but Michael stepped aside, throwing me off balance.

"It's all in the footwork, William," Michael snickered as I stumbled forward. "Who wants to be on my team?" he called.

We played soccer every day at recess. It was the most fun any of us could remember. Michael was very competitive, and I thought he was a real show off. Even so, we became friends. He was also competitive with schoolwork, and I was glad to give him a run for the money. Since Francis was in a different room for primary one, Michael and I ended up studying together and challenging one another.

Lunchtime was another break from the work of the day. We liked to go and look at the road that went through the town of Nyigeri.

"I heard that sometimes cars come through this way," Michael said. He kicked at the gravel lining the edge of the packed dirt, sending up a little puff of dust.

"I would love to see a car!" I replied.

"Someday, I'm gonna *drive* one!" Michael replied, eager to top me in even our imaginary activities.

My older brother came up behind us. "You kids haven't seen anything yet," he bragged. "I saw a jeep from the Ugandan army drive through here before."

"Aw, that must have been great," I mumbled enviously. After that, I made a mental note to keep an eye on the road, just in case.

After a full day of school, it was time to get back home. We had to be sure to get back before dark. Francis and I were exhausted at the end of every school day, and it did take some time for us to adjust to the rigorous schedule and the difficult academic work. Sometimes we began to think that it would be easier to go back to shepherding, but then we would remember how important it was to have an education. We were proud of our work, and we knew that somehow it was all dedicated to God. Abba's gift of cotton would someday bear fruit for the Lord.

CHAPTER FIVE

The Addis Ababa Agreement

The news spread like brushfire in the dry season. The air crackled with excitement and the sound of grownups talking together. I didn't quite understand the importance of what was about to happen, but I knew I was about to go on an adventure with my whole family. In fact, all of the families in the village would be going on this adventure, to a place called Chinyaquia. My father looked serious, and he was speaking rapidly to my mother, his hands accenting each syllable.

"I don't trust them, Anna," he said, striking the palm of his hand down on a table for emphasis. "Even when the British left in 1956, I knew deep down that they would plot against our people. There can never be unity between the North and the South—can the leopard change his spots?"

"Ajjugo," my mother placed her hand gently on Father's arm. "Can't we dare to feel hope for our people? Just for a little while?"

Father drew Mother close for a moment, as if to gain strength from her presence. "I really want to—you *know* I do," he said.

"Then hope," Mother replied. "But hope in the Lord. Just like it says in the Bible, there are some who trust in chariots, and some in horses; but we will remember the name of the Lord our God."

A trace of a smile softened Father's expression. "I knew there was a reason I married the preacher's daughter." He paused for a moment. "Thank God we have something more than politics to give us hope. I have to tell you, Anna, as much as I would like to believe in this agreement—well—I just can't. There's too much history telling me otherwise."

Now it was Mother's turn to look serious. "So what are we going to do, Ajjugo? What will this mean for the children?"

Father looked around to see several sets of eyes fixed upon him. He took that as his cue to change the subject. "What are we going to do?" He straightened his shoulders and grinned broadly. "Why, Anna, we're going to Chinyaquia, of course!"

The whole village was making preparations for the trip to Chinyaquia. Every Sudanese in exile who was able to make the journey was certain to be there. I could barely contain my excitement. People were singing and smiling, like they were making plans to attend a wedding party or a festival instead of some political ceremony. The mood was contagious, and I soon forgot my father's misgivings.

"Hey, Michael," I called, running to greet my school friend. "I heard there will be airplanes!"

Michael Longwa's mother had brought him to visit, and she stood nearby, talking with my mother.

"Rrrrrrrrrr!" Michael grabbed a toy car that he had made out of dried mud, sweeping it in a dramatic arc through the air. "There's gonna be jeeps, too! And trucks!"

"I can't wait! This is going to be really fun."

An older boy overheard us and leaned toward us. "There's gonna be *kuro* there, too," he smirked. "And you know what they do to little kids like you." He chuckled to himself as he sauntered away.

"Don't listen to him, William," Michael insisted. "He's just trying to scare us."

Kuro was one of the names that the Madi people had for Arabs. They were also called *More,* or *Kuturia.* The Arab people were mysterious to us. We didn't understand the way they thought or the reasons for their actions. I had never seen an Arab before, but I had heard lots of stories—and they were scary. There were tales handed down about the children who were stolen away and sold to slave traders in India, the Middle East, and the Americas. Even Mohammed the Prophet had owned slaves, so slavery was accepted by the Muslim people. Also, the attacks by the Islamic military regime from Khartoum were fresh in our minds. So the thought of actually seeing a *kuro* was a little frightening for a kid like me.

"I'm not scared," I replied. "My dad will protect us. And besides, this is a peace agreement."

Michael nodded. "I'm not scared, either. I'm going to have *fun!*"

He punctuated the word *fun* by shooting an airplane made of mud and straw into the air like a rocket. We both fell down laughing. It was going to be a great trip.

Our families were soon ready for the long trek to Chinyaquia, a small city on the border of Uganda and Sudan. The Ugandan military had an outpost there, and there was a small airstrip as well. Idi Amin Dada, the president of Uganda since a coup d'etat the year before, had agreed to host a meeting between Jaafar

Mohammed Nimieri, an Arab leader from Khartoum, and Joseph Lagu, an African leader, representing Southern Sudan. Michael and I couldn't wait to see all the soldiers and important people.

"Are we almost there, Dad?" I asked.

"Only about ten more miles," he replied gruffly.

"My feet are sore," I complained. My feet were getting swollen from walking so far without any shoes.

"Just be glad you don't have to carry your little brother," Mom chided. She handed me some fruit to quiet my grumbling.

Soon we were able to see the small town of Chinyaquia in the distance. Suddenly, a small airplane appeared! I watched entranced as the little craft circled and descended for a landing at the small white ribbon of airstrip. I forgot all about my sore feet.

"Look! An airplane!" I laughed with joy and hurried forward.

Michael kept up the pace and pointed a finger at a dark line near the horizon. "Jeeps! Look at all the jeeps!"

It was true. There were hundreds of military vehicles crossing the border from Sudan. The Islamic military was using German-made trucks. They were painted green and filled with Arabs!

"Look, Mom! Look at all the *kuro!* Those people are our enemies!"

Mother was quick to correct me. "Our *enemy* is Satan. You know that Jesus died for all of those Arabs just like He died for you and me. The Bible tells us that we ought to love the Arabs and pray for them, too. Right, Ajjugo?"

Father's eyes met mine. His expression was stern. "Your mother is right. I don't want to hear you talking that way. I know you have heard me say that I don't trust these people. The Bible never said I needed to *trust* anybody—but it does say that it's wrong to speak evil of somebody made in God's image."

I felt my face flush. "I'm sorry," I mumbled.

As we approached the town, we realized that it was packed shoulder to shoulder with refugees, and the people from our village were jostling and crowding for a place near the podium that had been set up for the ceremony. The sun was white-hot, and the glare made me squint through the shimmering haze. I tried to jump up in the air to get a better view, but mostly what I saw was people—lots of hot, dusty people.

Idi Amin Dada had mobilized all the refugees within walking distance of the border town to witness an agreement. The agreement, signed in Addis Ababa, Ethiopia, was supposed to grant political autonomy to the Africans of Southern Sudan. The civil war had reached a bit of an impasse, and the Khartoum government was tired of trying to put down the rebels. At the moment, it seemed to be in their best interest to make some sort of concession. All of the Sudanese refugees cherished the possibility that this might mean that they could return to the homes that they had longed to see for so many years.

"There's Idi Amin!" I heard people murmur in the crowd around me. I looked up and saw a large African man in full military dress. The Ugandan military men who accompanied him wore fatigues and carried rifles.

Soon after Mr. Amin ascended the platform, Joseph Lagu and Jaafar Mohammed Nimieri arrived, smiling and waving to the crowd. They were also dressed in military fatigues, and although they were opponents, they certainly seemed to be friendly enough.

"I heard Nimieri didn't even sign at Addis Ababa," a man in the crowd whispered to my father.

"True enough," Father replied. "Another negotiator signed in his place."

"That doesn't seem like a very good sign."

"Perhaps not."

"An agreement of convenience will be broken when it no longer serves the interests of Khartoum."

Father nodded slowly. "We have seen that before . . ."

The conversation was cut short by cheers from the excited crowd. With great fanfare, Lagu and Nimieri were preparing to cut a red ribbon, a symbol of the opening of Southern Sudan to her returning people. As the fragments of the delicate ribbon fluttered to the ground, a great roar erupted. It was an emotional moment for everyone. Under the new agreement, Southern Sudan would have the authority to govern her own affairs without interference from the North. For millions of Sudanese refugees, it was a chance to go home at long last.

A throng of people pushed their way to the border. Parents hoisted young children up on shoulders to see, often for the first time, their homeland. I felt the pull of home on my heart at that moment as well. Even though I never thought of myself as a "refugee," I always knew that someday I would return to my real home country. Just like my headmaster at the Nyigeri School had said, I knew that it would be up to me to do my part to rebuild Sudan.

I looked up at my father as he drank in the sight before us. I wondered what he was thinking. Then the muscle in his jaw tightened, and he turned around briskly.

"Time to go," he said simply.

While others in the group that had traveled from our village talked excitedly amongst themselves, my dad remained silent. Mom didn't say anything to him; she just walked by his side. I figured she knew what he was thinking, as she usually did. What I didn't know was how much our lives were about to change.

That evening, back in Ambuluwa, we were all thoroughly exhausted. My feet were cracked and bleeding. Even so, there was so much excitement that I didn't want to go to sleep. My oldest sisters, Angela and Jemima, were lost in animated conversation. They had formed a little circle together with their boyfriends; occasionally one or the other of them would run over and say something to our parents. Even from where I was sitting, I could see how much they were smiling. I thought they looked especially pretty when they smiled like that.

In fact, it seemed that the only people in the village who were serious and subdued were my parents. My father in particular was unusually quiet.

Eventually, the thrill of the day's events gave way to weariness, and everyone finally settled into their homes for the night. I fell into a deep, dreamless sleep.

It was mid-March in 1972, and I had only been in school at Nyigeri for one half of a semester when the Addis Ababa Agreement took effect. I had only just begun to make new friends at the school and learn to read and write. The next day at school, I began to understand what was about to happen to our community and our school.

The headmaster gathered all of us together after the morning prayers. He looked excited. "Children," he announced, "I have something important to tell you."

The students listened attentively as our favorite teacher began to speak. "How many of you saw the ribbon-cutting ceremony at Chinyaquia?"

Every hand shot up.

"That's wonderful. Remember what you saw. It was a historic event! How many of you know what the Addis Ababa agreement means?"

A few hands waved in the air, mostly from the primary three students. Even though I thought I understood what it meant, I wanted to hear what the headmaster had to say, so I kept my hand down.

"Who can tell us what it means?"

"We get to go back to the Sudan!" one of the boys from my brother's class yelled out.

A murmur rose from the group of students. "Quiet! I didn't give permission for everyone to speak . . . That's better." The headmaster wiped his brow with a handkerchief. "What this agreement means is that the war is over. The government in Khartoum has agreed to allow all of us in the South to have a say in how we will be governed. That is certainly something to celebrate." He cleared his throat and looked around at the student body. "I want to tell you all how much I have enjoyed teaching you." His voice faltered.

Francis elbowed me. "He looks like he is about to cry," he whispered.

"How many of you children will be leaving your villages?"

Again, hands shot up all over the group of students. Suddenly, I had a bad feeling in the pit of my stomach.

I elbowed Francis back. "Is everybody leaving?" I gasped.

Francis nodded slowly.

"What about us?" I demanded.

Francis just looked at me and shrugged.

The headmaster continued his speech. "I will be leaving as well. Today will be my last day teaching at this school. May God bless all of you children. Now, I would like to speak privately to all the students in primary three."

My head was spinning with a sudden realization. The students were leaving. The headmaster was leaving. *What would become of my school?*

What a difference a day could make! That treaty had changed everything! No wonder my father had looked so serious. I wondered if we would be leaving Ambuluwa, too. I didn't want to leave our village; it was the only home I had ever known. I just didn't know what to think.

During our lunch break, I sat down with Michael Longwa. We had gotten to be pretty good friends.

"So, William," Michael said between bites of lunch, "when is your family leaving?"

I didn't know what to say. "I'm not sure; Abba didn't tell us." Actually, I was pretty sure that the Levi family wasn't going anywhere soon.

"Mama and I are leaving tomorrow," Michael said casually. "We're going back to the Mali Township, back to the old village."

"Tomorrow?" was all I could manage. "Oh."

"Your family used to live not too far from our family," Michael continued. "I know because Mama told me."

"Maybe we'll see each other again when we get there."

"Sure!" Michael got up and brushed the crumbs from his lap. "It will be great."

I wasn't so sure. I wasn't so sure if I would ever see any of my new friends again.

After school, I walked back with Francis, my big brother, Odu, and some boys from our village. I wasn't feeling too well. Odu came up behind me and gave me a little push.

"Hey, little brother, hurry up! What's eating you?"

"Are we going back to the Sudan?" I asked.

"*I* am," my brother replied smugly.

"What do you mean?"

"All the boys from primary three have been invited to go to a boarding school at Loa. There's a big Catholic Church there, and they're taking in students. The school starts at primary four, so only those of us who are graduating get to go. That's what the headmaster told us."

"What about me?" I demanded. I was beginning to feel a little bit fearful. My best friend, my favorite teacher, and now even my brother was deserting me.

"Haven't you heard? The school at Nyigeri is closing down."

"Why?" I couldn't believe it.

"Think about it." My brother spoke more gently this time, feeling my confusion. "The students are gone. The headmaster is gone. The teachers are all leaving. What's left?"

Finally, everything became clear to me. I began to cry. Within days, the school I had been so blessed to attend would be closing its doors forever. I might never get another chance to go to school!

I walked the rest of the way home with an ache in my heart. How could I ever see my dreams come true?

That night, as every night, we prayed together as a family. Then my father told us his decision. We would not be leaving Ambuluwa. Our family had invested many years into our home and farm, and we were secure. My father did not want to risk losing everything to return to Sudan prematurely. Yes, there was a cease-fire, but would it hold? My father was very protective of our family, and his decision was to wait and see how things turned out.

"Dad," I asked, "why aren't we going back to Sudan?"

My parents exchanged glances. I'm sure that they had been expecting us to ask that question before long.

"William," Dad began, "this hasn't been an easy decision for us, but it is a decision we are making for the benefit of the whole family."

"How can it be a benefit? I can't go to school anymore!"

"Don't interrupt!" Mom interjected sternly.

"You know how much I love my country," Father continued, "but I love my family even more. I don't think it is safe to return to Sudan. Every agreement the Arabs have entered into, they have broken. I worked among them when I was a young man, and I saw and heard things that have left me cynical, I admit. Mark my words; it is only a matter of time before Khartoum violates this agreement. I have broken my back working hard to make a life of safety here in Uganda for us. I plan to stay here until I believe it is safe for you kids to return."

"But what will I do? How can I make a difference for our family and our country if I can't go to school?"

"You will need to work as a shepherd again. It was good enough for King David; it is good enough for you. Besides, you can't make a difference for anything if you are dead."

I just didn't understand it. Father had told us that times were different now, that we needed an education to make a difference. He told us that he didn't want us to end up as uneducated farmers with no influence in modern society. But now he was telling me that I had to give up my dream of an education to take care of sheep and goats. It just didn't make sense.

Mother was the one to break up the family meeting. "Time for all of you to go to bed," she insisted. Her face looked suddenly drawn and old. "I'm not feeling too well tonight, and I want to lie down."

That was the end of the discussion.

CHAPTER SIX

Changes

The changes came quickly, and they pummeled me full force like heavy droplets from a sudden squall during the rainy season. Like a new river in the desert, they cut a path into the very fabric of my life. I could no longer go to school. My friend, Michael Longwa, had left with his mother to return to the Sudan. My big brother, Michael Odu, was packing to go with his friends from primary three to the secondary boarding school far away in Loa. Neighbors had left their homes eerily vacant in the rush to return from exile. But worst of all, my mama was sick—very sick.

We had no way of knowing what was wrong with Mama, and there was no medical care available near our home. We only knew that she was gravely ill, and we needed to care for her in whatever way we could. Severe headaches, weakness, and pain left Mama bed bound and unable to go about her usual activities. It fell to me to pick up some extra chores around the house and to tend to Mama's needs when she asked me. I didn't mind doing extra work, because I knew she would have done anything she could to help any of us kids.

One afternoon when I came in to check on Mama, I saw Angela and Jemima bent over Mama's bed, murmuring quietly. I felt a sudden surge of anxiety. *Is Mama OK?* I hurried over to the bedside and was relieved to see that she was smiling. Her smile was weak and fragile, but I could see that it was genuine. I exhaled with relief.

"Ajjugo," Mama called out. "Fetch Francis and Rose and William and all. It's time."

Time for what? I wondered.

My abba came in, and soon the whole family was gathered about. Mama kept right on smiling. Jemima and Angela were giggling, and when I looked up I saw their fiancés standing at the doorway, watching the gathering.

"You tell them, Ajjugo," Mama said.

Tell them what? I wondered. All the secrecy had me feeling anxious.

Abba cleared his throat and looked around the room. "Children," he announced, "say hello to your new older brothers."

My oldest sisters ran to the doorway, and I suddenly understood. Jemima and Angela were getting married. More changes! The two young men at our doorway were not strangers to us; they had worked side by side with our family in our little village for many years. We already loved them like brothers—but I for one was not ready to give them my sisters!

One of my new brothers-to-be addressed my parents respectfully. "Abba," he said with a nod. "Mama," he said, smiling at my mother. "We will be leaving for the Sudan as soon as possible."

As my father gathered the two new families together to pray a blessing on them, I felt like my world was spinning in slow motion. I couldn't believe that my own family was being torn apart and Mama and Abba were doing nothing to stop it! They could not allow my sisters to move to the Sudan. It was just not possible!

In those days, there were no telephones, no e-mails, no roads, and no transportation. Odu, Jemima, and Angela might as well have been leaving for another planet. We would have no contact with them after they left. And yet, Mama was smiling.

I turned away so she would not see the tears that slipped hot and silent down my cheeks. But she knew anyway.

"William," Mama called gently.

The others had hurried off, chattering happily and making plans for the trip back home to Sudan, leaving me alone in the room with Mama.

"Yes, Mama," I replied glumly.

"Do you want to tell me something?"

I looked at her, and I saw sympathy in her eyes. For a moment I marveled that her eyes were still so luminous and expressive set in a face gaunt with illness. The last thing I wanted to do was to burden her with my sadness. "No, Mama," I mumbled. "It's nothing."

"It's OK to feel sad about your sisters, honey. I know they raised you since you were a baby. They love you like you were their own child, you know that. But their place is with their new family now."

"Yes, Mama."

"Be happy for them, honey. It isn't easy for them to leave."

"OK, Mama." I said it, but it was hard to feel it. I could still remember how my sisters used to carry me on a sling on their backs as they worked. I remembered how they fed me and taught me and took care of me all those years. It was just plain hard to feel happy for them when they were leaving me.

When my older sisters and brothers left, Ambuluwa truly seemed like a ghost town. Without Mama or the other men of the community to help him, Abba was overwhelmed with work. Francis and I weren't old enough to do a man's work, and it took both of us, and Rose besides, just to get Mama's work done. Our life in the wilderness was just about over. My father realized that we needed to get help for Mama, too. The only way to do that was to leave our beloved home.

I was sitting next to Mama, trying to get her to eat some porridge when Abba came in and gathered what was left of our family around. "Anna," he said softly, "try to eat something."

Mama just nodded and then turned her head from the spoon that I offered her. I looked up at Abba and shook my head. "She only ate a couple of bites, Abba."

Father sat down by the bed and stroked Mama's hair. "I've made a decision," he said. "We're leaving Ambuluwa."

Mama didn't say anything but nodded her assent. As usual, she had known what her husband was going to say. Rose, Francis, and I didn't argue. Ambuluwa was not the place we had come to love anymore. It was returning to the jungle day by day, and now the forest would reclaim it.

"Where will we go, Abba?" Little Rose had never known any other home.

"We will go to back to Nyigeri, near the main road. From there, we can bring your mother to the UN hospital. Maybe they can help her there."

Although the school in Nyigeri was now closed, people still lived there, and its proximity to the main road into the Sudan made travel and communication possible. Since it was near the border, it was a safe spot to live. If trouble arose in Uganda, it would be easy to slip back across the border and head to Nimule. I knew my father had considered all of these factors carefully.

By the time we closed down the farm in Ambuluwa and gathered all of our belongings for the move, I was glad to be going. I was happy to be near people again, but mostly I was relieved that Mama would be getting help soon. I was beginning to fear for her life.

As soon as we had settled in to our new home, the whole family set off to the UN hospital in Nimule, South Sudan. The doctors wanted my mama to stay in the hospital, so for the first time in my life, I went home without her.

None of us had much to say on the road back to our new home in Nyigeri. We were all wondering if we would ever see Mama alive again. I lived in Nyigeri for a little over a year, and it was not a happy time for me. My mother spent six long months in the hospital, and for much of that time we really felt that we would lose her. But God was merciful to our family, and Mama began to improve.

Eventually, she was well enough to return to Nyigeri, although she hadn't yet returned to her former health. We were very thankful to have her back home with us.

My sister, Jemima, lived with her husband, Albereto Kenyi, in Loa, and when my mama had been home from the hospital for a time, she came to visit. It was wonderful to see the joy on Mama's face when she saw her daughter again.

"Jemima! I have missed you so much!" It was gratifying to see Mama able to stand and embrace her younger daughter. "What news do you have from Loa? How is your brother Odu? Is he doing well in school?"

A shadow passed over Jemima's face, but she quickly covered it with a smile. "I have the best news for you, Mama!" she cried. "I'm going to have a baby!"

"Ajjugo, did you hear? We're going to be grandparents!" Mama's smile was so bright that I had to laugh with joy. It was so good to see my sister make Mama smile like that.

Father came up and slapped Albereto on the back. "Congratulations, son! It's about time!" He pulled up some chairs and the family sat down together to talk. Father turned to Jemima. "So, Jemima, tell us . . . how is your brother doing?"

Jemima and Albereto exchanged glances. From their moment of hesitation I gathered that the news was not going to be good.

Finally, Albereto took the initiative to speak up. "Ajjugo, I have to say that Odu is one of the reasons we came to visit today. I'm sorry, but we have to spoil your good news with some bad."

I heard Mama catch her breath. "Is he OK? Is he hurt?"

Albereto shook his head. "I know that you were counting on me to keep him in line, because we live near the school in Loa. I haven't lived up to your expectations." Albereto looked chagrined, and I could see that he felt in some way responsible for Odu's behavior. "Michael has left Loa."

"What?" My father was stunned. "Odu has left Loa? What kind of rebellion is this? He knows that this family has invested everything in his education. Where has he gone?"

Jemima answered. "I am hoping this is only youthful foolishness. Perhaps he will come back to school. He has gotten involved with some bad friends, and they are involved in drinking and chasing girls. He and some other boys just dropped out of school. We couldn't stop him."

It was depressing to watch the happiness on Mama's face fade to tears. We had all placed so much hope in my brother Michael's education. Now he had left school, and we feared that his life was headed in the wrong direction. I wondered if he had felt too much pressure to succeed.

Father spoke next. "I went through some troubled times myself at his age. It was your grandfather Vuni who came alongside me and gave me some direction."

He glanced at Mama and smiled. "I took his advice, and then married his daughter. We will pray that Odu will accept advice and find his way again. I'm sure that he will come back to us when this time passes. Don't blame yourself, Albereto—he will make his own choices."

Father set the tone for the rest of the visit, and after the disturbing news about my brother, we all were determined to dwell on the happy news of my sister's first child. Eventually, Father's prediction was fulfilled. Although he didn't complete his schooling, Odu did return and claim his important place in our family. But at the time, the thought of my brother throwing away the very thing that I so desperately wanted filled me with conflicting emotions. I loved my brother dearly, but it hardly seemed fair that he had the chance to go to school while I was doomed to stay in Nyigeri with no future that I could see. How I wished I could have been in Odu's place at the boarding school in Loa.

The abandoned school in Nyigeri was a constant reminder that my education had stalled terribly. I was already ten years old, and I knew that if I didn't finish primary school I would have no hope for the future. My only lot in life would be farming, and I would be forced to go wherever the political situation demanded—growing enough food to survive and running from the GOS. I respected farming, and I was not afraid to work with my hands, but even Father was quick to agree that simple subsistence farming would soon become obsolete in our rapidly changing world.

As time passed, I began to despair of ever achieving my goals. It was my two sisters, Angela and Jemima, who finally brought some hope back into my life. Jemima and Albereto had settled near Loa. Angela and her new husband Korica were going to live in Bori near Opari, a region where some of Mother's relatives lived. My uncle Ezekiel and my maternal grandfather were both teachers at the Opari Elementary School, a new school that had opened up since the return of large groups of refugees. Since Loa was near Uganda, Jemima was willing to take me with her and on to Angela's home. Angela was willing to take me up to Nyakaningwa, a village in the Opari district, where my aunt and uncle could look after me. If I went with them, I would be able to attend school again at last.

I didn't hesitate. I knew what I wanted to do, and I begged my father to let me go. At first, he was adamantly opposed to the idea. He was afraid to let me leave Uganda by myself since I was only ten, and he believed that my place at that age was with my own parents. But he also knew that my options were terribly limited in Nyigeri. My big sisters argued on my behalf, reminding our father that he himself had told us many times how valuable an education could be. In fact, it was because of his words that I was so eager to pursue an education in the first place. Besides, with Odu out of school, the family hopes would have to rest on me, the younger son.

Reluctant though he was, Father eventually relented. I was soon on my way back to the Sudan. I didn't realize it at the time, but leaving for Opari would mark one of the greatest changes of all in my life. That decision charted the course for my future and shaped the person I was to become in many different ways. It was a choice leading to independence, education, and great personal pain. The upheavals that I would experience in my life were only just beginning. God would use the changes to break my heart and shape my soul. It was to be an increasingly difficult process, but like clay in the hands of the Potter, I would be crushed, cast, and molded into something useful for my Creator.

CHAPTER SEVEN

The Bible or the Axe

I left my parents' home with gifts of cloth and peanut butter to bring to my relatives. I was proud that they trusted me to be the bearer of greetings and gifts all the way from Uganda. I hadn't seen my uncle for many years, and I had never met his wife or any of my cousins, but that didn't matter. In our large extended family and beyond we treated one another as if we were the closest of kin. Even a stranger well met would be long remembered in our culture. We were a people who supported each other from community to community with open-handed hospitality. For that reason, I didn't feel awkward when I was received graciously into the home of my uncle. It was the most natural thing in the world for us.

Grandfather Vuni and Uncle Ezekiel welcomed me, and they both thought that it was a great idea for me to come to pursue my education.

"Good to see you again, little William," Grandfather smiled. "You too, Angela, and it's great to see you and your new husband back here where you belong."

We sat down to a festive dinner, with more relatives than I had seen in years. I explained the purpose of my visit between mouthfuls. "I want to go to school again, Grandpa. Our school closed down in Nyigeri."

Grandfather nodded. "We heard about that. Heard your father won't be coming back home, either. I wish he would." There was no condemnation in his voice; it was merely a statement of fact. "There isn't much left in Nyigeri."

That was certainly true. "He doesn't trust the government. He thinks everyone will only have to run again in a few years."

Grandfather shrugged. "He's probably right. But in the meantime, I'm going to stay home as long as I can. Who knows, maybe things will turn out all right."

We discussed the latest political events for a while, and then the conversation turned back to me.

"It's been a while since you were in school," my uncle remarked. "You should repeat primary grade one."

I stiffened at the suggestion. I knew that time was working against me. "I'll be fine," I insisted. "Just give me a chance and I'll prove it to you. Please let me start grade two—I'm nearly eleven!"

Uncle looked doubtful, but he decided to give me a chance. "I'll tell you what," he said, "You can start primary two. After a month or so, we will evaluate your performance. If you do well, you can stay. If not, you will be held back."

The plan was reasonable, and I could do nothing but agree. "I promise you I will do my best. It will work out."

It was with great relief that I began my schooling in grade two at the Opari School in Nyakaningwa, a village that boasted a population of nearly 1,000. Since it was near the borderlands of two neighboring tribes, many residents spoke both Madi and Ocholi. It was practically cosmopolitan! Sturdy brick frame buildings topped with thatch lined the single main road—a dirt road that wound its way from Torit to Nimule-Juba in Southern Sudan. Big flatbed trucks or Land Rovers would occasionally rumble past on the rutted thoroughfare; and usually the vehicles would be coated with a thick layer of dust since they dislodged great clouds of the stuff as they traveled. Local traffic was accomplished with bicycles or on foot. There was no electrical lighting, so we relied on kerosene lamps to ward off the dark, and our water was pumped by hand. Still in all, it was a big city to me. The school building consisted of a single structure divided into three rooms, each with a blackboard. It was very similar in design to my old school in Uganda, except that it was less than a mile from where I was staying. I was glad that I wouldn't have to run seven miles through the jungle to get to class!

I lived with my Uncle Ezekiel, his wife, Marietta, and their new baby boy, Kanga Wilson, and two other older daughters, Rose and Josephine. Besides her own three children, Aunt Marietta took care of me and my cousin, Moses, as well as Letiyo, a niece from her side of the family. It must have been difficult for her to have to take responsibility for three children who were not her own; It was certainly difficult for us to adjust to life in a household run by someone other than our own mothers. I did my best to be obedient to my surrogate parents and to do everything that was expected of me.

Our lives soon settled into a predictable routine. We arose at around seven in the morning and then went to the well to wash up and fetch the drinking water. Sometimes I washed and ironed my uncle's clothing so that he would be ready for a day of teaching. At school, he taught math, geography, and hygiene. I sat with my cousin, Moses, in primary two. After school, there were always gardening chores waiting to be done as soon as homework was complete. Sometimes Aunt Marietta would ask me to watch the babies for her. In the evenings, my uncle would often bring home piles of paperwork. He would sit down after supper by the light of a lamp to mark papers and prepare lesson plans. I was fascinated by the textbooks that he read, and I began to read them, too. Although most of the material was beyond my understanding, the knowledge that I gleaned was enough to keep me motivated. The success I began to experience academically was my reward, and my reason to endure. Endurance, as it turned out, was increasingly important in my new life in Nyakaningwa.

I soon found out that my uncle and the other teachers at school were having trouble. The newly autonomous Southern government based in Juba was responsible for handling the money for education. Unfortunately, the Islamic government from the North had little funds budgeted for Southern Sudanese education. The money that they did release through Juba passed through many hands, mostly those of corrupt officials. So, even though the Juba-based government was administered by Southerners, it did little to actually help the governed. As a result of these abuses of power, the teachers at our school went for months at a time with no pay and no funds for supplies. It was purely an exercise in self-sacrifice for the teachers, who freely gave up time that they could have spent growing food for their families. Occasionally, some staff workers from UNICEF would come by to provide us with books, papers, and pencils. The UN relief did help some, but I began to see the strain building in my uncle's home. Feeding all of us was a burden.

Aunt Marietta asked us to do a full load of farming chores in addition to our school and homework duties. I was used to farm work, so I just did what I had to do without complaining. I didn't blame my aunt for making us work for our share of the food, especially since my uncle spent all day teaching us without pay. Moses and Letiyo had a tougher time adjusting to the workload. They felt that our aunt was far too strict and making us work too hard. They were determined to tell their parents that she was mistreating them. They both eventually ended up going home to their own villages and giving up their schooling. I must admit that there were many times when I felt like going back to Uganda, but I just gritted my teeth and kept on going, despite the hardships and the feelings of homesickness.

Finally, the teachers got together and explained to the parents of the village that they were not being paid much, if at all. They held a community meeting to try to solve the problem, with the fate of the school ultimately at stake. It would have to be closed down if the teachers could not afford to feed their families. There was a big crowd at the meeting, with families attending from miles around. Everyone had a stake in the success of the Opari Elementary School.

Working together, we came up with an unusual plan. Every Friday, the students were required to dedicate two hours to a physical education curriculum. Gym class was everyone's favorite, but that was about to change. Instead of the usual running races and soccer games, it was decided that students would need to go and clear land

and plant crops. There were three to four hundred students in the school, and they all worked together with their instructors clearing, plowing, and planting a very large parcel of unused land. It was definitely a different sort of PE class. Every week this large group of children worked hard planting cassava, grain, sorghum, beans, sesame, millet, sweet potatoes, tomatoes, and all sorts of green vegetables. It was a huge and exhausting task.

By October, we had reaped a huge harvest. There was enough food for all of the teachers to eat at last. We had a wonderful celebration, attended by parents and teachers alike. We came to realize that we didn't need money from Khartoum to educate ourselves. We didn't need the money siphoned off by corrupt officials in Juba to feed ourselves. We learned that we needed to work together as parents, teachers, and students to achieve our common goals. This was a great lesson for me, but it did not come without a price. The work was very difficult, and it did create some dissent. Some students felt that they should not have to do farm work, and they wanted to arrange a protest. Although a full-scale protest never materialized, there were bad feelings among many of the students who resented being pressed into service for the sake of their education. But in the end, the majority of students were successful and the school enjoyed the fruits of our labors.

During the week, I worked hard to complete my studies and grow food. On Sundays, I had the opportunity to attend the first real church I had ever seen. The African Inland Church, like the school building, was a simple structure. Grandfather had worked hard to restore the building, because it had stood idle while congregants spent several long years in exile. The roof was made of thatch and the walls were plastered with muddy clay. Baked bricks added strength to the structure, and glass-less windows let in natural light. The church stood on a hill near the Kulo-jobi River, just a stone's throw from the school compound. I loved going to that small, simple structure each Sunday morning. We didn't need an ornate cathedral or elaborate stained glass, because the beauty for our call to worship came from God's world all around us. The Opari region was lush and beautiful, with soaring mountains and rushing streams. I loved walking to church on Sundays, enjoying the sights and sounds of the countryside and taking a break from my farming work. But the best part about going to church was hearing my grandfather preach. His sermons were quite different from the classes that he taught in Christian Education at the school. He really made the Bible lessons come alive in a way that made me want to apply them to my life.

My grandfather, the Reverend Andrew Vuni, was the most prominent of all the village elders, and people often sought his counsel. The force of his convictions and the power of the Holy Spirit in his life brought admiration and respect from all who knew him—including me. Even though he was a kindly grandfather to me, there was something about him that commanded a response of more than mere affection. In my mind's eye, I could imagine him dressed in robes and sandals, holding the staff of an Old Testament prophet in one hand and the scrolls of the Torah in the other. In a way, he was like a modern-day prophet, bringing the Word of the Lord before his congregation and serving up a fiery rebuke to all who strayed into the idolatry of worldliness. Instead of a flowing beard and untamed hair, he sported a clean-shaven face and a close-cropped head of snowy white hair. Instead of home-spun robes, he wore slacks and a short sleeved shirt. Although he was an old man then, his dark skin was smooth, and his slender frame stood erect. His rough hands bore testimony to many years of hard work cultivating rice and bananas and of raising flocks of sheep and goats. But it was my grandfather's eyes that I recall most clearly. Those eyes were serious, sober, and penetrating—some-how those dark brown eyes could convey both a stern warning and gentle compassion at the same time. He was average height in stature, but he was an impressive man. I was proud to have him as my teacher and my pastor. Under his tutelage, I decided to dedi-cate my life to Yeshua in a real and personal way.

When I came to faith, I wanted to be baptized right away. But the African Inland Church still held to a very ancient practice that is seldom followed today. In the early days of the Church, new believers went through a period of intense study as catechumen while they prepared for baptism. This period of time often took several years. In fact, many early Christians were martyred before they qualified for baptism. Ancient church writings describe these believers as having been "baptized with blood," and their require-ment for baptism by the church was considered to be fulfilled. Grandfather's church required a three-year period of study and preparation prior to baptism, so I was enrolled in a class with sev-eral other church members toward this end. Grandfather Vuni was our teacher.

"Today we will be reading from the book of Ephesians, chap-ter six."

Pages rustled as students, young and old, turned to the passage we were about to study. It was a warm, tropical evening, and I enjoyed the cool of the cement floor and the gentle breeze that often passed through the screened windows. One of the older students stood to read the passage aloud.

"Finally, be strong in the Lord, and in the strength of His might. Put on the full armor of God, that you may be able to stand firm against the schemes of the devil. For our struggle is not against flesh and blood, but against the rulers, against the powers, against the world forces of this darkness, against the spiritual forces of wickedness in the heavenly places. Therefore, take up the full armor of God, that you may be able to resist in the evil day, and having done everything, to stand firm."[9]

The room fell quiet as the baptismal students struggled to absorb the words of the passage and to grasp their meaning. Grandfather looked around the room, studying faces.

"There is an enemy," he said. "There is one who would erase the name of Yeshua from our country and would gladly shed our blood to gain his ground. Who can name our enemy?"

Several sets of eyes looked up at the pastor. It was clear that everyone in the room knew who was seeking to destroy us. A hand went up.

"The Muslims of Khartoum are our enemies. They would like to drive Christians from this country."

A murmur of agreement filled the room, until my grandfather silenced it with a wave of his hand.

"No, you are wrong." Grandfather spoke sharply, frustrated that his students were so slow to comprehend the meaning of the scripture they had just read. "Don't you understand? Our enemy is not human. We do not struggle against flesh and blood but against spiritual powers. The one who opposes us is much greater than any mortal man, and he wants to destroy Muslims and Christians alike. But it is the name of Yeshua that he cannot abide."

Nobody wanted to ask a question; we were all trying hard to understand without looking stupid. Fortunately, the Reverend Vuni continued his explanation.

"Satan is our enemy. He blinds the eyes of the Muslim to the gospel message. They are left in darkness, bound by the chains of sin. He has beaten them already. He deceives human leaders into declaring war on the innocent, spreading genocide and persecution against God's children. But greater is He that is in us than he that is in the world. Praise God! Satan can kill our bodies, but he can never devour our souls in hell."

All this talk of malevolent spiritual forces made me feel a little frightened. I was glad I was going to heaven, but I didn't want to get killed and get there before my time. Hesitantly, I raised my hand.

"Since God is greater than the devil, why doesn't He just fight him? He would surely win, wouldn't He?"

Grandfather smiled. "He already did. The battle has been won and in the most unexpected way."

"What do you mean?"

"The cross, of course. The cross has made it possible for us to pass over from death to life. It's as simple as trusting in Yeshua. Sin, death, and hell have no power over us."

"So why does the Bible tell us to stand firm against the schemes of the devil? Didn't you just say that the battle is over?"

"The battle is won, but it is not over—not until Christ returns to claim His kingdom. We must fight, but our warfare is spiritual. You can't fight a spiritual enemy with physical weapons."

"How do you fight a spirit? Is there a special ritual for that?" One of the older students was looking a bit perplexed as he tried to figure out how to fight something he couldn't see. That was something only shamans were trained to do.

Grandfather was treading on delicate ground, and he knew it. Witchcraft was a very real influence among my people, and it was not unusual even for Christians to be involved with the superstitions of traditional magic. Many shamanistic rituals were thought to ward off evil spirits, and my grandfather wanted to make a very clear distinction between the Christian view of spiritual evil and the animist way.

"There is no ritual, there is no magic. There is only the Sword of the Spirit, which is the Word of God."

"You mean the Bible is your weapon?"

"Exactly!" Grandfather's eyes brightened as he sensed that his students were beginning to grasp his message. "The Bible is sharper than any two-edged sword. Reading it and meditating on it brings power from the Holy Spirit. Prayer and constant connection with God will guard your heart and your mind. You will be given strength to face whatever enemy may come."

"But what if the soldiers try to kill me?"

"To live is Christ . . . to die is gain. I'm not saying that it is wrong to fight in the military. But the ultimate battle is way beyond that."

I didn't fully understand all of that at the time, but now I know how carefully I was being prepared for the real battles that were to come. Grandfather had lived through a lot of trouble, and, like my father, I'm sure he suspected that we hadn't seen the end of it. He wanted all of us to understand that our earthly enemies were just people who needed God's love. I could choose to dispatch them to eternal damnation with a bullet or a sword, or I could serve them and reach out to them with the redeeming message of the Gospel of Christ. In choosing the latter, he wanted me to know that I would have to be prepared to sacrifice my life for my enemies, just as Christ did when He died for the redemption of men who hated Him. He wanted us all to understand that the war and the corruption and the hunger and the pain and the hatred were just symptoms of the disease of sin. God's overarching plan, I would come to understand, is not about me or my comfort. It is about His redemptive plan.

Our little class continued, and I gradually came to understand more about the Scriptures. I moved beyond the familiar stories of the patriarchs and the miracles of Christ and into the more complex ideas of theology, church polity, and Christian living. I had so much to learn. For three years I dedicated myself to studying the Scriptures.

As my education through the primary school progressed, I found that I could read and understand with increasing ability. God really confirmed that my decision to pursue an education was the right one. With flowering literacy came flowering spiritual growth for me. I will never forget the day that I received my baptism. It was a pivotal experience in my life, defining the man I was to become. The decision that was put before me tested everything that my father and my grandfather had so carefully taught me.

It was December of 1977, and the quiet, brown waters of the Kulo-jobi River lapped and eddied along rocky banks that had been exposed by the long dry season. The dry season was the time of baptism in most villages, because that was when the waters were calm. In August, torrential rains would swell the riverbed, and the Kulo-jobi would rage and boil again. It wouldn't do to have congregants swept away by the currents.

I stood on the shore as a skinny boy of thirteen that December, feeling the packed dirt beneath my bare feet. It was a happy feeling. Tall grasses bent and rustled as a warm breath of dry air soughed across the savanna lands, mingling the scents of sun-dappled vegetation and hot earth. The mountains stood out in sharp relief in the blue sky beyond the wooded riverbanks. It was easy to think about God's great love for me as I drank in the beauty of my surroundings.

I barely noticed the others from my baptismal group as they gathered by the river. The mood was reverent, and people spoke only in whispers as we all waited for the ceremony to begin. Finally, my grandfather appeared and stood beneath a huge old tree by the riverbank to address the congregation. As he spoke, I studied the water that flowed gently behind him. I was about to venture into that water to be immersed! The river was muddy this time of year, and I hoped that there was nothing sinister lurking in the shallows. Alligators, snakes, and even sharp rocks might be waiting for me there, but Grandfather didn't seem to be even a little bit concerned.

I shook off my childish fears and began to listen to the sermon. It was time to become a man and a full member of the church. I wanted to be ready.

Once again, the text for Grandfather's sermon was from Ephesians. He spoke of the struggles that we would endure if we chose to cast our lot with Jesus Christ.

"Yeshua was a man acquainted with grief," he said. "If you wish to partake of His glory, you must understand that you will be asked to partake of His suffering."

The congregants nodded at Grandfather's words. Every single person there knew what it was like to be targeted for persecution.

"Are you willing to lay down your lives for the sake of the gospel?"

It was quiet except for the cheerful song of a colorful bird and the chirping of insects in the grass. Each person pondered Grandfather's words, fully understanding that they might eventually be called upon to do just that. Grandfather surveyed the crowd before him, love and pain mingled in his expression.

"A good soldier must be prepared to die. But we have God's armor, protecting our eternal spirit against the devil's schemes."

I was too young to completely understand the implications of Grandfather's words. Yes, we had lived as refugees, and I knew that boys like me were sometimes stolen from refugee camps to become slaves. I also knew something of war, and I knew that my own father believed that our current peace agreement was a fragile one. But I didn't really imagine that I would ever be asked to deny Christ or face death. Grandfather, though, knew from experience that some would die for their convictions, and he had been working to prepare his congregation for just such a possibility.

"Put on the helmet of salvation, and the breastplate of righteousness," he continued. "Make sure your feet are shod with the preparation of the gospel of peace."

I looked down at my toes. Little puffs of dirt swirled up between them as I dug them into the dirt of the riverbank. I tried to imagine that I was wearing gospel shoes. The image was an odd one, but I understood that the scripture wasn't talking about real shoes or real armor. The war, though, was very real.

"Most importantly, learn to wield the Sword of the Spirit, which is the Word of God." Grandfather was finished with his sermon, and we all sang a hymn. It was time for the baptismal ceremony to take place.

Murmurs of excitement rose all around me as everyone jostled for a better view. It was a special time for everyone, because most families had at least one member preparing for this sacrament. When my name was finally called, I walked toward the great tree that served as a podium for our outdoor gathering. Its branches spread lazily overhead, swaying softly in the breeze. Great roots twisted into the riverbank at crazy angles, jutting up like solid benches, perfect for sitting on.

Grandfather looked into my eyes, and I sensed that he was studying my face very carefully. He was searching for something in my expression, but I wasn't sure what that something could be.

"William Ochan Levi," he said. "Your enemy will come."

I nodded dumbly. Without a word, Grandfather produced an axe and placed it on a broad root of the great tree. Next to it, he placed the Bible. Then he turned and focused his gaze on me once again.

"When your enemy comes to destroy you, which weapon will you choose?"

Would it be the Bible or the axe? I was taken aback by the question. If my enemies were coming toward me, preparing to kill me, I would certainly want to have that broad, sharp axe in my hand. I could almost feel the heft of the smooth wooden handle, worn by years of hewing trees. The sharp head of the axe was a perfect counterbalance to the haft, and I knew what it felt like to send the sharp steel ringing into a sturdy trunk. Surely the axe would give me a fighting chance against the swords of the jihad. *For we battle not against flesh and blood.* . . . The words of my scripture lessons flooded my mind with a new clarity. Suddenly, I understood that I would never be able to fight my enemy with a weapon of steel.

Almost as if by instinct, my hand reached for the Bible. Grandfather smiled, and I thought I detected a fleeting expression of relief.

"You have chosen the right way," he said at last.

We waded together into the murky water, and I no longer thought of snakes and alligators. I knew that I would have to trust God for my life, just as I trusted Him for my soul. I emerged from the water a changed man.

CHAPTER EIGHT

Juba

The Ugandan dictator, Idi Amin, fell from power shortly after my graduation from Opari Elementary School. I was busy selling grain to pay tuition costs that spring, and the currency of trade often includes news that travels faster than goods. When I heard the rumors, I knew immediately that the fall of Amin would spell certain disaster for the refugees who were still living in Uganda, including my parents. It was time for my family to return to the Sudan, no matter what the risk. I literally dropped everything to rush to Uganda to help my family make their escape, and I was none too soon. Thousands of Idi Amin's ex-soldiers as well as civilians of Uganda and Sudanese refugees were flooding across the border into the Sudan. Armed thugs roamed the streets of Ugandan villages, killing indiscriminately. It was a time of bloody chaos, but my parents and I were able to bring my younger siblings and some belongings across the border to safety in Nimule.

Nimule was a hilly, craggy hamlet overlooking the Ugandan border just at the spot where the River Nile makes its crossing into the Sudan. The only road for miles around threaded a path into the little border town, and Nimule was soon desperately overcrowded with refugees. My parents were among the many who stayed briefly before making plans to find a more permanent home in Sudan. My father still lived in fear of the Islamic regime that continued to dominate his native country, but the threat of renewed persecution and civil war in Sudan was not as imminent as the threat from Uganda's descent into lawlessness. Once again, our family would be forced to make a new start in the wilderness.

At that time, I learned of my acceptance into the middle school at Nimule. I was thrilled, of course, but I had to wait for eight months for the school to open. That provided me with the opportunity to help my parents find a new home. My father settled on a place called Corom, meaning, "Men are equal." It was a fine spot, surrounded by four mountains and adorned with mahogany trees. My brothers, Michael Odu and Francis, joined me, and we worked hard to plow the fertile soil and build a new house for our parents. Mama and Abba were very pleased to see how much we had grown and how skilled we had become since they had seen us last. As our little farm took shape, my older brother, Michael Odu, was reunited with his elementary school sweetheart, Katherine, and they decided to marry and settle there with our parents in Corom. Michael Odu's youthful rebellion was a thing of the past and he took his rightful place as the oldest son. Of the many Ugandan refugees who came up to build homes, one was the natural father of my adopted brother, Francis. It was a difficult reunion for Francis, who had been abandoned by this man so long ago, but he was able to forgive. They were finally able to lay aside the hurt of the past and find reconciliation during this time of rebuilding.

With my family safely settled in the wilderness of Corom, I was able to enter middle school in Nimule with a sense of relief. Like most middle schools, the Nimule school was a boarding school of necessity. Most students had to travel quite a distance from the homes of their parents to attend such a regional school, and only the most serious students continued education into the secondary levels. Life was tough in the Sudan then as it is now, and education was a prize obtained only with great effort. So, for those of us at the middle school, it came as a great disappointment that school was declared over for the year in January due to a lack of food. The policy of the Khartoum-based Government of Sudan toward the Southern schools was to cut off their supplies in order to discourage southern Christians from pursuing a higher education. Uneducated people are always easier to control and manipulate, and they generally don't pose a threat to the regime.

I was terribly discouraged when I returned to Corom. I felt that the Government of Sudan had once again successfully sabotaged my education. It was obvious that I could not return to Nimule. With the foreshortened school years, I would be an adult before I would be able to attend high school! And so, after some deliberation, it was decided that I ought to head for Juba, a bona-fide city some 120 miles north of Corom. Juba was a diverse and wealthy city of merchants and traders. The schools there were the best to be found in the southern portion of the country.

Those were the events that led to my arrival in Juba, all alone and looking for a way to provide for myself through the remainder of my middle school and high school years. Juba, the capitol of the "autonomous" southern portion of Sudan, was truly a large city. It was the first real city I had ever seen. There were cars, markets, buildings, and people from many different cultures and walks of life. I was enthralled, and I wanted to explore the whole town, but that would have to come later. I had lots of work to do before I could even think of playing the tourist. I needed to find a job, a place to live, and a middle school that would accept me into their program! My parents had helped me find a place to start—I had gifts to bring for my mother's cousin, Gerelina, and her husband, Nicodemous. I could count on a welcome from them.

I was glad to discover that my mother's cousin had a son my age named James. Gerelina greeted me warmly and invited me to stay with her son, James, until I could settle in to my own accommodations. I accepted gratefully. The following day, James offered to show me around the Juba area. We set out early at my request.

"So, James, which of these buildings is the school?"

I craned my neck to take in the vast expanse of large structures, rising from the streets of Juba as far as the eye could see. It was quite a contrast from the towns I was used to, where the only public buildings were the church and the school.

"Several of these are schools, but I go to that one." James pointed out one of the structures nearby. "Its called Buluk Intermediate School. I hope you get admitted there. If you do, we could study together."

"That would be great!" I agreed enthusiastically. "Of course I need to find a job first. I can't go to any of these schools unless I can pay for it."

"Well, if you want a job, you should take a look at the business district." James motioned for me to follow him. "Come on, I'll show you where I work."

I shuffled along behind my second cousin, taking in the sights. I hoped that he could give me some good advice about local jobs, because I knew that I couldn't ask the Nicodemous family to support me. Life in the city was a lot different from life on the farm, where extra hands were always needed. Although I was only a middle schooler, I knew that I would really need to be self-sufficient for the first time in my life.

James stopped at a large, open-air market. It was crammed with ranks of dusty people haggling and milling about. The air was heavy with the smell of spices and leather and ripe produce.

"This is Konyo-konyo," he said proudly. "I work here."

I was impressed by the sheer size and the conspicuous wealth of the marketplace. "Which shop is yours?"

James indicated a small grocery store. "I sell tea to the customers who come here to buy groceries. It's good business."

"What are my chances of getting a job in a place like that?"

"Well, first things first." James looked at me and frowned slightly. "You don't speak Juba Arabic and that could be a problem."

"What do you mean? You speak English, don't you?"

"Well, yes . . . in the South we do learn English in school. But most of the merchants are of an Arab background, and they only speak Arabic. It would be hard to get a job in the market if you can't speak Juba Arabic. You need to learn the language first."

James spent the morning introducing me to downtown Juba and explaining the ins and outs of city life. Of course, James couldn't spend too much of his time helping me find work, so I immediately began my search for work on my own. Juba had a large number of expatriates from around the world, and the majority of these spoke English. I figured I could find a job with someone who spoke English, but I wasn't sure what skills I had to offer. My only real skill was farming, and that wasn't very marketable in the city. Juba was a town that ran on commerce, and I had no business skills. Even so, I knew I could work as an errand boy for a businessman if the opportunity arose.

With that in mind, I began to wander through the streets of downtown Juba, passing stall after stall of merchants hawking their wares. The colorful awnings, the strange smells, and the profusion of exotic items for sale were mesmerizing. For a while, I forgot my mission and enjoyed a bit of window-shopping. Suddenly, I was surprised by a voice calling my name.

"William!" The voice was familiar, but I couldn't place it right away. I turned around to see a young man waving to me from a nearby stall. Could it be? It was Michael Longwa, my childhood friend! He looked almost the same, except that he had grown into a broad-shouldered, muscular young teen. He smiled broadly and waved again.

I hurried over to the stall where Michael was at work as a salesman. "Michael, it's so great to see you again!"

"Likewise! What are you doing here?"

"I came to go to school. I just arrived here in town."

"I'm going to school, too. Oh, just a minute . . .," Michael turned from me and began assisting a customer, speaking in rapid-fire

Arabic. I was impressed. The customer completed his purchase and was soon on his way.

"Wow, Michael, you speak Arabic really well."

"Yeah, you have to speak Arabic if you want to work for the businessmen. They all use Arabic in the marketplace."

"So I've heard. I can only speak a few phrases in Arabic. Where can I find a job around here where I can speak English?"

Michael thought for a while. "Well," he replied, "there are a lot of American missionaries working all over Juba. Maybe you could get a job working for them. Your English is really excellent, so I'm sure that would be a plus. I think if they have a job opening, they would take you."

Michael excused himself from his stall with another flurry of Arabic. "I told the boss I was going to take my lunch break," he said with a smile.

We stopped for lunch in the Konyo-konyo market and had a good time catching up on the years since we had last seen each other back in Uganda. First grade seemed like several lifetimes ago, although it had only been a few short years. Michael told me where I could find the missionary quarter, where there was a compound housing the Summer Institute of Linguistics, or SIL. I decided I would try to find a job there.

"I think that is the right decision, but be careful." Michael gave me a warning glance. "Remember, this is Juba."

I thanked Michael for the lunch and for the advice and went on my way. I wondered why my friend should caution me as he did. Was it dangerous to associate with missionaries? I had not experienced any religious persecution in the villages—was there something different about big cities like Juba?

I approached the SIL compound with a mixture of hope and unease. I noticed a Land Cruiser just leaving the compound and hailed the occupants to a stop. I explained my situation to the missionaries and asked if they could offer me a job. The woman in the Land Cruiser leaned out to get a better look at me.

"What kind of skills do you have?" she asked.

"I come from a farm," I replied. "I am good at gardening and tending sheep."

The couple paused for a while and looked at each other. After a while, they shook their heads. "Sorry, we can't help you right now," the woman replied. "We don't really have a job for you."

As the Land Cruiser drove away, I felt my chances of finding work dwindle. In truth, it was the first attempt I had made to find a job, but my first attempt had been a failure. I tried not to allow myself to imagine what would happen to me if I could not get a job in Juba.

I spent nearly two months pounding the pavement in Juba, every day asking for work and every day being turned away. It was a lonely time that tried my faith nearly to the breaking point. The people of Juba lived a life that I had not even been aware of before. There was material wealth in an abundance that made me wonder if God had been holding out on me. It didn't make sense to me that the people who did not believe in Jesus were so wealthy and successful, while I was barely surviving. Arabic seemed to be the language of acceptance, intellect, and success, while English-speakers were marginalized. The mosques seemed to be the home of the powerful and the elite, while Christian churches were poor and grudgingly tolerated. I became angry with God and bitter toward the people who refused to hire me. I began to question the teachings of my father and grandfather. Somehow, it seemed to me that God was not being true to His word. He was not taking care of me.

Despite my bitterness, I turned to the Bible for comfort. It was all I had, and it was all I knew. As I read, I came across Matthew 6:25–34. I knew I was wrong to worry about what to eat, where to sleep, and whether I would go to school. I was trusting in myself instead of believing in God. The Scriptures told me, "Seek ye first the Kingdom of God, and His righteousness; and all these things shall be added unto you."[10] I understood then that I needed to attend to my spiritual life first and trust God to take care of the details.

After a time of prayer, I went to listen to the Reverend Benjamin. Pastor Ben could often be found preaching at an open air gathering in downtown Juba. That particular day, he was preaching that Jesus is the same yesterday, today, and forever. He emphasized that the power of the cross does not change depending on time or circumstance. He encouraged us to bring our burdens to the cross and offered to pray for any who were in need. I went forward to request prayer and Pastor Ben prayed for me. He told me not to lose heart and invited me to attend the Juba Christian Center where he was ministering.

Two days after my encounter with Pastor Ben, I received word from my mother's cousin, Gerelina, that my father had arrived in Juba to see how I was adjusting to city life. Unfortunately, he had fallen ill after his long trip from Corom and had to be sent to the hospital for a couple of days. I found my father recovering at the Juba regional hospital. I was so happy to see him, and I told him everything that had happened since my arrival in Juba. He listened carefully, and he prayed over me. He encouraged me to trust in God's provision, as he himself had learned to do through many years of exile and uncertainty.

Since it was a Sunday, we decided to attend church together at the All Saints Cathedral. I didn't normally attend church there, but it was near enough to the hospital that we could make the service as soon as he was discharged, because he was feeling much better. Of course, God had a reason for bringing us there on that day. After the service, I noticed a foreign couple looking at me as if they had seen me before. They came up to me and introduced them-selves as Chuck and Patsy Ohrenschall from the USA.

"Aren't you the boy who came by the SIL compound to look for a job?" Patsy asked.

"Yes, that was me."

"Are you still looking for work?"

"Yes, I haven't found anything yet."

Chuck extended his hand and I shook it. "It turns out that we need a gardener to manage the property for the SIL compound. We're going to be out of the country for a while. Do you think you could handle the maintenance around the place?"

Of course I could! It was something that I was well qualified to do. I was so glad that my father was there to see the nearly imme-diate answer to our prayers.

School had already begun, but now that I had an income, I was ready to register for classes immediately. I was able to skip level two and register in intermediate level three at Buluk Intermediate. I found myself in the same class as my old friend, Michael Longwa! But God wasn't finished answering all of my prayers yet. Pastor Ben heard that I was working at the SIL as a gardener and had been accepted at the school. He offered me and my friend, Severino, a two-bedroom apartment at the Juba Christian Center. To pay for the room, we were required to clean the church and maintain the landscaping of the grounds. All of my prayers were answered even more generously than I could have imagined or believed. God's hand in these provisions for me was even more evident because of the trials, disappointment, and doubt I had gone through in the two months since my arrival in Juba. God was not slow to provide for me, He only wanted me to learn to depend on Him. It was a lesson I would cling to from that time and to this very day.

The next few months were very productive for me. Michael and I often studied together, and my friend, Severino, and I worked together at the Juba Christian Center and the SIL. Both school and work were going very well for all of us. Sometimes we would join our new friend and mentor Pastor Ben as he conducted open-air revival meetings in the streets of Juba. Michael dreamed of becoming a minister himself, and I think he learned a lot from all the preaching that we heard in those days. In retrospect, I can see how Pastor Ben was making the most of the time that he had to teach us boys and to reach out to the citizens of Juba. He knew what was coming, and he was preparing us in the only way that he knew how.

It started at the end of 1981. The time had come for Michael and me to prepare for the Senior Secondary School entrance examinations. What should have been a time of academic testing for young students became a time of political maneuvering and discrimination. The Islamic regime based in Khartoum set out to undermine the educational system of the south portion of Sudan. Their goal was to impose Islamic rules in all the schools, starting with the Arabic language. The Addis-Ababa agreement of 1972 had specified that Southerners would be allowed to conduct their education in English. Khartoum broke this agreement with a unilateral decree that all students must be tested in the Arabic language—starting immediately. This was to be a prelude to the introduction of compulsory Koranic education. There was, however, a special "exemption" for those of us who had been taught English as our second language. In our villages, English had been the unifying language of the educated people, since there were so many different tribal tongues. For that reason, I sought out the exemption and was asked to sign exemption documents with several other students who found themselves in my situation.

When the examination time came, I was well prepared. I had studied hard and I had documents confirming my exemption from the Arabic language section. For one full week we were tested. I did my very best work in English, math, science, geography, and all the subjects that we had prepared for. I never even entered the room for Arabic testing, because I was exempt from that portion. But when the results of the examinations were in, I was shocked to find that I had failed to qualify for further schooling. Even though I had received near perfect scores on the tests that I had taken, my "exemption" was in reality an automatic failure in the Arabic language test. I was not being exempted from a required portion of the test; I was simply being exempted from a future in the educational system of the Sudan.

I was emboldened by anger at the injustice done to me and to others who had no Arabic skills. I sought out the local office of the regional minister of education; the results of my examination folded tightly in my fist.

"I would like to lodge a complaint," I said as respectfully as I could.

"What is the problem, boy?"

I thrust the examination results onto the desk of the bored administrator. "I was exempted from Arabic. Why am I being denied further schooling?" I demanded.

"Looks like you failed Arabic."

"I didn't even *take* Arabic! I was exempted! Just look at my other scores. I am more than qualified for admittance to Juba Day Secondary School."

The administrator glanced at my paperwork, his face blandly expressionless. "Well, my hands are tied here. All decisions of this nature are handled up in Khartoum. You'll have to take the matter to them."

Of course he knew I couldn't take any matter to Khartoum; and if I did, he knew they would do nothing. So he felt perfectly justified as he sent me away. I tried speaking to the headmaster of the Juba Day Secondary School as well, with similar results.

I was despondent. I understood then that I was being discriminated against and there was absolutely nothing that I could do about it. I couldn't understand why God would provide a way for me to live in Juba and then take away my very reason for living there. Something was terribly wrong. Even so, the lesson I had so recently learned about trusting God had not been forgotten. I went to my employers at the SIL and to Pastor Ben to ask for prayer and whatever assistance they could give me.

After the adults had prayed for me, Pastor Ben spoke frankly to me. "William, you might as well know that going to the Juba Day School will not be the answer to our prayers."

I must have looked puzzled, because he was quick to explain.

"Khartoum is tightening its grip on the public schools. Before long, they will have you boys memorizing the Koran. Your friend, Michael, speaks Arabic really well, but I predict he won't be welcome in the public schools for long, either. Oh, it's coming."

"What's coming?"

"The persecution. The changes. I hear the rumors." Pastor Ben used to be a military man, so he kept up on politics. "Khartoum is ready to make a move."

I didn't like the sound of that, so I tried to focus on the present. "What should I do now, then?"

Pastor Ben motioned for all the grown ups to gather around. "We will pray that William will be able to attend a Christian high school."

A Christian high school? Was it possible that Pastor Ben was unaware of the fact that a Christian high school did not even exist? Pastor Ben simply ignored the absurdity of his request and led all of us in fervent prayer that I would be admitted to the nonexistent Christian high school.

Irony of ironies, a Christian high school *did* exist, in Khartoum, of all places. The elite of the ruling Muslim class had been sending their children to the Comboni Catholic School in Khartoum for over fifty years. The Verona Fathers were a group of Italian men with excellent skills in the areas of science and mathematics. Their school was a preparatory school for medicine and engineering students, and it was the best in the country. Although the Islamic regime rejected the teachings of Christ upon which the school was founded, they used it to advance their own children. As it turned out, the Verona Fathers had a plan to open a brand new Comboni school in Juba to benefit the Christian children who had no other hope of education.

Testing took place immediately. The Comboni School did not accept the Sudan Intermediate School Certificate that I had so recently failed to obtain. Three hundred students took entrance exams, and Severino and I were among only eighty students to make the cut. That is how I was accepted into an elite high school without taking Arabic. God did not just protect my future by providing me with a Christian high school; He put me in the best school in the nation and provided me with tuition.

Work was hard at the Comboni School, but I enjoyed it thoroughly. It was great to have my friend and roommate, Severino, to study with. The next year, I was happy to see Michael Longwa at Comboni. He had quit the Juba Day School and decided that the Christian school was superior in every way. Another friend from our old village, Gosh, arrived in Juba to pursue his education as well. My group of friends was growing even as my education was flourishing. My cousin, the Reverend John, also ended up nearby, pastoring the African Inland Church. When we didn't attend the Juba Christian Center on Sundays, we enjoyed visiting my cousin John's church. It was a great time for me, but there was trouble on the horizon, and the clouds of a great storm were gathering fast.

During my high school years, the government of Jaafar Mohammed Nimieri was slowly dismantling the Addis-Ababa accord of 1972.onomy of the South was being dissolved step by step. Nimieri divided the South into three separate states in order to rend the tenuous unity between the tribes. The eight years of Southern sovereignty had done much to restore democracy and freedom in the South, but it had also created regional differences that were ripe for exploitation. The regions of Upper Nile, Bahr El Gazal, Jongolei, and Lake in the Southern Province were largely populated by the Dinka, Shilluk, and Nuer tribes. The two Equatorial Provinces (East and West) were home to the smaller tribes of the Madis, Acholis, Latukas, Zandes, Bari, Muru, Kakwas, Taposa, and others. The Equatorial Provinces were more affluent, and the regional governments were based there, in Juba. The separation of the South into the three provinces was very effective in stirring up old tribal rivalries.

The next step in Nimieri's plan was to move the ministry of education, natural resources, mining, and wildlife to central government control. To reinforce this power bid, he imposed military rule in the South and made a daring move to reshuffle the veteran army of the South Sudan who had fought in the Anya-Nya movement. The regime was poised to conscript all Southern boys born in the year 1964 and up to bolster the Islamic army and suppress any opposition to the new regime. Not unexpectedly, there was an uproar in the Southern army and in the Southern churches as freedoms were slowly stripped away.

There was a military mutiny at Bor, in Jongolei, where the former Anya-Nya army refused to surrender their guns and be re-billeted in the North. They fled into Ethiopia. The rebellion became "official" when the regime attacked their position in the Boma hills and killed eighteen soldiers.

Dr. John Garang, a professor of military academics at Khartoum University, was commissioned by President Nimieri to go to Bor and convince the rebels to lay down their arms and accept their new commission in the Northern Islamic army. Since Dr. Garang was himself a Southerner from Bor, it was believed that he would have the ability to influence the rebels. Instead, Dr. Garang took the opportunity to leave the Islamic regime forever. He joined the ranks of the rebels at Bor and founded the Sudan People's Liberation Army, or SPLA, of which he was the commander-in-chief.

Many Southerners from Equatoria were not happy with the formation of the SPLA, because Dr. Garang was a Dinka. Some Dinkas were filled with pride and believed that their tribe was destined for greatness. So squabbling between ethnic groups divided churches and provinces as Nimieri plotted to impose Shari'a law throughout the South.

People who were focused on petty racial differences failed to see the monstrous danger that would crush them all. Shari'a was the real danger. Churches bickering about local power didn't realize that they would soon have to apply for permission from the Islamic magistrate to congregate in their own buildings. They didn't understand that the Koran would be taught in the public schools and that the Bible would be banned. The churches would be shut down, and the missionary organizations would be forced to leave.

The Comboni Secondary School would shut down if it failed to change its curriculum in accordance with Shari'a law.

Tribes complaining about territorial issues failed to realize that their own young men would be conscripted into the Islamic army. Their enemies would be their own brothers and sisters. To be a good citizen, they would have to take the jihad oath. They didn't understand that land owned by non-Muslims would be confiscated, as Christians would not be allowed to own property unless they paid impossibly heavy taxes. They didn't realize that all of the natural resources in the South, including land, wildlife, water, and minerals, would be controlled by Islamic law and the tribes would have no rights over their own ancestral inheritance. Instead, they were riled up about which tribe ought to have the most power.

Jaafar Mohammed Nimieri had planned well, and the pieces were all falling into place. It was time to move.

CHAPTER NINE

Shari'a

Shari'a came suddenly, though not unexpectedly. One day we had some illusion of freedom and the next day we had none. It was almost funny how the new military leadership put a positive spin on the whole thing. They accused the Christian leaders from the free government of being "soft on crime." The Shari'a, they explained, would rid the people of the scourges of alcohol, prostitution, immorality, and all sorts of petty crimes. Christians, they insisted, were hypocrites who failed to enforce the moral code that they claimed to believe in. The fundamental principle of Shari'a is that freedom disturbs the moral order and fosters crimes against Islam. Therefore, freedom must be ended, along with the permissive Christian philosophy of government. And both were summarily eliminated.

It didn't take long before I began to see the results of Shari'a. There was a sudden rise in the number of amputees as petty thievery was met with machete justice. A man's hand for a loaf of bread seemed a price too high to pay. But who would dare to say so? The pain of the new law was felt by Muslims and Christians alike. Most of the Muslims were moderates who didn't particularly welcome the religious police into their lives. But they were cowed by the pressure to conform to the Shari'a, because the edicts came from their own mosques. At least the Christians had some reason to expect that some of the laws would not apply to them.

Through the early days of the Shari'a, Pastor Ben kept up his evangelistic efforts. He had developed a program of street preaching that he took to downtown Juba's business district. People from the congregation would accompany him to a street corner, singing songs in Arabic and attracting groups of onlookers. After the singing, Pastor Ben would deliver a gospel message and an invitation to attend the local church. It was a popular ministry, and I enjoyed going along and singing songs for the people who stopped to listen. But it soon became apparent that the military rulers were going to apply the law across the board, and we found that we were bound by the rules of the religious police just as our Muslim friends and neighbors were. We began to realize that we would be forced to protest the Shari'a if we hoped to retain some measure of our religious freedom. But protest was a dangerous thing.

Pastor Ben was an ex-Anya-Nya military man turned preacher. As such, he was under constant surveillance. His outspoken criticism of Shari'a and his defiant street preaching made him and the Juba Christian Center itself prime targets of the Islamic government. We were all considered to be enemies of the State. Pastor Ben and his family were in grave danger, and he knew it.

"Hello, is anyone here?" I was just stopping by to visit the pastor after school one day, but the church office seemed strangely quiet.

There was a shuffling noise and a "click" that came from the small storage room behind the desk, and then a nervous-looking Pastor Ben peeped out from behind the door.

"Oh, it's only you," he said, obviously relieved. He ducked back into the closet-sized room. "You can come out now."

Some of the men from the church emerged from their hiding spot in the storage room.

"We thought you might be someone else," one whispered.

I must have looked mystified, so Pastor Ben gestured for me to sit down with the rest of the group. "You're old enough to hear this, William," he said. "This is going to affect you and all the students your age. We were just listening to . . . the radio."

He didn't have to explain further. I knew that the men weren't listening to the latest music. Listening to the radio meant listening to forbidden message of the Sudan People's Liberation Army, or SPLA. The SPLA was a new entity that had arisen from and mutinied against the tired and divided Anya-Nya movement. While the Anya- Nya movement had called for Southern autonomy, the SPLA, headed by Dr. John Garang, wanted a unified Sudan under a secular, democratic government. This message appealed to many disaffected and marginalized Muslim groups as well as the majority of Christians and animists. For this reason, the SPLA was considered to be very dangerous and treasonous to the General Nimieri and his jihad forces. Just listening to news of the SPLA would be considered a criminal act.

Pastor Ben leaned back in his chair, folding and unfolding his hands as he shook his head. "It has really started."

What has started? I wondered to myself. I didn't dare ask.

"Where should we stand on this issue?" one of the church elders mused. "We need to pray for wisdom."

Pastor Ben frowned. "I hate this, but I know it has become necessary. When there is war, we can't remain neutral. We have to stand up for what is right."

War! So that was what the men were so nervous about.

"Perhaps the war won't touch Juba," another elder remarked. "We could just try to wait this thing out."

"The last war was seventeen years long! There's no way we are going to come out of this thing unscathed—or have you forgotten living in Uganda?"

In bits and pieces, I learned the story. Since 1972, when General Nimieri had signed the peace agreement at Addis Ababa, oil had been discovered in the southern district of Bentu. Nimieri had used the time of peace to arrange a division of the Southern territories, and then he had followed up with the unjust imposition of Islamic Law and martial rule. He had also signed the Egyptian-Sudan integration law that allowed Egyptian government to build the Jongolei Canal into the Southern territory. The canal would drain 90 % of the Nile water from the Sudd region into Egypt, with catastrophic results for the people and the ecosystem of that region. Of course, the Southern leadership had not been consulted in the matter. The "autonomy" of the South was nothing but a cruel joke. General Nimieri was exploiting ethnic hatred and religious extremism to make a grab for the resources of the South while oppressing or eliminating her people. It was bound to spark a resurgence of the civil war, and it finally had. The first shots of renewed war had just been fired. Dr. Garang's troops had just attacked some exploration and construction companies that were involved in digging the Jongolei Canal. The attacks were meant to be taken as a declaration that their activities were illegal and their assets would be targeted for destruction unless the construction was stopped. Finally there could be no doubt why Nimieri had been building oil refineries in the North. He was making his move to completely conquer the Africans of the Southern Sudan. The men of the church had been listening as the SPLA broadcast an invitation to join the resistance.

"Look, Sudan is for all the people, not just for the radical Muslim elite." Pastor Ben had obviously been thinking about this for a long time. "Here in Juba, we have people from different tribes and different religions. We were all happy to live together until the Shari'a came."

"Nimieri wants to stir up hate, and that's wrong."

"But he will do it if he can. When he calls for a jihad, many of the Muslims who support us now will feel it is their duty to side with him—even those who hate him and his Shari'a."

"I say we fight with the SPLA."

"No, that makes us just as bad as Nimieri is."

"Not if we are defending our right to freedom—and maybe even our right to stay alive if we choose to keep our faith."

My head was swimming as I listened to my elders discuss the breakout of the new civil war. Everything my grandfather had taught me about spiritual warfare told me that physical war was wrong. I had chosen to fight my battles with the Sword of the Spirit, the Word of God! But now it seemed like things were more complicated than I had originally thought. I knew that I would eventually be called upon to choose a weapon, just as I was called upon to choose at the time of my baptism. Would I choose the Bible when the time came? I wasn't so sure anymore.

One by one, the church elders left for home, but I stayed behind. I was troubled, and I had a few questions for Pastor Ben. The pastor looked pretty troubled himself.

"So, William, what are you thinking?"

I paused for a moment, because I was thinking so many different thoughts at once. "The Bible instructs us to obey the laws, doesn't it?"

Ben nodded.

"Doesn't all authority—even bad authority—have some sort of mandate from God that we have to respect?"

"Yes, that is true."

"Do you think it is right to fight against our own government?"

The pastor chuckled softly. "You ask some pretty tough questions for a kid." He rocked back in his chair again, looking beyond me. I hoped he could see some answers. "The issue of respect for the laws is easy to answer. We respect and obey all laws, even unfair ones, unless they go against God's law. Just like Paul, we shouldn't stop preaching the gospel just because Caesar tells us to. We can be good citizens and still protest laws that go against God's principles."

"But what about war?"

"We're all going to have a choice to make and soon. Believe me; I have been wrestling with this choice for a long time, because I saw it coming." Ben allowed his shoulders to slump just slightly, betraying the helplessness that he tried not to feel. "This war is about a lot of things, and people might respond different ways for different reasons."

I was not sure what he was getting at and I told him so.

"Well, you could say the war is about religious rights and persecution and that would be true. Nimieri's ilk is all about forcing extremist views down everybody's throats and killing off the infidels. But it wouldn't be the whole story. It's about greed, it's about power, and it's still about slavery. We can't forget that they are slavers, and they still think of us as slaves. The oil fields found in the South were just like a match in this huge powder keg."

"OK, so there are lots of reasons for the war. How does that influence the decision to fight?"

"People have their own reasons for fighting. Some people just plain enjoy the killing. The jihadists think they do Allah's will. Some Christians think that they are saving the faith from certain destruction. People will fight for their homes and their property, too. Sometimes it just comes down to kill or be killed."

"Are any of those reasons right?"

"I don't know. But sometimes fighting is just inevitable. All I can say now is that life under Nimieri has become intolerable. I don't think that those who choose to fight are doing wrong."

"Thanks, Pastor Ben." I stood to leave the darkening room that was the church office. "Sorry to keep you so late."

I left the church in a state of agitation. Pastor Ben hadn't really answered my questions; he had only managed to raise more pressing ones. He didn't condemn those who were leaving to join the SPLA; that much was certain. But it seemed like I was going to be wrestling with a very personal decision all by myself. There weren't really any black and white answers to count on. I didn't get much sleep that night.

The next day at high school, everyone seemed to have heard wildly different stories about the war. The Verona Fathers had to be stern to keep the classrooms orderly, although they were probably just as preoccupied with the news of the day as their students were. We tolerated lessons with restless anticipation of the lunch break in mind. At the bell, the gossip boiled over like an unwatched pot; knots of students gathered and scattered as each new bit of information was passed along. Since most of us were boys in our teens, it was immediately apparent what war would mean for our lives. My friends and I were sure that things would go from bad to worse.

"Did you hear?" Michael leaned close to spread the news. "The garrison for the GOS is recruiting boys for the jihad. They want everyone eighteen and up."

"No way!" Gosh's jaw was set in angry defiance. "I will never fight for Nimieri. I would join the SPLA!"

"Not so loud—you want somebody to hear you say that?"

"I don't care. They kill our people and force their ways on all of us. The SPLA is our only hope for freedom."

"Calm down," I said. "You are letting your emotions cloud your thinking. We are still students now, and our school is still open. We have time to think and plan."

"No, Gosh is right. We are all at the age of conscription now. They will try to force us to fight our own families. What choice is there but to join the other side? We have to do something!"

"I understand your point," I countered, "but rushing off to join the SPLA isn't necessarily the best thing for us to do."

"Well, do you have a better plan?"

"Not yet, but we can think of something." I felt the anger and the fear as much as any of my friends, but I still held the picture in my mind of the Bible and the axe resting on calm tree roots by the banks of the Kulo-jobi River. I could see my hand reaching out to choose the Bible—a sword of division, of judgment, and of reconciliation all at the same time. I still struggled to understand the meaning of that choice in a time of war.

"We do have a year before we graduate," Gosh conceded. "Maybe we should keep on studying and by then things might be better."

Michael had been sitting silently, which was unusual for him. I figured he was thinking hard. "I still want to go to seminary after high school," he mused. "I won't be able to do that here, and I sure won't be able to do that if I'm drafted into the jihad. Of course, I can't exactly get ordained by the SPLA, either."

Gosh smiled grimly. "We don't really have too many choices. I guess we should try to get our education while we can, though."

"Of course we should. But that doesn't mean we have to give up and do nothing!" I was starting to get an idea. I had been thinking of my discussion with Pastor Ben. I felt confident that Paul's example of civil disobedience in the New Testament provided a course of action that would be both peaceful and just. We could arrange a protest!

"Listen, guys," I began. "We have a whole school full of kids our own age. If we all get together to protest the Islamic Law, what can they do? It would look bad for them if they publicly attacked a group of peaceful teenagers."

Michael's eyes narrowed. "I wouldn't be too sure of that, William. I heard that the GOS troops attacked another high school protest. They might choose to make an example of us."

"Michael is right. They think that anyone who disagrees with them is in league with the SPLA."

"That is pretty paranoid, don't you think?"

"Maybe so. Or maybe it's just an excuse to shut people up."

"Well, I still think we should try something. The Shari'a is illegal, and it goes against the treaty. We can protest on the grounds that Nimieri should not break his own agreement. If he stops the Shari'a, maybe this war can be over very soon."

"We can only hope and pray that they will listen."

For the next several months, I worked together with some other students to arrange some peaceful protests. Our goal was simply to state our request that religious autonomy and self-governance ought to be restored in compliance with the 1972 treaty. It was an opinion that enjoyed broad support across religious lines. Even as we worked out our political agendas, we redoubled our efforts to complete high school in a hurry. We knew that if the Verona Fathers had to leave Sudan, we would be out of luck. We were determined to sit for our final exams while we still could. It was exhausting work, but times were desperate. Every day saw the ranks of jihad soldiers swell, often with forcible conscription. Every day also saw the disappearance of adults that we knew. We didn't dare ask where they were going, because it was dangerous for us to be aware of anyone who would join the resistance.

One afternoon in 1984, Michael, Gosh, and I organized what was to be our last peaceful protest, although we didn't know it at the time. The war had been going on for nearly a year, and the situation in Juba was becoming increasingly uncomfortable for us. As usual, we gathered together to pray. We asked God to grant us the freedom to worship Him and the freedom to speak the gospel message. God heard that prayer and He showed me the freedom that I possessed already—just not in the way I had expected.

A large group of students armed with signs and slogans streamed out into the streets of Juba on that day. The mood was peaceful and perhaps a bit naive in its hopefulness. As hundreds of young people filled the downtown area, onlookers glanced, and then averted their eyes as if to hide any treasonous thought that may have arisen in their hearts. Only the sun dared to look boldly down on us, and we were warmed by its apparent approval.

We hadn't been out long when the chants of protest died down to a scattered few and finally silence. The GOS military forces were headed our way.

As soon as we saw the armed men in their dusty fatigues, we knew we were in trouble. I didn't turn around, but I could hear the rapid footfalls of kids running away as the slow crunch of boots approached. One of the ranking officers stepped forward, his face stern and without compassion.

"Who is in charge here?" he barked.

His words sent another flurry of students running in all directions. Apparently, he wasn't interested in protesters who ran away, because the soldiers stood their ground.

"I am," I said.

Only then did I dare to look around me. I found that I was all alone, except for my friends Gosh and Michael, who stood by me. The commander gestured to a group of soldiers, and I felt a pair of hands grab my arms from behind. I was jerked back with a rough tug.

"You are all under arrest."

I made brief eye contact with Gosh and then Michael as we were taken away. I was relieved to see defiance in their gaze instead of defeat. There was not yet time for fear, though that would come soon.

We rode separately back to the ghost house, a place where prisoners were kept for crimes of conscience. It was a simple cinderblock building, nondescript in every way. I tried to read the expressions of my captors, hoping to glean some insight into my fate at their hands. I was not rewarded. Faces revealed boredom, sly amusement, or thinly disguised disdain. My enemy had come for me, and I didn't have an axe to wield. I did, however, have a Bible in my pocket. If they took that away, I had another copy in my heart. It was then that I began to have a glimmer of understanding of my role in this conflict. I didn't have to choose my weapon—God had chosen it for me.

The torture began right away. I was led into a dark room that smelled of damp uncleanness and cigarette smoke. The blow to my face knocked me to my hands and knees.

"You!" I felt a fist grab at my shirt, pulling me up to a kneeling position. "What do you know about the SPLA?"

I knew what the SPLA was and what their goals were, but that was about all. "I don't know anything about the SPLA," I replied.

"Liar!" The word struck me just as my face received another forceful blow. "Who are the SPLA operatives in Juba?"

I tasted blood as I opened my mouth to reply. "I'm not involved with the SPLA. I am a peaceful student, demonstrating in favor of the peace agreement." It was the truth, and I had nothing else to say.

The commanding officer gave a grunt of disgust as he waved to his men. "Take care of him," he said. Then he turned to me and lowered his voice menacingly. "Whatever you know, we'll find out." With that, he left the small cell.

For the soldiers, the fun was just beginning. I guessed that their job was to break my will, a task that they would apparently relish. They were practically gleeful as they measured and cut strips of cable. It was time for a beating.

They stripped me and humiliated me as the blows fell like rain on my exposed skin. I steeled myself against the searing pain in my body, but it was more difficult to steel my soul against the insults and intimidation. Silently, I recited scripture to try to keep my own feelings of hatred at bay. My mind felt numb, and I struggled to grasp some shred of the gospel to carry me through.

"How can you stand to be a Jewish dog?" one soldier kicked me as if to emphasize my inferiority. "Do you enjoy being a *kafir* pig?" The soldiers laughed and brought down the cable again and again.

Suddenly, the abuse stopped. One of the soldiers leaned forward, exhaling the smoky contents of his lungs into my face. "You can make the beating stop," he said. "It is very easy. Only speak *Shahada*. Then you will be one of us. You will join jihad."

They wanted me to confess Islam. Of course, that was something I could never do. If I did, not only would I betray my own faith and conscience, but I would also be obliged to kill my own people and burn down their villages. I would just have to accept the torture.

"Jesus said, 'I am the Way, the Truth, and the Life . . . no one comes to the Father except through Me. He that believes in Me, though he were dead, yet shall he live.'"[11] I tried to reply to their demands with scripture. I knew that in the face of brutality, I was being called upon to be a witness for my faith.

Dear Lord, I prayed, *don't leave me. Tell me what to say.*

After the soldiers tired of their sport, they left me alone in the darkness. I stretched my body out on the floor, feeling the gritty coolness of dirty cement against my wounds. I was too exhausted to remember any more.

I was awakened with a sharp kick in my flank. It was still dark in the little room, and I was terribly disoriented. I couldn't tell if it was day or night in the midst of the gloom. I did know, however, that it was time for my daily torture.

This time, it was time to raise the stakes. The soldiers twisted long strips of wire between my fingers as I watched with dull detachment. I didn't have the energy to feel horrified or outraged as they swung the loose ends of the cable around a beam in the ceiling. With a jarring snap, one of the soldiers pulled the cable taut. My arms shot upwards, pulling my body up by the fingers. Intense nausea swept over me as fingers dislocated and a bone snapped from the unnatural weight it was suddenly forced to bear. As I dangled from cable-strangled fingers, the guards again began to whip me. Once again the soldiers insisted that the pain would stop as soon as I would recite *Shahada*. Again, I refused.

I recited scripture over and over again. Psalm 23, John 3:16, the Beatitudes . . . when presence of mind allowed, I managed to explain snatches of the gospel message. *Love your enemies . . . pray for those who persecute you . . .* I had to fight to speak those words. But still the punishment came.

I specifically recall that the story of Shadrach, Meshach, and Abednigo came to my mind many times throughout my ordeal. I imagined the three young men standing in the fiery furnace because of their stand for God. They didn't know if they would survive the flames. They believed that God was able to deliver them, but they understood that He might not choose to do so. Even so, they made it known to the king that they would never deny their God. They simply could not bow down to Nebuchadnezzar's golden image. If I recited the words of the *Shahada*, I would become a Muslim. That act would relieve my body from the torture. My will was weakening.

I tried to picture myself in the fiery furnace. The burning pain of buffalo hide whips licked against my skin like flame. Then I remembered that there was a fourth person in the furnace that day, and the fourth man was in appearance like the Son of God. I came to understand that my only weapon was a spiritual one, and that I was using it to fight for my very soul. How could I fear men who could destroy my body rather than God, who could destroy my eternal soul? I would not recite *Shahada*.

I couldn't say how long I remained in the ghost house, not exactly anyway. But eventually, the abuses stopped. They were satisfied that I really didn't know anything useful. It was obvious that I was not a danger to their regime.

As I waited for my release, I recalled the prayer that I had prayed with my three friends just before our capture and imprisonment. We had prayed earnestly that God would grant us the freedom to worship Him. In that moment, I understood that God had answered my prayer. I was free to worship now, and I always had been. Now I knew that nothing could force me to do otherwise—not even death.

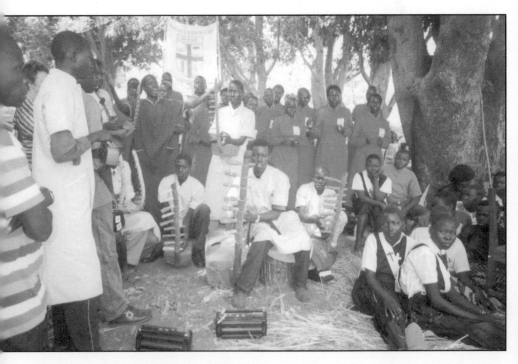

The Evangelical Choirs in Adumani refugee camp worship together with handmade harps. Courtesy Rev. Enoka Dumo.

William graduates from NJIT in 1992. Courtesy William Levi.

The Levi family reunion after 18 years of exile, Kiriadongo refugee camp, Uganda, 2003. Courtesy of Joseph Levi, for ON Missions.

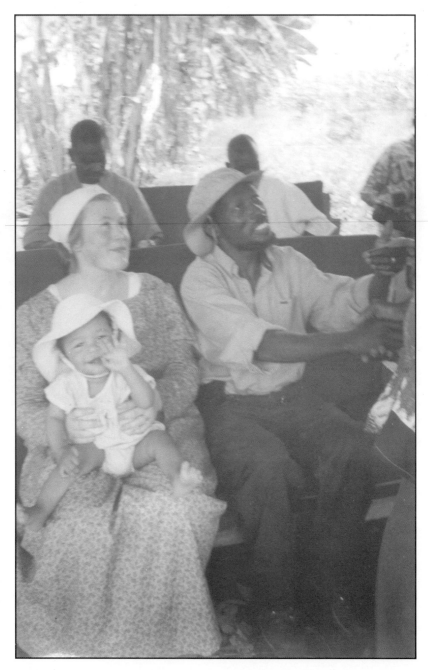

William, Hannah, and Abijah Levi greet refugees in Kiriadongo, Uganda, 2003. Courtesy Joseph Levi, for ON Missions.

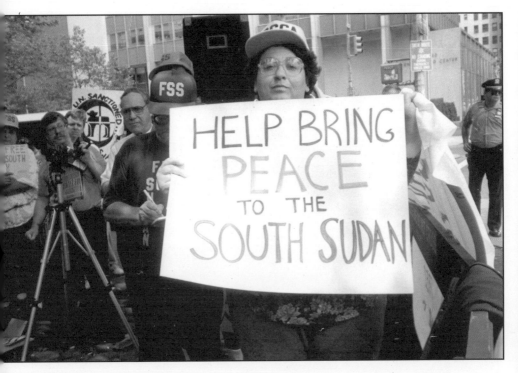

Protestors demonstrate for peace in the Sudan in front of the UN building in
New York City, July 31, 1993. Courtesy ON Missions.

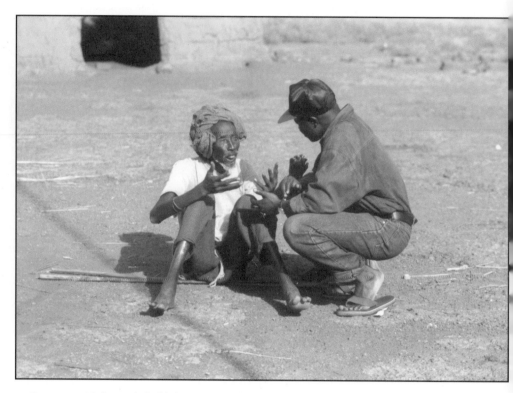

Operation Nehemiah field director Michael Longwa reaches out to help a blind man in Tonj, New Sudan. Courtesy ON Missions.

Islamic jihad soldiers captured by the SPLA, Tonj, New Sudan. They are listening to Rev. Michael Longwa pray for them. Courtesy ON Missions.

Michael, Palma, and David Longwa family photo. Michael is field director of Operation Nehemiah Missions based in Kampala, Uganda.
Courtesy ON Missions.

The Reverend Michael Longwa preaches to over 70,000 people in Madras, India.
Courtesy Beth Israel Messianic Congregation/ON Missions.

From left to right: William Levi, Dr. John Garang, Steven Wondu, and Paul Liben, Arlington, VA, 1995. Courtesy ON Missions.

The Reverend John, his wife Sue, and their children. Reverend John is the
Director of the Operation Nehemiah Internet Café in Kampala, Uganda.
Courtesy of Reverend John.

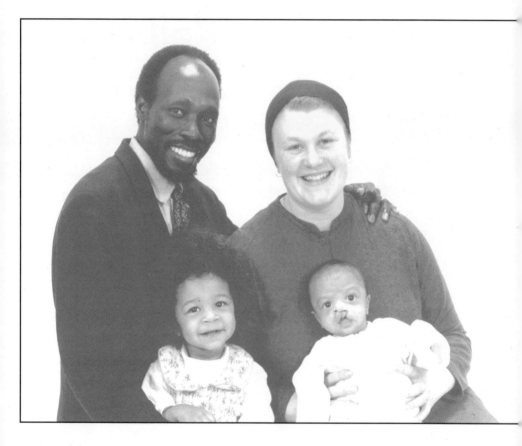

The Levi Family
(William, Hannah, and two children)

CHAPTER TEN

Close Call in Kapoeta

The white haze of the noontime sun was painfully bright to eyes that had become accustomed to the constant gloom of the prison. I stood for a moment, disoriented by the sights and sounds of the city. How long had I been locked up? It couldn't have been more than a couple of weeks, but it seemed like time had somehow been suspended. I felt like I was sleepwalking, unsure if I was really headed back to my Juba apartment. The dust was real enough, and the spicy smells from the marketplace were just as I had remembered. It wasn't until my hand stretched out to open the door to my own room that I realized I was definitely awake. A stabbing pain shot through my hand and up my wrist as my broken and swollen fingers fumbled with the latch. I winced and struggled to push open the door with my forearms instead. It would be some time before I could be back at work attending to the landscaping or holding a pencil at the high school.

"William, thank God you're OK!" I recognized Michael's voice immediately. "I heard the news that they let you go. Thank God!"

My old friend looked bruised and disheveled, but his broad shoulders were unbent and his smile was as genuine as ever. "They let me out this morning, too."

"Can you believe this, Michael?"

"They want to make an example of us. They want everybody to be afraid to speak up; it doesn't matter if you are just a student. Nobody can disagree with the Shari'a law."

"They beat me in there. They wanted me to become a Muslim and join their jihad."

"You didn't give in, did you?"

"Of course not! I could never deny my faith!"

"Me neither. These guys just don't take 'no' for an answer. It was like the inquisition in there for me. They kept on telling me that I had to give them information about the SPLA."

"I'm sure they knew we weren't SPLA members. Otherwise, they wouldn't have let us go. But to be honest, I'm still scared. Do you think they can force us to join the Islamic army?"

"They can kill us if we refuse, that's for sure."

"I would rather die than kill one of my own brothers."

"Me too. There is no way I would agree to fight my own people. I would die first."

"That may be what they have in mind."

"So what do we do now, join the SPLA?"

The idea was tempting, but I shook my head. Many Christians had already gone off to fight in the guerrilla-style warfare that was being waged against the military regime, but I felt a different call. "We could, but I don't think that is what God wants for me. I don't condemn those who fight, but I really believe that I must love my enemy. The Sword of the Spirit has got to be my weapon."

"Well, we can't stay here anymore, that's for sure. The school is going to be shut down, and they'll just round us up and try to force us to fight."

"You're right. We have to get out of here while we can. Maybe I should go back to Corom."

"That is just another dead end for you, there's no way you could ever finish your education if you go back to your village. Same for me."

I thought for a while. The heat of the day was making my swollen hands throb. I had to go lie down in my own bed and rest. But an idea had come to my mind.

"Michael, why don't you and Gosh come over tonight? I think I have a plan."

I was sore and exhausted, and it felt good to be back in my apartment after the torture and humiliation of the prison house. Gingerly, I rinsed my wounds with cold water and straightened out my bent fingers the best that I could. I changed out of my dusty and torn clothing and sank down onto my cot. I must have slept through the entire day, because the next thing I remember was a knock on the door. My head pounded and my vision blurred as I stood up to answer. I could barely walk, because my whole body was stiff as a board. It was Michael and Gosh, and they had brought some food.

"Come on in."

"Thought you could use some supper," Gosh offered.

"Thanks."

My stomach was sour from being empty for so long. The pain in my hands lent an edge of nausea to the discomfort. We gave thanks for God's mercy in letting us go free, and then we ate in silence. We all felt discouraged because the prospects for our future just didn't look too good at that moment. But at least we were alive and free—for now.

"So William, what is your plan?"

"If you have any brilliant ideas, we're with you."

"Well, we already know that we cannot complete our education here."

Gosh and Michael nodded their agreement.

"What use are we without education? Our people will have no one to lead them."

"No one but the military," Michael added.

"That's right. The military leaders are educated, but they will get old or maybe get killed. What will we do when none of us from the South has an education?"

Gosh shook his head. "Nothing, I guess."

"We will be farmers or soldiers—nothing more. There is no way we can help our people that way."

"We will just be forced to live under the Shari'a law." Michael smiled grimly. "That hasn't worked out well so far."

"That's for sure," I agreed. "If we want to preserve our way of life, our faith, and our people, we have only one choice. We have to get out of the country and get an education."

There was silence for a moment as we all considered the implications of my plan. It was definitely risky, but if it was successful, the benefit would be great.

"Where do you think we should go?" Gosh wondered.

"Kenya. I've already considered a route."

Michael Longwa smiled. "I have a brother in Kenya! Mark left for Kenya a year ago to get his pastoral degree, and we can join him up there. Maybe we can all get a fresh start there, and Mark will help us adjust with life in Nairobi. I think that would be a great idea!"

Gosh looked a bit more serious. "You know, William, the SPLA has camps across the Kenyan border. How would it look, three guys like us crossing into Kenya?"

"I know. It would look like we were going to join the SPLA." That was the one concern I hadn't mentioned.

"If they catch us . . ."

"It is a risk we have to take." I was determined to make our escape work. "We have to have a story to tell in case we get captured. We can tell them that we are headed to visit your brother."

"Do you think they'll buy that?"

"Usually they separate prisoners for interrogation. If we rehearse our story ahead of time, our stories will all match. But that is plan B. Plan A is that we don't get caught."

Gosh was looking more and more doubtful. "I prefer plan A," he commented.

"Yeah, me too." Michael laughed in spite of himself. He was not the type to worry.

"What route do you think is best?" Gosh asked.

"Well, the entire border is pretty well patrolled, so we would arouse less suspicion if we head through a border town. If we were SPLA, we wouldn't travel through the towns; it would be too obvious. I think we should go to Kapoeta. From there, we could hire transportation to the Kenyan interior."

"Sounds reasonable," Michael mused. "It would be easier than going across the border on foot. I've saved up some money to bring, and whatever is left over I could use for tuition at the seminary."

"I'm in," Gosh agreed. "I can't think of a better idea. We sure can't go to Uganda these days with all the random killings going on."

"Then it's decided. We'll leave for Kenya as soon as we can take care of business here in Juba."

We wasted no time in taking care of loose ends. We said our good-byes to good friends we had come to know. Our friend, Pastor Ben, and his family had already left town. Ben planned to join the SPLA in the capacity of a military chaplain. Many students were headed back to their hometowns. As it turned out, there wasn't much left to leave behind. Our school was closing down.

Soon I found myself back in Corom, explaining to my parents that I would be leaving the country. The tensions of Shari'a were already being felt even in our remote village; my parents knew that open warfare could not be far behind. To them, this knowledge was just another fact of life. My parents were very realistic, and they had learned to deal with oppression and war in a practical, no-nonsense way. It was just a matter of survival for us. Our lives had been lived on the move as refugees for so long that my flight to Kenya to finish school didn't seem like anything new to my family. The fact that my trip would be risky and dangerous was acknowledged, but not dwelt upon. Everyone agreed that my idea was a good one, and my family supported my decision fully.

Our trip to Kapoeta was relatively uneventful. We purchased seats in a crowded, open-topped Austin lorry, carrying sheep, grain, and farmers to Kapoeta. We brought next to nothing in the way of personal belongings, but we had some cash (280 Sudanese pounds) and our Bibles with us. We put Michael Longwa in charge of the money since he had been working as a cashier in Juba. I was assigned the responsibility of decision-making and leadership, while Gosh was given the responsibility of monitoring trip logistics. When we arrived in the small border town, we had suffered nothing worse than a bumpy ride.

One of my uncles, Abednego Vuni, was a pastor in Kapoeta. He was out of town, but his youngest daughter, Naima, happened to be visiting when we arrived in Kapoeta that night. She quietly welcomed us into the house, but she was curious. She couldn't help wondering why we were in Kapoeta. Since it was vacation time for the local schools, Naima asked us if her father had commissioned us to come and serve in the church. Even though she was my cousin, I decided not to reveal the full scope of our plans. I just told her that we wanted to travel to Kenya to see Michael's brother, Mark. She seemed content with my explanation and did not press for further details. The rest of the evening was spent in pleasant company.

When we left my uncle's home the following morning, we put our heads together, planning the best way to make our next move. We knew that the difficult part of the journey was yet to come. Even though we were a mere stone's throw from Kenya, getting across the border would be tricky.

"This place is crawling with GOS military," Michael whispered.

It was true. Dusty olive green lorries prowled the streets, and soldiers with AK-47s slung across their shoulders seemed to be everywhere.

"You're right," Gosh agreed. "We're going to have to be extra careful what we say and who we talk to."

"Let's go over our story again, in case we're questioned," I suggested.

We rehearsed the story one more time. *We are heading out to visit Michael's brother in Kenya. We plan to come back soon. We don't know anything about the SPLA, and Shari'a law doesn't matter much to us. We just want to visit with family and friends abroad.*

"OK, what do we do now?"

"We need to hire a lorry to take us in to Kenya. We have to act casual and be careful what we say."

"Just ignore the soldiers; act like you don't care about them."

This, of course, was easier said than done. We kept together, chatting casually, but still feeling pretty nervous. Anyone might be a spy, and although there was a constant stream of travelers through Kapoeta, we knew that we could easily arouse suspicion. We purchased lunch at a crowded stall and kept our ears open for possible contacts. With a few discreet inquiries, we soon found what we were looking for.

Michael was the outgoing one; he was a smooth talker who always seemed to gain a good reception with people. We let him do the bargaining while we hung back, trying to blend into the crowd. He found someone who was willing to sell us berths on a lorry bound for Kenya. It was leaving town that afternoon. We were all pretty relieved that things were going so smoothly. If things continued to go well, we figured to be in Kenya by nightfall.

That afternoon, we headed downtown to catch our ride. *So far, so good.*

We didn't notice the gradual movement of men in olive drab until we were surrounded. With the cold steel of GOS assault rifles pressed against our backs, we were led away. The lorry would be leaving without us.

I can hardly recall our trip to the military barracks. I was numb with dread, because I knew that we had been branded as SPLA operatives. Too late, I realized that they would never believe a word we would say, no matter how similar our stories sounded. If they thought we were planning to join the SPLA, as they obviously did, we were lost. Being an SPLA member, of course, was a capitol offense. By the way, they didn't care much if they were wrong. If we weren't SPLA members, they wouldn't feel any remorse from our deaths. Our lives were utterly unimportant to them, whether we were telling the truth or not. A few more dead Christians could only be a good thing in their way of thinking, especially if the dead Christians were young males who had the potential to lead or fight. It was then that I understood that Michael, Gosh, and I were dead men.

It's funny what you think about when you know you are marked for death. Perversely, I was filled with regret that I would not be able to go to school. When you are seventeen, you have your whole life ahead of you; but for me, the desire to finish school was the first thing that came to my mind. Michael and Gosh were silent—I wondered what they were thinking. From their somber expressions, I knew that they were fully aware of the seriousness of our situation.

As expected, the three of us were separated for interrogation. If we had any hope at all, it was for all of us to stick to the story that we had planned. If any of us admitted that we planned to leave Sudan permanently, it would be a death sentence. Leaving the country was tantamount to siding with the SPLA. Even so, there was little hope that we would be believed, no matter what we said.

I was led into a small room without windows. It was empty except for a couple of folding chairs and a light fixture. I was directed to one of the chairs with a shove. The chair tipped back with a lurch as I sat down hard. My thoughts finally cleared enough for me to breathe out a prayer. *Lord, help me.* It was all I could manage under the circumstances, but God understands the inaudible cries of our spirit and knows what we would ask even before we can form the thoughts in our consciousness.

My thoughts were jolted into focus with a sharp blow to my face. An army officer was bending over me, threatening me with his gun.

"Why do you join the SPLA?"

It was not a question I could really answer. I wasn't joining the SPLA, but they would not believe that. I remained silent.

"Answer me! Who are you planning to meet when you join the SPLA?" The officer who questioned me narrowed his eyes, his face betraying no sign of compassion.

"I am not joining the SPLA. I am a high school student, but my school was closed down. My friends and I were planning to visit family in Kenya. That's all."

The officer didn't like my answer. I felt another blow land on my cheek. "I want names of your SPLA contacts! Tell me who supports the SPLA and maybe you will live!"

I could answer honestly, but it was no use. "I don't have SPLA contacts. I don't know anything."

Of course, I knew many people who supported the SPLA ideologically—that would include most Southerners. But he probably already knew that.

"*Kafir*! You infidel traitor." The officer's face expressed his unfeigned disdain. "You and your friends will go to Juba tonight. There you will be tried as traitors. The penalty is death."

My interrogator turned on his heel and left me alone in the little room, guarded by an armed soldier. Although I had already imagined the worst, it was very unsettling to have my fears confirmed. I was going to be tried for treason as an SPLA operative. The trial would be a mere formality, and I would be executed, along with my two best friends. While I was alone in my cell, I had a little time to gather my thoughts and pray. I prayed for myself, my friends, and my family. I prayed for my people and my country. I prayed that I wouldn't be tortured again.

As I despaired of any escape from execution, my prayers seemed to bounce off of the ceiling and fall flat on the dirty cement floor. But I knew that God could really hear, and some hope remained for me.

That evening, my friends and I were herded onto a lorry as prisoners. Several soldiers accompanied us aboard, bound for Juba. There, we would be recognized as the student leaders who had protested Shari'a, which would certainly not help our case in our trial for treason. Our only hope for life would be conversion to Islam and a pledge of service to the jihad, but for us death would be the preferred option. We allowed our eyes to meet briefly, communicating volumes before we looked down again. We didn't dare speak to one another in the presence of our captors. I could see

Michael's lips moving slightly, and I knew that he was praying silently. I closed my eyes and joined in, agreeing in wordless prayer. The dusk was passing to darkness as the lorry jolted forward on the road to Juba.

Gradually, the faces of my friends faded to outlines and then shadows as the light waned. I could hear the shuffling of feet as soldiers and prisoners shifted positions in the hard seats, and I could see the occasional flare of red when one of the soldiers took a drag on his cigarette. Although I was exhausted, there was no way to rest. My mind continued to form prayers, sometimes coherent and sometimes not. Occasionally, rough spots on the road would jolt painfully up my spine as the lorry's wheels dipped and bounced. The constant grating noise from the old diesel engine made my head ache and my ears ring.

I can't say how long we had been traveling that way, perhaps three or four hours, when the lorry's engine noises increased in pitch from a grate to a whine. I could feel a new vibration shake the old truck so that my teeth rattled. Over the din, I could hear the soldiers complaining to one another in Arabic. Then, without warning, the engine shuddered and died. The lorry ground to a halt along the rough path that served for a road. It was a moonless night, black as pitch. There was cursing and more shuffling of feet as the soldiers pulled on the parking brake and lifted the hood. I heard the driver call to the cigarette-smoking soldier, something about a light. Inexplicably, the soldiers who had been guarding us hopped off of the lorry and went around to the front of the vehicle to help inspect the engine. Miraculously, we were left unguarded for a moment.

We needed no further prompting to know that this was our chance to survive. Without a word, we jumped from the back of the lorry and started to run blind into the darkness. In the few seconds it took for the soldiers to register the sound of our feet hitting the ground, we had already made some distance. There was shouting and confusion among the soldiers, and a few seconds later we heard reports from assault rifles. Although the shots were fired in our general direction, there was no way the soldiers could see and aim accurately in the blackness. We were all fast runners, used to running through the wilderness. Raw fear lent us speed and sharpened our senses as we ran. I could hear my friends nearby, crashing through the underbrush, and I used the sound to guide me.

In the back of my mind it registered that the shouts of the soldiers were increasingly distant. I knew they were giving chase, but they were running blind, too. We had a head start, and we were running for our lives—without guns and gear to weigh us down. I can't say how long the soldiers chased us, but I know we kept running long after they had turned back. They were probably more concerned about the inconvenience of spending the night in the middle of nowhere with a broken lorry. It would be a long walk for them in the morning if they couldn't repair it.

We ran until we thought our lungs would explode from exertion, and then we gradually slowed to a walk before daring to stop.

"Where are we?" I managed, scarcely able to spare the breath to speak. We had come to a clearing, and there were only a few landmarks, revealing themselves as dark upon dark in the starlight. I guessed that we had been running for a few miles.

"I know," Michael panted. "We are only a few more miles from the town of Torit."

"You can lead us?" Gosh asked.

"Yes, my mother's house isn't far."

"Thank God."

"Amen to that. Let's go."

We traveled quickly and carefully, sticking close behind Michael. Although we had run for several miles, we didn't feel tired. The buzz of adrenaline kept us hyper-alert as we headed back, escaping certain death. Time seemed suspended as we traveled, but it couldn't have been too long before we reached Michael's mother's house. The three of us knocked on the door to awaken Michael's mother, because it was the middle of the night.

Michael's older brother, Wilson, opened the door. We saw that the house was lit, and it was full of people crying and praying, with their faces to the floor. Michael's relatives looked up, and from their expressions it seemed as if they had just seen a ghost—or more correctly, three ghosts.

"Michael!" His mother ran to embrace him, tears streaming down her face. She held him close and sobbed.

"Praise God!" someone exclaimed. "It's them! They're alive!"

Spontaneous shouts of praise rose up from the impromptu prayer meeting. Their prayers had just been answered.

"We heard word from Kapoeta," one of the people explained. "It was just rumors. They said you were captured. We were told that you had probably already been executed. We were all here praying for you until we could hear more news."

"God spared us," I replied. "We were about to be executed."

The people gathered around us as we recounted the amazing events of the day. It could not have been coincidental that a houseful of people had been interceding for us at the very moment that the lorry's engine died. God had brought the truck to a stop at the darkest hour of the night, within running distance of that very house. The added miracle of being abandoned by the soldiers if ever so briefly to check the engine only confirmed that God had been protecting us. The gathering of tears and intercession was immediately transformed into a time of thanksgiving and relief.

The flood of emotions that washed over us diffused the tension that had kept us going for so long. When the tears subsided, we were drained and exhausted. Our sleep that night was deep.

When we awakened the next morning, Michael's mother provided us with breakfast. Although she was grateful that her son was still alive, it was obvious that she was angry. After we had eaten, she spoke her mind.

"William," she said sternly, "I hold you responsible for this reckless idea. My son was nearly killed."

I couldn't blame Mrs. Longwa for feeling upset. Her husband, a pastor, had been murdered by jihad forces two years after Michael was born. Michael was her baby boy, and she couldn't bear the thought that the same fate might befall him.

"I'm sorry," was all I could say in reply.

In truth, I was sorry we had been caught, but I still believed that escape was our only viable option. There were many who planned to just maintain the peace and get by, hoping to live through the troubles unmolested. Mrs. Longwa was hoping to do just that. From past experience, I thought that her particular mindset was dangerously naïve. It was like sitting in the middle of a lion's den, hoping the beasts weren't too hungry. Eventually, you will get eaten. Similarly, everyone in the South of Sudan would discover that the time to take defensive action was past, and they would be running for their lives again. Personally, I planned to be out of the country before I was forced to run, kill, or be killed.

Gosh and I thanked Mrs. Longwa, and said goodbye to Michael. Michael's mother forbade him from trying to escape again. He was planning to lay low for a while and see what would happen. He respected his mother's wishes and trusted that God would provide a way for him to attend seminary some day in the future. We wished them the best and headed back to Corom.

After a couple days with my family, Gosh and I also parted company. He went to Moli where his family was staying at the time. Word of our ordeal had traveled quickly, so my parents were not surprised to see me. My father came out to welcome me, draping his arm around my shoulders.

"I'm sorry you didn't make it to Kenya," he said. "The Lord has other plans for you this time."

"I'm not sure what to do," I admitted.

"You can start by thanking God for protecting you," he said with a grin. "I'm not afraid for you, because nothing will happen to you unless God permits it. I believe that with all of my heart. That's how I keep going in times like this."

"Believe me," I replied, "I'm learning to understand that more each day. But how do I know what God has planned for me? I have so many decisions to make."

Father looked sober. "That isn't easy, you're right. Sometimes you just have to pray and then make the best decision that you can. I think God honors that."

I paused for a moment. "I've been thinking—I feel like if I try to escape again, it will have to be alone. I can't take the responsibility for the lives of my friends."

"That sounds reasonable. Besides, it may be easier to escape if you go alone. You would be less likely to be noticed."

"But what should I do now? I need your advice."

Father nodded. "You have had a very close call. I can see why you feel uncertain."

He thought for a moment. "I will ask your grandfather and your uncle to come and talk this through with us. God uses the wise counsel of men when decisions are tough. I think they can help you to make the right decision."

"Thanks, Abba."

I felt relieved. I was grateful that my father was willing to help me despite the difficulty instead of reacting emotionally like Michael's mother had. I knew I could count on him and Grandfather to give me their best advice.

As we walked into my parents' house, I relished the welcome I received. For one day, I would enjoy the comfort of my family once again. Their familiar faces were so precious to me, especially after having come so close to losing my earthly life. There would be time enough for difficult decisions in the morning.

CHAPTER ELEVEN

The Eye of the Enemy

W hen morning came, my family gathered as promised to help me decide what to do next. We reviewed my options systematically, and the first decision that I felt absolutely certain about was that I needed to complete my education if I ever hoped to really help my family and my nation. With that decided, it was immediately clear that I would have to leave the Sudan, because all of the educational opportunities in my native country had been closed to me. It was also evident that I could only travel to a country adjoining my own without due process from the authorities—and I was quite sure they wouldn't grant me leave to travel abroad. That left me with an increasingly limited set of options.

"What about Kenya?" I looked around the room, my eyes resting on the concerned faces of my uncle, my father, and my grandfather in turn.

Their expressions were grave as they considered that option. We had already determined that I could not head for exile in

Uganda. Ever since the fall of Idi Amin Dada, Uganda had become a bloody killing field. With rampant and random violence, no one could be safe in Uganda any more. Kenya, however, was relatively stable politically. But would it be possible for me to escape through another border town like Kapoeta?

"Out of the question," my father replied.

"I have to agree with Ajjugo," my uncle added. "The entire Kenyan border is crawling with GOS military. Everyone knows that the SPLA uses Kenya and Ethiopia for their bases, and Kapoeta is a border town adjacent to both countries. That gives the GOS surveillance reason for very high alert in that whole area. If they think you are crossing to join up with the opposition . . ."

"Yeah, I found out the hard way. I'll be blessed if all they do is kill me."

Truth be told, I already knew that Kenya was not a viable plan. After my capture at Kapoeta, it was obvious that the military had stepped up security there to the extent that crossing into Kenya was a fool's errand. The border routes were carefully guarded because they expected boys like me to head that way. *They expected it.*

"What *don't* they expect?" I mused.

"What do you mean?"

"The GOS. What *don't* they expect me to do?" I was thinking of a plan, and it was just crazy enough that it made my heart race. I smiled grimly. "They won't expect me to walk through the very eye of my enemy."

My father sought my gaze and found it. He knew I was thinking of something we hadn't discussed before. "What is your plan?"

I paused for a moment. "It isn't quite a plan yet, but I do have an idea. Where are the military units stationed?"

Grandfather leaned forward. "They're all over the place!"

Father smiled. "They're all over *South* Sudan . . ." He was beginning to see where I was going with this.

"How many people head to Khartoum to join the SPLA?"

"Khartoum!" Grandfather sputtered. "That is the headquarters of the GOS! No one in their right mind would go there to escape from the jihad forces!"

"My point exactly. They would never expect me to make my escape via Khartoum. They would never suppose that I was an SPLA agent if I traveled openly and boldly to the Muslim capitol."

Uncle nodded slowly, letting his mind process this new option. "Where would you go from there? You can't stay there, you know."

"You could travel north to Egypt," Grandfather suggested.

"Of course! There are many Sudanese students on scholarship in Cairo, and many businessmen travel there as well."

"No one would accuse you of joining the SPLA by crossing the Egyptian border. Perhaps you could find work there and wait for the situation to improve."

I nodded, wondering briefly what I could do in Egypt. My Arabic wasn't too great, but maybe I could work as a laborer until . . . until what? In my heart, I knew that I ultimately wanted to reach the United States. But I knew that religious freedom and economic opportunity were a world away. I remembered the song I had learned in primary school back in the Ugandan wilderness. It was a song about learning English and getting an education so that I would be able to help my people. Even then, I knew it would take a miracle for me to escape the destiny of so many of my classmates. For us, life was war and survival. Still, I dared to hope for a nobler purpose in my life. The first step was getting out of the country.

"I will travel north and escape to Egypt," I said. "From there, I will wait for the Lord's direction."

Murmurs of assent arose around me. It was decided.

"Mama, I need to tell you something."

As Mama passed by the open doorway, I motioned for her to come closer. From the look on her face, I knew that she already had a pretty good idea what it was that I was about to say. It was hard to tell my mother that I would be leaving again. Even though she understood the peril that we all faced, it was very difficult for her to accept my decision to leave, especially after my run-in with the military in Kapoeta. She listened quietly as I explained my plan.

"From Egypt," I concluded, "I hope I will be able to get a visa to travel to the United States. The universities there are the very best in the world and people have freedom to think as they please. When I get a good education, I will be able to help the family."

Mama looked uncertain. She had no knowledge of geography at all. She couldn't really picture in her mind where I might be headed. All she knew was that the US was somewhere very far away.

"You will come back as soon as you can, right, William?"

"Yes, Mama," I replied quietly. I avoided the directness of her gaze. "As soon as I can."

That night, my father took me aside. We stepped outside into the warmth of the evening air. The lingering scent of firewood mixed with the earthy musk of the tall grasses and tilled fields surrounding the village. I breathed in, memorizing the sensation of living with my family in the Sudan. My father rested his strong arm loosely across my shoulder. We were silent for a while, each of us wrestling with emotions both deep and unsettling.

"William," my father spoke at last, "you know we might never see you again."

Of course I knew.

"Your mother and I want you to know that we love you, and our prayers will follow you even when we don't know where your path has taken you."

I nodded silently.

"You will always be with your family, because your family is the Body of Christ. Wherever you go, find your family first."

My abba was releasing me, and I knew that this was difficult for him, as it was for me. I listened carefully to his words, because I knew in my heart that I might never receive counsel from my father again. That thought entered my soul like a great weight, crushing my spirit with its gravity.

"In the book of Timothy, God gives us instructions on how to live within our family," my father continued. "Rebuke not an elder, but entreat him as a father; and the younger men as brothers. Treat the elder women as mothers, the younger as sisters. Fellow Christians, wherever you are, will be your fathers, mothers, brothers, and sisters. They must accept you for our sake, and you must accept them on our behalf."

"Tell Mama not to worry about me," I replied with a bit more bravado than I felt. "I will be careful, and God will be watching over me. She will be proud of me some day."

Abba chuckled. "You know she is proud of you already. Don't you worry about Mama. She may fret about you children sometimes, but she is a lot tougher than you think."

It would have been unnecessary for us to say how much we would miss each other—we were already feeling the pain of separation. Our lives had been shaped by the politics of a godless generation, and now the storm around us was tearing me from everything I had known. Separation was inevitable; it would come by death or by distance. We could only hold to the belief that we would be together again in the arms of the Savior if our paths failed to cross again here on Earth.

Word travels fast in the small, close-knit communities of the South Sudan. Over the next couple of days, well-wishers from every family had stopped me to express their interest in the success of my journey. I spent my remaining time in Corom visiting with relatives. The following Sunday, my last at home with my friends and family, Grandfather's little church was packed. At the end of the service, I was asked to stand up and share a brief testimony. As I stood at the front of the little church, I looked out over a small sea of familiar faces.

These are my people, I thought. I was overwhelmed with a feeling of love for them, and I gathered renewed strength in the knowledge that it was for them that God was calling me out of Africa. I addressed the crowd from my heart.

"Brothers and sisters," I began, "God is calling me to leave my precious homeland. I will be facing uncertainty and danger. But those of you who remain behind will also be facing tremendous difficulty."

There were heads nodding across the room, as many understood what lay ahead.

"When I received my baptism," I gestured toward my grandfather, "the Reverend Vuni asked me to make a choice. He asked me to choose the weapon I would use to face my enemy—the Bible . . . or the axe. I chose the Bible, which is sharper than any two-edged sword."

A few amens rose from the congregation.

"I don't have to tell you all what kind of enemy we are facing. The Government Of Sudan has imposed the Shari'a on all of us. They want to force us to learn the Koran in school. But we all know that something worse is coming. They want our land, and they don't want any of us to remain here to live on it." I paused, but the congregation was silent. "What can we do?"

The question "what can we do" was not simply a rhetorical one. We were all searching for practical answers every day. Some buried their heads in the sand, hoping that the jihad would simply go away and everything would be OK. Some joined up with the SPLA, hoping to preserve freedom through guerilla style warfare. After that, the options became even more limited.

"I believe that God has called me to use the Scriptures to fight this war. I feel that God has a plan for me, and I believe He will use me somehow to bless you, my people. I don't know how that will happen, but for me it will not happen through violence. For that reason, I must leave you. I beg you all to pray for me, and I will pray for you all as well. Goodbye to you all. May God bless you."

The congregation prayed for me, and Grandfather pronounced the Aaronic blessing over me.

The Lord bless you and keep you . . ." The whole congregation joined in the familiar words, and I soaked in every syllable. *Please be gracious to me and give me peace*, I prayed.

All too soon it was time to leave Corom. My family sold a field full of crops for cash, enough to purchase a one-way airplane ticket to Khartoum with some left over. I was grateful for my parents' sacrifice, and I told them so. Then I said goodbye to Abba and Mama. That was the last time I ever saw them on this earth.

As the little propeller plane flew at a low altitude over the South of Sudan, I kept my face pressed to the coolness of the double-paned window. I watched as the green of the savanna and the gently rolling foothills gave way to flat, featureless desert. In the distance, the Nile River snaked ever northward, bordered on each side by verdant patches of irrigated farmland. The glare of hazy sunlight reflecting off the sand and refracting through suspended dust made my eyes ache and my head throb. Still, I kept my forehead pressed to the glass. The pressure on my skin counterbalanced the heaviness in my heart. It was a relief to me that no one seated near me was eager to talk.

Eventually, the hum of the engines and the vibration of the narrow but comfortable seat lulled me to sleep. When I awoke, I was in another world. I was in Khartoum.

I had been right about Khartoum. I was unnoticed and unmolested. From there, I caught a train to Wadi Halfa, a small boarder town in the northern desert between the Sudan and Egypt. I had to lie low for a couple of days, feeling sick and exhausted from stress and some type of flu bug. Travelers of every description frequented the town, and I was able to purchase a ticket on a steamer bound up the Nile toward Egypt with no difficulty. It was a crowded, unregulated ship, typical of those used in developing nations, and I had the cheapest berth available. We were herded aboard like so many cattle, but I didn't care. I was bound for Egypt.

The engines chugged, and the big ship creaked and groaned to life. With a great heave, we headed north through the confluence of the Nile. It was a slow boat; there was no doubt about that. I had nothing to do but watch Sudan go by. At first it was fascinating to watch the banks of the Nile pass by, patches of green on either side giving way to shimmering white desert. But after a long while, the scenery all started to look the same. I was bored and uncomfortable, so I took to reading my Bible and singing softly to myself to pass the time. I spent two days aboard the steamer, with nowhere to lie down to rest. It was blisteringly hot beneath the desert sun, and the crush of merchants and traders aboard ship only made things worse. Most of the time, I kept to the upper deck, which at least provided me with fresh air and a place to sit.

It was a relief to disembark in Aswan, Egypt. I changed the little money that remained into Egyptian pounds and purchased a train ticket to Cairo. My escape from Sudan had been blessedly uneventful, and for the moment, I was safe. I was just another face in the crowd, jostling for a seat on the crowded train. The air was hot, dusty, and close, and the limited seating made my legs ache, but all of that didn't matter. I was headed for a new life, wherever God would lead me.

CHAPTER TWELVE
Hotel Baghdad

I breathed a sigh of relief when my train finally rumbled to a stop in Cairo. It was a great metropolis, bustling with strangers speaking a language I could barely understand; but to me it was a first step on my journey to freedom. *Thank You, Father, for keeping me safe so far.*

I found myself in the Attaba section of Cairo, with only a couple of Egyptian pounds in my pocket. I was exhausted and hungry, with nowhere to go. I wandered through mazes of narrow, winding streets, taking in the sights and sounds of the city as I fought off the heaviness of fatigue that weighed down each step. I knew I would have to find a place to stay and someone to help me find work—but where? I didn't know anyone in the whole of Egypt.

Lord, I prayed, *I'm counting on You. Show me where to go. I really need Your help . . .*

I wasn't quite sure if the quickness of my pulse was due to the excitement of adventure or the anxiety of uncertainty, but I took a deep breath and tried to focus. The ground seemed to spin and sway as crowds of people passed by in every direction with swirls of colorful clothing and hints of exotic scents. When I looked up, I saw a dusty sign hanging from a dilapidated old building. "Hotel Baghdad," it proclaimed in English. I decided to go inside.

As my eyes adjusted to the darkness, I could appreciate that at one time this five-story structure had been a fine hotel. For now, I was just grateful to discover that this dingy old place was somewhere that I could afford to stay, at least for a day or two. My room was a tiny cubicle furnished only with a cot. The cot had only a plain cotton mattress with no sheets or bedding. That fact was most likely a blessing in disguise, because the place was absolutely filthy. Bedding would surely have been heavily infested with a variety of vermin. There was no running water, and the toilet facilities made me shudder. It is true that I have never been acquainted with luxurious living, but I have always been scrupulous about cleanliness and hygiene.

Beggars can't be choosers, I thought to myself as I finally lay down to rest. Indeed, I was fortunate to have a place to lay my head. I had no more time or reason to reflect on my surroundings as much needed sleep overcame me.

The following day dawned dusty and hot. Dust motes hung lazily in the haze of morning light, like an unspoken challenge to face the difficulties that promised to lie ahead. I made my way down to the lobby feeling a bit dazed and unsure of myself.

Suddenly, I felt a jovial handclap on my shoulder, rousing me from my reverie.

"Welcome to Hotel Baghdad," a stranger boomed, extending his hand in greeting. "You look like you aren't from around here."

I looked up and attempted a smile. "Yeah. My name is William. I came up from the Sudan."

"So, what brings you to Cairo?"

I was a little wary of confiding in this man. He looked like he might be Arab or perhaps Persian, but he seemed friendly enough. I decided to risk it.

"I'm on my way to America. I'm looking for freedom."

The man chuckled. "That's a big step for a young kid like yourself. How old are you, sixteen?"

"I'm eighteen," I replied.

Bit by bit, my story came out. I explained the situation in the Sudan and told him that I was fleeing because of my Christian faith.

"I feel that God's weapons are spiritual. I can't join the jihad and fight my own people, and I don't wish to take up arms with the SPLA, either," I explained. "God has given me a different path to follow, with God's Word as my weapon. That's how I ended up here in Cairo."

The man was quiet for a moment. "You truly are a stranger in a strange land, William," he replied at last. "So am I. I am also a Christian believer. I came here from Iraq. Things aren't so great for Christians there, either."

"At least we know that this world is not our true home," I replied.

"Well said!" The Iraqi man paused and glanced up at a sign hanging above the registration desk. "Baghdad," he said softly, "reminds me of my home in Iraq." A shadow passed over the man's features for a moment, and then his face brightened again. "This isn't exactly the Ritz, is it, my brother?"

I had to laugh, and I assured him that I had no intention of staying at the Ritz anyway. We spoke together for a while, and I marveled that God had provided me with a fellow Christian who could speak English just exactly when and where I needed him— right in the middle of a ramshackle flophouse in Cairo!

"Listen, William," he said after a time, "I know someone who may be able to help you. There is an Anglican Church by the name of All Saints Cathedral not too far from here. Maybe they could help you find a place to stay and some work to do."

I thanked him with all my heart, and the fresh hope he had given me lightened my steps. I soon found myself at the entrance to All Saints Cathedral.

Once again, God provided for me in a miraculous way. The pastor of All Saints Cathedral was aware of a group of South Sudanese students who were attending Cairo University on scholarship. These students came from Christian families and were likely to be willing to take me in.

When I arrived at the apartment where the students lived, a young man named Martin greeted me. He introduced me to his roommates. I was happy to discover that the students all spoke Madi! These young men had all grown up not far from my own village. God was truly good to me. My new roommates were curious about my reasons for leaving Sudan, and they gathered around to ask questions.

"William, why are you in Cairo?" one queried. "You don't attend university here."

Another was equally skeptical. "Are you sure you know what you are doing?" he asked.

"Why leave home with nowhere to go? You don't know what might happen to you!" another enjoined. "You are lucky we are here to help you out."

"Yes, and of course you will have to help out with the expenses."

I assured them I would help with expenses and began to explain my reasons for leaving my home. I soon found that my new roommates were unaware of the trouble that was brewing in the Sudan. They had special scholarships from the South Sudan government, and they had been isolated in their own world at the university. Even worse, I discovered that they had abandoned their Christian faith and were only superficially interested in following God, if at all. Their lifestyle was similar to what might be found on fraternity row in the United States. The pursuit of alcohol and women was more important in their lives than the pursuit of holiness. I would soon find out just how difficult it could be to keep myself pure in such an environment, as a young teenager so far from home.

In the evening, it was not unusual to find my new friends drinking beer.

"Have one, William!"

"Uh, no thanks, I'd rather not," I replied.

"I'd rather not," my friends mocked, chuckling amongst themselves. "For Pete's sake, William, one beer won't kill you!"

"Actually, it might," replied another, looking a bit more sober than he was. "But I'm just going to have to take my chances."

I was perplexed. "What do you mean? Beer might kill you?"

"Yeah. Don't you know?"

"Know what?"

"The religious police. They poison the beer."

"What?" I couldn't believe what I was hearing. "That can't possibly be true!"

"Oh, yes it is," they replied. "Some of the super-religious ones hate drunkards so much that they sneak around putting poison in beer. We know of people who have died from drinking it."

"And you still drink it? Aren't you afraid?"

"Well, it isn't every beer. We figure the chances of getting poisoned are pretty low."

"Yeah, we're not afraid to drink. Everything in life has some risk involved. Why give up our fun?"

I didn't know what to think. I had always respected the Muslim stand against drunkenness, but this was shocking. My friends seemed to be willing to risk their lives for a few hours of fun. Were the pleasures of drink really worth such a high price? I have to admit there were times when I was tempted to find out.

One night while my friends were drinking there was a knock at the door. It was a prostitute, offering her services to all of us. I was stunned to discover that my friends entertained such women from time to time. These beautiful young women were willing to give themselves away for as little as two Egyptian pounds. It was an offer almost too good to resist. In my pocket I could feel a few Egyptian pounds that I had received from my new job in a downtown supermarket. More than enough to pay what this woman was asking. Enough to make me forget my loneliness, if only for an hour. None of my companions would judge me, as they were emptying their pockets themselves. My family never needed to know. But God would know. I could not sin against my own body. It was a difficult decision, but I knew what I would have to do. I would have to make a stand against the wrong decisions that were being made.

"Friends, you know that in the Book of Proverbs it says that you are not to join yourself to a prostitute."

"You've got to be kidding!"

"No, I'm serious. God does not want us to dishonor our bodies in this way. Our bodies are meant to be His temple."

"Mind your own business, you little prude."

"Yeah, you don't have to be such a religious fanatic. We're not doing anything wrong."

"You think just because you can't have any fun, we shouldn't, either."

"But . . ." I had barely opened my mouth to protest when I was interrupted again.

"Maybe William isn't a man at all!" one of my roommates re-marked sarcastically.

Now it was getting personal. My friends were laughing and making rude comments. I didn't know how to respond.

"Yeah, right . . ." another laughed, "or maybe he's the kind of man that doesn't prefer women!"

By this time, everyone was enjoying a good laugh, except, of course, me. My face burned with embarrassment and fury. Invol-untarily, my fists clenched and unclenched as I resisted the sudden urge to respond in kind and escalate the disagreement. To them it was all a bit of harmless fun at my expense, but I was feeling the pain of ridicule. I knew that if I wanted to maintain my witness for Christ, I would just have to let it go. But how could I remain friends with young men who rejected the values of their Christian faith so completely? I needed some time to pray and ask God for help. I remembered that we ought to give thanks in all circumstances, so I thanked God for His wisdom in providing me with roommates from among my own people. OK, I'll admit that I was a little hesitant about the prayer of thanksgiving at first, but I knew what God would have me do.

God, I prayed, *please bless each and every one of my friends from the Sudan. Please give me a spirit of love instead of bitterness. Show me what to do!*

God gave me a desire to reach out to my roommates, and He gave me the idea to reach out to a prostitute at the same time. He showed me that He loved prostitutes and prodigals, and I knew He wanted me to feel the same way. Before long, I had a plan in my mind of what to do the next time a prostitute showed up at our door. I just needed to get my roommates to agree to try it.

After our argument had blown over, I approached my friends with my idea. "Guys, I have an idea of how we can help the next prostitute who knocks on our door," I began.

"You mean you plan to buy what she's selling?" A snicker passed through the group of men.

"No, I'm serious," I replied. "Just hear me out."

"OK, William," Martin agreed. "We're listening."

I looked around the room. Everyone's eyes were on me but expressions revealed skepticism.

"Do you think the prostitutes want to do what they are doing?" I asked.

"It's just a job," someone replied. "They're working girls."

"Yeah. They are happy for the business. They need the money."

"Do you really believe that your own mothers and sisters would be happy if they had to sell themselves just to survive?"

Nobody had an answer for that one. My roommates suddenly appeared to be very interested in looking at their shoes.

"I say that the next prostitute that comes by we give her some money but we don't take advantage of her. Then we'll see what happens."

"What?" This idea was clearly something that sounded totally outrageous. "She will laugh at us—she will think we are fools!"

"Maybe so, but give me a chance. If she laughs at us, I will never complain to you about this again."

My roommates were intrigued by my crazy plan. Actually, they probably were only interested in watching me make a fool of myself, but at least they were listening. We agreed to try my little experiment at the next available opportunity. We didn't have to wait long, because that very week another prostitute knocked on our door soliciting business. I invited her in.

"Would you like something to drink?" I offered her some hot tea as she slipped into our apartment.

She nodded but kept her eyes lowered and her veil wrapped tightly around her head and shoulders. My roommates' eyes were fixed on me, registering an expression somewhere between morbid curiosity and disbelief. Quietly, they took their seats within easy earshot.

"Have a seat." I motioned to an empty chair near our common table.

The woman reminded me of a shadow sinking in the twilight as she obliged. She dared a glance at my face, as if to question the terms of our encounter. Ever so slightly, her eyes moved to calculate the number of men in our group. With any luck, this would be the only door she would have to knock on this night. I smiled at her, in a ridiculous attempt to feel more at ease, and I took a seat across from hers.

"Ahem." I cleared my throat nervously, without risking a glance at my friends. I figured they would be smirking at me. "I am wondering," I began, "how a fine Muslim woman like you came to visit us tonight in this way. Please tell us about yourself."

The woman stiffened in her chair and her complexion paled a bit. This was certainly not a part of the bargain.

"What do you want from me?" she demanded. Her nostrils flared slightly, like a spooked horse, and I could tell by the pulse at her neck that her heart was pounding. She had good reason to be terrified. The only thing worse that the abuse and indignity she suffered from her customers was the prospect of being brought to justice in the courts of Islam. I suspected that if she were ever caught the law would not be too forgiving.

"You are informants!" She declared. "I will not speak to you."

"I give you my word, we will not turn you in. We do not wish any harm to come to you. In fact, we want to help you. I am a Christian. My beliefs allow intimacy only within the sacred bonds of marriage. I would never take advantage of you. We only wish to hear your story, you are safe."

The woman's shoulders relaxed a bit and her gaze dropped to hands that were folded primly in her lap.

She pinched her lips tightly together. "I have children, you know."

"Go on."

"I love my children more than life . . ." She looked around the room, seeking empathy—or at least understanding. "I must care for them. What can I do?"

It was not a question meant for answering. Postures shifted uncomfortably as my roommates tried not to think of how they took advantage of women like her. Slowly, the woman's story came out. It was not easy for us to hear or for her to tell. My friends remained silent as stones.

I turned to her and extended my hand in friendship. "We will ask nothing from you tonight. You don't need to sell yourself to us.'"

I gathered together ten Egyptian pounds and pressed them into her hand. "On behalf of all the young men in this room, take this money and go home to feed your children. This is the beginning of good things happening in your life."

The woman initially stared at me with her mouth agape, and then her slight frame was racked by uncontrollable sobs. Tears filled her dark eyes until they slipped slowly from her lashes. She never had reason to expect kindness from anyone, especially men.

"God loves you, that is why we are helping you," I said. "Jesus can bring you forgiveness and healing. But you must want to change your life. With God, all things are possible. Would you like me to pray with you?"

"Oh, yes," she whispered, "I do want to change my life."

She dried her eyes, accepted my prayers and the money gratefully, and left in peace. My friends were stunned and convicted by what they had seen. It was a while after the woman had left before anyone found the courage to speak. Finally, one of my friends took the initiative. Grinning sheepishly, he slapped me on the back.

"William," he said, "I hate to admit it—but I guess you were right."

"Yeah. Maybe you aren't such a fanatic after all."

The episode with the prostitute proved to be a real turning point in the lives of several of my friends. It was quite disturbing for them to see the consequences of their own sin in the life of a poor, destitute mother. The Holy Spirit convicted them of their need to live lives of compassion and purity. Some prayed for salvation and some re-dedicated their lives back to Jesus.

Thank You, Father, I prayed again, *for Your wisdom in sending me roommates from among my own people.* This time, there was no hesitation in my prayer of thanksgiving. I was reminded once again how God has a good plan for everything in my life. The discomfort I had experienced due to the ridicule of my friends was totally eclipsed by the joy of seeing Christ at work in their lives. I wish I could report that all of my Sudanese roommates had a complete change of heart, but that was not the case. There was still tension and still disagreements. I was acutely aware of the fact that I was depending on their hospitality, since I was not attending the university as they were. My job at the supermarket didn't pay much; it was barely enough to help out with the expenses. I began to realize that there was no way I could afford to purchase the necessary visas and airfare to reach the United States at the rate I was going. I began to sense restlessness in my spirit, and I knew that I would need to make a change soon.

CHAPTER THIRTEEN
Mme. Seiko

For two more months, I threw myself into my job at the supermarket with vigor. My relationship with my roommates had improved, and I was still able to pay my share of the expenses. Even so, I knew in my heart that the time had come for me to move on. The students I was living with had helped me when I had nowhere else to go, but they had not planned to take me in permanently. Finding another apartment in Cairo would be costly. Work at the grocery didn't pay well, and my back ached from standing at the register for twelve hours every day. I felt like I was in a holding pattern, unsure of the next step God would have me to take. I knew that I had served God's purpose as a witness among my new friends from the Sudan, and that knowledge confirmed in my heart that a new purpose was coming soon.

I was at work one day, feeling unsure—and feeling pretty sore—when I took a brief break from register duty. I pressed my hands to my lower back to work out the tension and let out a little groan.

"Hey William," I heard someone say. "Are you having a rough day?"

It was Edward Ibrahim, a repairman who often came to the supermarket when the old refrigeration system went on the blink. He was a Coptic believer who was outgoing and helpful, and I enjoyed talking to him whenever he stopped by.

"Good morning, Edward," I replied with a bit more cheerfulness than I felt at that moment. "My back is just acting up today. It bothers me when I stand here too long. I guess I'm not cut out for this type of work."

"Why not look for a new job?" Mr. Ibrahim suggested. "You are young and educated. I'm sure you could find something that suits you better."

"Well, your suggestion does make sense, but I don't have any brilliant ideas. I haven't been in Cairo for long, you know. Plus, I don't really speak Arabic too well. I can't read and write in Arabic, either. Around here, that makes me illiterate."

"You can read and write in English, can't you?"

"Yes, I can."

"Are you good at math?"

"Pretty good, yes."

Mr. Ibrahim paused for a moment, resting his hand on his tool belt. "I know a lady who needs someone who can read and write in English, but she lives outside of Cairo a fair distance."

I was interested. My restlessness was something I could not ignore. Plus, with the salary I was earning at the market, I would never save up enough to get out of Egypt. I wondered if God was about to show me a new direction to take.

"Tell me about it."

"Her name is Madame Seiko. She's a Japanese lady, and she runs a farm. You can tell her that I'm willing to vouch for you, and she'll listen to you. You're a good kid; I don't think you will have any trouble there.

I thought for a moment, gathering resolve. "Thanks, Mr. Ibrahim, I think I'll do that."

My friend gave me the information that I needed and then turned back to his efforts at refrigerator repair.

Shortly after our discussion in the supermarket, I found myself on a train headed for Madame Seiko's house. Mrs. Seiko raised dairy cows in the countryside near Cairo. As soon as I saw the farm, I immediately felt at home. All of my life I had cared for animals and worked the land. That little bit of familiarity caused a twinge of homesickness to darken my mood. Although I had only been away from my homeland for a few brief months, I had a bitter realization that I may never see my home or my family again. I remembered the look on my mother's face as she gave me her blessing for my journey to freedom, knowing full well that she might never see me again. Even though my emotions were in some turmoil, I approached Mrs. Seiko with confidence to ask for employment. I was certain that working on a farm again would be good for me, and I looked forward to using my English skills in a new way.

As it turned out, Madame Seiko was eager to hire me. "So William, when can you start work?" Mrs. Seiko, a sharp businesswoman, was always quick to get to the point.

"I can begin right away, but . . ." I hesitated. There was a request I needed to make, and I didn't know if my prospective employer would be too happy about it. "I can only work for you if I can take Sundays off."

Although Madame Seiko was married to a Muslim man and was therefore considered to be a Muslim herself, she really cared very little for religion of any sort. Friday was the expected day of religious observance in this Muslim community, and I knew it might throw things off schedule if she were to grant my request. Even so, I knew I could not compromise on this issue, because I was sure that I would be devastated without any contact with fellow believers. Mrs. Seiko was silent for a moment, considering my unorthodox request. Finally, she acquiesced.

"Very well William," she said, "I see no reason why you should not live as your religion dictates."

"Thank you, Madame," I replied. "I promise to do my best for you and the farm."

True to my word, I began working right away and was quick to learn the skills I was required to master. It was comforting in a way to work once again in an agricultural setting. I was thankful that God had provided me with another job. Just as I had found more than I bargained for with my wayward roommates in Cairo, I soon discovered that life in this rural community was going to be a real test of my Christian faith.

The problems started the very first week. As the other farm workers were entering the compound for another day of hard work, it was immediately evident to them that I was headed elsewhere. Since my boss had approved my Sunday departure, I felt that I had nothing to hide. As I walked two miles to the train station to make the trip to Cairo for worship, I was feeling pretty happy. I was eager to spend the day at church. But by the time I got back from the city it was already dark, and it was pretty late by the time I finished the long hike from the station back to the compound. Rumors spread quickly in a small town, especially about a foreigner. The other men had noticed that I didn't show up for work at all that Sunday, and it didn't take them too long to find out why.

"*Kafir!*" The word hissed from man to man as I passed by to get to my work the following Monday. Although I was not fluent in Arabic, the word sent chills down my spine. The other men were calling me an "infidel," someone who was worthy of being stoned to death.

"You are a lazy dog, *kafir*," one of the men yelled from across the barn. He stared at me with violence in his eyes as he approached. "You refuse to work like a man on Sunday, and instead you go to wallow in your filthy idolatry."

I stood frozen in my tracks, my eyes searching quickly for a way to escape. I did not want a confrontation; especially in the darkness of the barn with so many sharp farming tools within easy reach of anyone who wanted to harm me. A couple of men, also interested in avoiding trouble, hurriedly quit the scene as if they suddenly remembered how much work they had waiting for them.

Another farmhand spat in my direction. "Who do you think you are?" He stepped forward, and his muscular forearms tightened menacingly. "You take a job that should have belonged to one of us, and then you go to lie around with those western devils while we do your work!"

I shuffled backward toward the barn door, not daring to turn my back on the men. I hoped that I looked calm, but my alarm must have been obvious to them as they moved slowly toward me. *Lord, help me,* I prayed silently. I knew that I was no match for the two angry men, and I didn't think any of the other workers would step in to defend me.

"William!" the commanding voice of Madame Seiko summoned me from outside the barn. "I have a job for you, come now."

The two farmhands scowled as they turned away, with a look that suggested to me that our little "discussion" was far from over.

Thank You, God, I breathed quietly, *for getting me out of that one!* "Yes, ma'am, Madam Seiko," I called. "I'll be right there!"

I hurried out of the barn, grateful for the bright sunshine and open space of the outdoors. I made a mental note to check carefully before going into the barn or other dark outbuildings. I had a feeling I was now a marked man. Mrs. Seiko stood near a new tractor, smiling proudly.

"My new tractor," she said. "I want you to learn how to use it. It will be your responsibility."

I looked up at the new piece of equipment appreciatively. It would be fun to learn how to operate and maintain, and I was already looking forward to the task of driving it. I was chosen for this special job because I was the only one able to read the English manuals that came with it. I took the instructional materials from Madame Seiko.

"I'll study these manuals right away, ma'am," I said.

I hopped up into the metal driver's seat and found that it was surprisingly comfortable. I paged through the glossy technical guide, noting each gauge and lever as I went along. It was absorbing, interesting material to me, and I soon had a good idea of how the big machine was supposed to work. It was a welcome diversion from the disturbing incident I had faced that morning. Before long, I was ready to take the tractor for a spin. I put the rig in gear, and soon I could feel the rumble of machinery vibrating up through my hands and down my whole body. I threw the gearshift into drive, and I was off.

The rest of that day was spent tilling the fields with the new tractor. I was careful to ride in neat, precise rows, keeping the plow lines perpendicular to the gentle slope of the terrain. The warm, freshly turned earth smelled comforting to me. The land was a good and constant gift from God, and honest labor would generally bear fruit even in the most troubling times. By the time night fell, I was ready to rest.

After supper, I retired to my quarters. They were spare, but clean and comfortable. I was able to spend some time reading my Bible and singing quietly to myself. After the frightening encounter with hostile Muslim farmhands, I understood that life on the compound was not going to be easy for me. I could not neglect to nurture my spirit, because I sensed that forces of darkness were preparing an attack. Forewarned is forearmed, and it was very clear that I would need to arm myself for a spiritual conflict in the days ahead.

Father, I know that these men are not my enemy. My true enemy is Satan. Please give me the strength to be a witness for You to these men. I know that You love them; help me to never return evil for evil so that You will be honored.

It was hard to feel God's love for men who hated me and hated my faith, but I understood even then that love is not a "feeling," it is a decision. Love is obedience to God's will toward other people.

As I tried to put away all bitter thoughts, I didn't realize that there was far worse yet to come. The remainder of the week was fairly uneventful. I took every opportunity to prove myself to the other workers. I worked very diligently and tried to help others at every opportunity. I felt like I needed to compensate somehow for my absence on Sunday and prove that I was not lazy. Some of the workers were grudgingly responsive, and I tried to fit in by speaking to them in Arabic. By listening and speaking, I began to feel a little bit more comfortable with the language, although I was still unable to read or write it.

Finally, the end of the week came; it was Friday, the Muslim day of prayer. I realized with sudden dismay that all of my hard work to fit in with the other workers would be tried to the breaking point on this day. When the call to mosque came, I felt my heart sink. What will the others think of me when I don't show up for prayers? Of course, I soon found out the answer to that question.

"Blasphemer!"

I looked up from my work to see the men returning from prayers. Their faces burned with indignation and disdain. "You blaspheme Allah by refusing his call to mosque!"

The man who had threatened me earlier that week confronted me. His beard trembled as he spat out the words, "There is no god but Allah, and Mohammed is his prophet! Do you believe this? Do you?"

I knew that I didn't really have the answer he was looking for, so I remained silent. I was sitting up in the tractor, so at least I felt safe from physical assault. I turned the key, and the motor rumbled to life. As I maneuvered the tractor toward the field, I could hear the epithets following me. I tried not to listen. The ethnic and religious insults were hurled at me like weapons. I was a pig . . . a dog . . . an infidel . . . a blasphemer. I should go back to Sudan where they would really "take care" of me.

Why God? Why are they doing this to me? I knew in my head that Jesus said, "I will never leave you nor forsake you,"[12] but in my heart, I felt very alone. Everything about me set me apart from my peers in the village. My appearance, my language, my culture, and especially my faith kept the others either at an arm's length or overtly hostile. I wondered what purpose God could have had in mind when He sent me to be the only Christian for miles around. Does God really work all things together for good to those who are called according to His purpose? To be honest, I was having doubts about that one. I was isolated, I was in danger, and I had nowhere else to go. *What can I do to get out of this situation?* I thought to myself. I couldn't go back to Sudan—I would be forcibly conscripted into the jihad. I couldn't go to the US—I didn't have the money or the proper paperwork. I couldn't even go back to Cairo—I couldn't live with the students again, and I would be unemployed. I missed my family terribly, and I knew that they had no idea where I was.

To make matters worse, the news about Sudan that I heard on the radio in bits and pieces wasn't good. Villages were being attacked and burned to the ground. Factions were fighting. Random shootings and violence were spreading throughout the region. I longed to know what had happened to my family members, but I had no way of finding out. Night after night, I found myself crying in the darkness of my little room, asking God to help me. It seemed like He just wasn't listening. As days became weeks, and weeks became months, I became increasingly depressed. I held on tightly to God and spent my evenings studying the Bible and praying. Life on the farm was becoming increasingly difficult for me.

There was a young man about my age named Nabil who didn't threaten me but would often argue with me about the errors of my ways. He was a sincere believer in Islam, and we had several discussions about issues of faith. Since I was progressing rapidly in my ability to speak and understand Arabic, I was able to converse with him fairly readily.

"William," he said, grasping my shoulder as if he was planning to shake some sense into me, "why do you refuse to accept that Mohammed is the seal of the prophets? Don't you see that to worship the man Issa is blasphemous? There is no god but Allah, and he will punish you for the worship of a man."

"You are correct about one thing, Nabil," I replied. "It is blasphemous to worship a mere man. But Issa—Yeshua—is not a mere man. He is God incarnate, God with us."

"Your Bible has been corrupted—it has been perverted. Although it does contain God's revelation, the Koran is God's pure word. It is the perfection and completion of the religions of the Jews and the Christians."

"Our Bible is very reliable!" I was feeling a little agitated. "There were hundreds of ancient prophecies about Issa from the Old Testament that came true many hundreds of years later! The historical accuracy of the Scriptures is being proven every day by archaeologists!"

"Christianity is propaganda of western missionaries. You are being brainwashed by the Europeans and the Americans. You should accept the true religion of your people—Islam!"

"My people are the Hebrews! They lived right here in Egypt!" I didn't like the implication that the Great *I Am* who revealed Himself to Moses not far from this very place was a "foreign" God. "And Jesus Christ came to save the whole world—not just Westerners, or Jews, or Africans—everyone! Jesus told us to go into the whole world to preach the gospel. The western missionaries are following the orders of a Jew who grew up right here in Egypt! Islam is not the 'true religion' of Africa or anywhere else, for that matter!"

It was beginning to be obvious that neither one of us was going to convince the other to change his beliefs, but at least we could have a discussion about the issues, and I was grateful for that. I was also grateful that my Arabic skills were improving to the point where I could converse fluently with Nabil. I felt like I was beginning to understand his beliefs more clearly, and I hoped he was beginning to understand mine. Although we did not agree, I felt that he was trying to help me in his own way. He believed that I would really be better off if I became a Muslim.

Although there was no intellectual temptation for me to accept Islam, the social pressure to become a Muslim was almost more than I could bear. While Nabil argued with my intellect, an older man named Saide argued with my heart. Saide was a relatively wealthy middle-aged family man. He wanted to take me under his wing and get me to listen to reason. He was a calm, friendly man, and he was very pragmatic.

"You know, William," he said to me, "I see that you are a hard-working young man. Madame Seiko has given you a lot of responsibility."

"Thanks," I mumbled, although I wasn't quite sure what he was getting at.

"Why do you insist on living the life of a *kafir* in our village? It will bring you only pain."

Well, he's got that much right, I thought to myself. I had plenty of pain and then some to spare.

"You are very young; you do not live with your people anymore." He leaned forward, his brow crinkled with earnest concern. "You could be happy here. You could have a nice car and a nice home. People would accept you if you would just accept Islam."

The way he said it made it seem so simple, like buying a new pair of shoes so as not to get blisters on your feet.

"I can't reject my faith," I replied. "It is everything to me. It is my life now and in eternity."

Saide laughed. "Allah will take care of you if you follow the Koran," he said. "Why worry about eternity when your life is so miserable today?"

I had to admit that he had a point there. "My life is not too great right now," I agreed.

"I have a beautiful daughter who is just seventeen. If you accept Islam, she could be your wife. You could have children, and you could have a good life. I will give you a car for your wedding. If life proves difficult for us here on the farm, we could all move to Fayum, the town in southwestern Egypt where my family came from before we moved here to work for Madame Seiko. What do you say?"

The beautiful daughter part sounded pretty good, and I was desperate for security and acceptance. Would I ever have a good life? Should I just give up trying to serve Yeshua and live in peace? Life in the little farming village of outside Cairo could be happy. I loved working the land and milking the cows. The families were close-knit and peaceful. It wasn't really so different from the life I had known with my own family in the wilderness of Uganda, after all. If I were to become a Muslim, I would be welcomed into the community and my skills would be valued instead of resented. The timeworn tactic of "good cop, bad cop" was definitely working on me. On one hand, the "bad cop" villagers would use threats to induce me to recant my faith in Christ. On the other hand, the "good cop" villagers were kind to me and offered me pleasant rewards as inducements to convert. Saide's offer of marriage and prosperity was very tempting.

At that point, I was so worn down that I was close to giving up and becoming a Muslim. Then I remembered the story of Jacob and Esau. Esau sold his birthright for a mere bowl of stew. The exchange was outrageously one-sided. How foolish Esau was to forfeit his blessing for a fleeting satisfaction! God spoke to me through this scripture story. Did I really want to trade my salvation for human acceptance? How could I sell my inheritance and forfeit my soul? I felt God's sharp rebuke. As worn and weary as I felt, and as much as I wanted a wife and family, I knew I would not—could not—give up my faith.

I said no to Saide's offer. I worked through the rest of the day like an automaton. My heart felt so heavy, and God seemed so far away. I didn't react at all when the farmhands insulted me. I didn't even have the heart to care. It was just another miserable day. I was so out of sorts after work that I didn't even think about carefully choosing my path home. I just walked in a direct path, without looking in every direction as had become my habit. My carelessness was a big mistake. Before I knew what was happening, I was ambushed.

"There's the blasphemer, let's get him!" someone yelled. "Yeah, the dog has become Madame Seiko's little pet! She lets him have the easy life, riding on the tractor and taking Sundays off."

I felt the first blows fall sharp and heavy on my chest and back. I tried to breathe, but the wind was knocked out of me. I struggled to twist free from the painful grip that twisted and bruised my flesh.

"You don't deserve to work here, *kafir*," a voice growled into my ear. "You don't even deserve to live!"

The beating I endured was horrible. But the physical pain was nothing compared to the dark shadow over my soul. Finally, I ran away. My breath came in quick, shallow sobs as I struggled to get back to my room. I fell exhausted into bed and slept a troubled sleep.

The one blessing I felt during this dark time was that Madame Seiko consistently treated me with fairness and respect. She kept her promise and allowed me to travel to Cairo each Sunday. As I rode the train toward Cairo, I felt a cloud of oppression lift from my shoulders. I was like a starving man as I entered the fellowship of the saints. For a few brief hours, I felt alive again. The trip back to the farm, however, was another story. I was practically sick with dread as I returned to my personal place of torment. Walking the final two miles back to the farm from the train station was like the walk of a condemned man to the gallows. I knew the persecution that awaited me when I returned would continue to escalate. I was beginning to fear for my life.

I will never forget what happened one Sunday night after I got off the train on my way back to the farm. The night was very dark, and I was tired. It was not just a physical exhaustion; it was a deep spiritual exhaustion that I felt down to the very core of my being. I just could not bear the thought of walking two miles through the darkness back to the farm. I felt like my hope was gone—and God had deserted me.

I can recall walking along the edge of a canal built to guide little rivers toward the farmland. In the dark, these irrigation routes could easily be followed back to the farm. As I walked slowly back toward the village, I suddenly felt so overwhelmed with despair that I absolutely could not take another step. My whole body began to tremble, and I sank to my knees right there where I was. I felt like my heart was broken beyond repair. Great sobs racked my shaking body. I just didn't feel like being alive any more.

Why God? Why have You left me here all alone?

I looked up into the blackness of the night, and tears streamed down my face like hot rivers.

Where are You, God? If You can hear me, please just let me die. I can't live like this any longer. Why have You forsaken me?

I just didn't have the strength of will to get back up on my feet to keep on walking, so I continued to cry and pray to God. I had no one else to talk to, no one who would care or even listen. The pain of missing my family was acute, and I had no one to call a friend. And so I stayed there, kneeling by the irrigation canal in the dark, pouring out my troubles to the God that I fervently hoped was still listening.

I can't say how long I knelt there, but after some time, I heard footsteps coming toward me. When I looked up I noticed a man approaching me. It was strange to see someone else along this rural path so late in the evening. The man was dressed in simple white clothing such as a Muslim farmer might wear. He was very close to me—too close—and I knew that he had seen me. I was terrified, but I was out in the open. I knew that I couldn't hide. What would he think of me?

"Why are you crying?" The man's question was not unkind.

"I . . ." I tried to compose myself and answer as politely as I could. "I'm praying. I feel like God has abandoned me and my people."

For some reason, I just blurted out the whole truth. I guess I needed to say it to somebody, even if it was a perfect stranger. "I told God that I might as well die if things go on the way they are."

The man looked at me quizzically. "Why not go to the mosque to pray?"

I caught my breath. I wondered if I ought to just reply, "Good idea!" and let it go at that. But I didn't want to lie to the man, so I answered him directly. What did I have to lose at this point, anyway?

"I do not go to mosque," I replied. "I worship the God of Abraham, Isaac, and Jacob. . . . I'm a Christian. He can hear me wherever I am—even out here—because my body is His temple."

I'm not sure what I expected the man in white to do or say in response to my confession. Whatever abuse he was going to give me, I just figured I would accept it along with the rest of my trials. But what he did say to me came as a complete shock.

"You have answered correctly," he responded calmly. "Don't be afraid, get up! The Lord is with you; He is closer to you than you think."

The man went on as I stared at him in disbelief. "Nothing will harm you and the Lord will be with you wherever you go."

I was at a complete loss for words. I just stared at the man, slack jawed and motionless.

"Get up and go now," he said. I did as I was told and hurried back to my temporary home at Madam Seiko's farm. As I went, my steps felt a bit lighter, and I allowed my heart to feel a new hope. Perhaps God had not forsaken me, after all.

CHAPTER FOURTEEN

An Unlikely Exit

I knew the time had come for me to resign from Madame Seiko's employ. I just couldn't continue living in the openly hostile environment of the farming village. I didn't have much money, and I had no definite long-term plans, but I felt that God was prompting me to head for Alexandria. I gave my notice and left the farm immediately. The oppressive spirit that had surrounded me in the small community faded with each mile and my heart felt lighter. I hadn't quite realized how depressed and discouraged I had become in that place. I shuddered as I thought of how close I had come to just giving up during my time at Mrs. Seiko's farm. Now my hope was renewed as my mind filled with plans to find a way to get a visa to the United States. But first, I needed to find a new job.

Alexandria, that ancient city, was a cosmopolitan port populated by thriving businessmen from around the world. There were plenty of construction projects and a bustling commerce near the docks. I was certain to be able to find work with decent pay in such a place. Unfortunately for me, many native Egyptians were also seeking work at the docks, and they didn't like to see a foreigner find a good job. I found myself being chased away from work by Egyptians who were jealous of the English skills that earned me favor with the foreign businessmen. The hostility became even more evident when they realized I was an "infidel" Christian. It was tough going, and I held several brief labor jobs until I met a fellow Sudanese Christian named Steven. He helped me find a job with a kindly developer who ran an Irish-British firm. He needed assistance wiring a high-rise building for electricity. My new employer was so generous that he paid me American dollars for my Egyptian pounds, an arrangement that was financially very favorable to me.

As I worked, I saved all the money that wasn't required for food or rent. When I wasn't working, I enjoyed hosting a Bible study in my modest apartment. My new friend, Steven, joined me, as well as men that I met from Ghana, Congo, Ethiopia, and other African nations. Life was difficult for me in Alexandria, but it was a big improvement over life in Cairo and the farm. The diversity of the city provided me with both protection and companionship.

Over time, Steven and I both had saved enough money to purchase airline tickets to the US. We were thrilled about the prospect of getting to freedom in America. But we soon found out that getting a visa wasn't that easy. The Americans required at least three thousand US dollars over and above airfares to grant a visa. That is a tremendous amount of money for a laborer working in a third world country to obtain. Steven and I didn't give up. We were determined to get a visa no matter what the cost. If we couldn't get to the States, perhaps we could get a visa to France or some other western nation. So we continued to save money and visit embassies, getting nowhere fast.

One weekend, Steven and I made the trip to Cairo, again with the intention of getting a visa. Finally, we heard the bad news from the Egyptian authorities. We would not be permitted to leave Egypt without express permission from the Sudanese embassy. That was the worst news possible! The Khartoum government ran the Sudanese embassy in Cairo, there was no way they would let a couple of Southern Christians like us get away. We were getting more and more discouraged and increasingly afraid of being sent back to the Sudan.

We were feeling pretty down when we headed for the train station to head back to Alexandria, empty-handed once again. As we were walking through the train terminal, I felt Steven's elbow jab my ribs.

"Hey, William! Look over there!"

I followed Steven's gaze and immediately realized what he was pointing at. There was a tall white guy at a nearby queue wearing a white jacket emblazoned in English with the words, "Jesus is Lord," on the back. We immediately guessed that the man was an American.

"Maybe he can help us," Steven said.

I shook my head at Steven's unrealistic suggestion. "What can some tourist do to help us?" I reasoned.

"He's a Christian, isn't he? Maybe we can talk to him."

I had my doubts, and I hung behind as Steven approached the stranger.

235

"What's up, man?" Steven asked, with his very best imitation of an American swagger.

It was ludicrous—with his thick African accent, no one would ever believe he was an American. The stranger turned and took in Steven's act with a look of bemusement. I was embarrassed for Steven and for myself.

"What can I do for you guys?" The American was clearly no fool. He immediately realized that we were up to something. But at least he was willing to hear us out.

I quickly stepped up and we introduced ourselves. We explained that we were Christians who were trying to make it to America where we could be educated and help our families who lived under the threat of war. The stranger listened sympathetically and then extended his hand to us.

"I'm Michael G. of Massachusetts, and I'll help you if I can. But just because I'm American doesn't mean I have any special influence at the US embassy."

"That may be true, but they might be at least willing to listen to you. As an American, you could speak for us. They only turn us away."

The American hesitated for a moment and then shrugged. "OK, I'll see what I can do for you; I guess it's worth a shot, anyway."

Michael was true to his word and went with us back to the Cairo embassies. While we were there, he was an advocate for us, and he was finally able to convince the Turkish embassy to grant us a tourist visa. It happened that Michael was planning to head through Turkey himself on his way to Asia.

It was a bona fide miracle. Why a stranger would be willing to change his plans to help a couple of guys he didn't even know was beyond my understanding. Why the Turks would give us a visa was beyond all of our understanding, but it happened. Before the truth of it had even sunk in, the three of us were on a flight to Istanbul.

The city of Istanbul was awe-inspiring. Ancient architecture dating from the days of the Byzantines graced the skyline with delicate spires and towering domes. Crowded open-air markets were filled to overflowing with colorful goods of fine quality. The men of the city seemed to be enjoying the sights as much as we were; they relaxed in the bazaars, chatting and sipping tea at a leisurely pace. Michael, Steven, and I enjoyed taking in the scenes all around us, even though none of us spoke any Turkish.

Michael parted company with us after a day or two of sightseeing. He was on his way to Japan to teach English there. We thanked him for his kindness and wished him well. He smiled and wished us well in return.

"I hope you guys find what you're looking for." He reached into his pocket and fished out a scrap of paper, scribbling a hasty note. "Here, William. If you ever make it to the States, give me a call."

"God bless you, Michael—I will." I slipped the paper into my wallet and waved goodbye to the young American. I was still amazed at the way God had provided a stranger to bring me out of Egypt.

While we were in Istanbul, I spent my time trying to work toward getting a visa to the West. I wasn't seeing the results that I hoped for, but I didn't give up. I wondered why God had brought me to Turkey, of all places, on a brief tourist visa. But I knew that God had a plan, as He always does. I just hadn't figured it out yet. I trusted my heavenly Father who had saved me from certain death in the Sudan and who had miraculously lifted me out of Egypt. I

237

was sure that His provision wasn't to lead me into a dead end. Steven and I parted company, and I devoted my time to working toward a visa. When I wasn't in some government agency filling out forms, I spent my time enjoying the atmosphere of the bazaar.

One beautiful morning I was sitting at the market having some tea when a young Turkish man approached me. He had heard me speaking English, and he was curious.

"Hello," he said, "may I sit here?" His words were clear and carefully pronounced, and I understood them quite readily. He introduced himself as Ahmet and explained that he would like to practice speaking English with me.

"Nice to meet you, Ahmet," I replied. "My name is William. I'm glad to have someone to talk to, because I'm here by myself."

Ahmet paused for a moment, scrutinizing my words. "You are not American or British, either. Where are you from?"

"I am from Africa; I'm here on a tourist visa."

Ahmet was intrigued. It was rare to see a black man in Turkey, and he had never spoken with an African before. "William from Africa, would you like to see our museum? I can explain everything to you in English."

I was delighted to have someone to show me the museum. It was a massive series of structures from antiquity, filled with artifacts of every description. I thanked Ahmet enthusiastically.

"It is my pleasure," he replied graciously. "You should see our great heritage since you are here, and I will be so glad to be able to speak English outside of the classroom."

Ahmet was a great tour guide. He was obviously very proud of his culture and of his city, and rightly so. The museum was spectacular. We stopped and admired the contents of each glass-enclosed showcase. I was amazed to see the arm of John the Baptist and the hairs of Mohammed, the Prophet of Islam. I wondered how the museum had determined these strange relics to be authentic. The buildings themselves were so fabulous that my senses were overwhelmed. Artistry was evident in even the smallest corners of the elaborately tiled structures. Azure, gilt, crimson, and alabaster melted into seamless mosaics beneath sumptuous vaulted domes. Arched windows, beautifully wrought, directed thoughts heavenward as they framed the vibrant sky. Ahmet described how these buildings were transformed into mosques with the rise of the Ottoman Empire. In Byzantium, they had been Eastern Orthodox churches.

My guide admitted that he knew little of the pre-Muslim history of Constantinople. I was able to explain to him what I knew about the history of the early Church in Asia Minor and how the churches in what is now modern-day Turkey were so important to the development of Christianity. Ahmet was surprised and pleased to find that I had learned about Turkish history even from a school in Africa. He listened politely to the information that I had learned as we continued to admire the ancient buildings.

Finally, we arrived at a display that was revered above the others. It was carefully protected, with security guards keeping watch nearby. Curious visitors leaned over velvet ropes to get a better look. The murmur of subdued voices rose above the cavernous quiet of the exhibit hall, so I knew that the crowd was excited. I wondered what artifact could generate such obvious enthusiasm.

"It is the sword of Mohammed the Prophet," Ahmed whispered. "With it he conquered Mecca and prepared the world for the coming of Islam."

I was both awed and troubled by what I saw. One piece of steel, wielded by a single man, truly changed history. I felt like I was looking back through time and the effect was dizzying. Something was bothering me, but I couldn't really put my finger on the source of my unease.

I was quiet as we quit the cool of the museum for the heat of the midday sun. My new friend, Ahmet, had showed me many wonders of the Muslim world, a counterpoint to the harsh fanaticism I had experienced in Africa. He was a man with an open mind and an open heart, and he was able to explain many of the intellectual and artistic triumphs of his culture. And yet at the end, there was the sword.

We stopped to rest over a steaming cup of tea beneath the shade of a brightly colored awning. A light breeze stirred the air and lifted the scent of the tea leaves all around us. The delicate fragrance served to calm my mind as I slowly breathed it in. I was lost in thought, trying to process the contradictions in my mind.

"What are you thinking?" Ahmet asked.

I looked up at my new friend. His eyes spoke sincerity, so I decided to trust him. "I guess I was thinking that Jesus never had a sword," I replied.

It was just a thought; I wasn't sure quite where I was headed with it. Just the same, I knew it was important.

Ahmet didn't understand what I was getting at. "Everyone carried swords in those days—that was the way of the world."

The way of the world. The sword has always been the way of the world. That was what my grandfather had tried to teach me so long ago at Opari. My jumbled thoughts began to make sense to me. Maybe I could explain it to Ahmet.

"That's true," I replied. "But a sword is the weapon of an earthly kingdom. God's kingdom *is not of this world.* That's why Jesus and Mohammed were so different."

"How do you mean? Jesus was also a great prophet, just like Mohammed."

"Jesus was different. He didn't need a sword of steel because His sword was within Himself. His sword was the Word of God. It was a different kind of weapon, serving a different purpose." I struggled to find the words to explain the fundamental other-ness of Christ.

Ahmet leaned toward me, wrestling with the dual task of understanding the English and understanding the strange new concepts he was hearing. "How could God's words be like a sword? I don't understand."

"In Islam, it is said that the Koran is the very word of God, brought to Earth by Mohammed, is that not so?" I tried to explain my thoughts in the context of what I knew Ahmet believed.

"Yes, of course I believe that." Ahmet nodded vigorously. "It is said that the word of God, the Koran, has always existed in heaven, but it was not known on Earth until it was revealed to the prophet."

"In Christianity, Jesus is called the Word of God. It is said that the Word of God, Jesus, has always existed in heaven, but was not known on Earth until He was revealed in human form. 'In the beginning was the Word, and the Word was with God, and the

Word was God. . . . And the Word became flesh and dwelt among us' (John 3:16, 1:14). That is from the *Injil*, from the Book of John."

"We accept the *Injil*, but I don't understand. Can a book be God? How could a book become flesh?" Ahmet's brow wrinkled as he tried to understand my explanation. "Do you worship a book?"

This was going to be hard to explain. "We don't worship the Bible, just like you don't worship the Koran. But the substance of the Scripture, the Word, is part of God. We believe that Jesus, the Word, is the same nature as God."

"This is a difficult thing," Ahmet mused. "There is only one God."

"You are right. There is only one God," I replied. We certainly agreed on that point. "But Christians believe that one God exists in three persons, just like water exists in three forms. You may see steam, ice, and clear liquid, but you would call all of them equally water."

"That is true enough. But I still don't understand the part about God's Word being turned into flesh."

"This verse is speaking of Jesus. We believe that Jesus always has existed as God—that He is the Word of God that created the universe and that He came to Earth as a man. He came so that we could know God personally and be certain of our place in heaven."

Ahmet looked startled. "How can anyone know God personally? Allah does not stoop so low. And how can anyone ever be sure of their eternal destiny, unless they die a martyr? Allah gives no guarantees but has mercy on those he pleases."

Finally I understood what had been bothering me. People always try to turn God into the ruler of an earthly kingdom, but God's plan is not about ruling the world. It is about ruling our hearts. With that sudden insight, I thought I could explain myself more clearly. "That is the heart of the difference between our faiths. You cannot know Allah personally, and the kingdom of Islam is ruled on Earth by the Shari'a—and by the sword. You have said this yourself. The Christian concept of God is very personal. Jesus walks with us, loves us, and relates to us—and His kingdom is in heaven. He assures us of our place in that kingdom forever. You will never need an earthly weapon to defend a heavenly kingdom."

Ahmet thought about my explanation for a while before framing his reply. "I see what you are saying, but one thing in particular troubles me. You have said that you can be certain of going to heaven. What do you have to do to gain entrance to your heaven? Allah weighs our submission to the five pillars of Islam. This is an ideal way to live, and I do my best. No one can be sure if Allah will find them to be good enough, but we try."

That was an easy question for me to answer. "You are right that God weighs our submission to Himself. But God demands perfection. God says, 'Be perfect, as I am perfect.'[13] But no man on Earth can be perfect."

"So you depend on Allah's mercy, too. You never know if you are good enough."

"Yes and no. Christians depend on God's mercy. But we don't need to be good enough, because Jesus Christ was perfect. He sacrificed Himself to take the punishment that we deserved. Now when we call on Jesus, God sees only His perfection. That is how we are assured of our place in heaven."

I knew that the claim of a free gift of perfection would seem outrageous to Ahmet. It was just too amazing—too generous. From the look on his face, I could tell that my friend was trying hard to wrap his mind around the implications. "Can that be true? God gives you His own perfection? Do you still believe in submission to God?"

"Of course we believe in submission to God. But we are free from uncertainty and imperfection because of the gospel of Jesus. You could say that our *Shahada* is from a prayer of Jesus; 'Now this is eternal life: that they may know you, the only true God, and Jesus Christ, whom you have sent.'[14] Jesus states very clearly that He gives eternal life freely to those who accept Him.

"As for *Salat,* we have the charge: 'Pray without ceasing.'[15] For us the call to prayer is twenty-four hours a day—and God understands every language, even the unspoken language of our hearts.

"Our *Hajj* is everywhere, all the time—because God's Spirit lives inside of us. Our bodies are His temples.

"We also believe in fasting and almsgiving. But Jesus said that the greatest law is to love God with all your heart and to love others as ourselves."

"So, there are many of the same ideas, but it all depends on Jesus," Ahmet concluded.

"Exactly. Everything we believe depends on Jesus—who He is and what He has done for us."

Ahmet was silent for a time, thoughtfully draining the dregs of his teacup. "I would like to learn more about Jesus," he said.

I was dumbstruck. I was beginning to see why God had picked me up out of Egypt and dropped me down in Istanbul. His reason was Ahmet. There was no other explanation for my increasingly unbelievable odyssey.

I only saw Ahmet that one day and the next I was off to Ankara. But on that day, Ahmet heard the gospel of Christ and believed. All I could do was direct him to the only church that existed in Istanbul at the time, an international church run by Canadians. The Lord truly works in mysterious ways.

My joy for Ahmet was real, but it was quickly overshadowed in my mind by concern for my own predicament. When I left for Ankara, I only had ten days left on my tourist visa, and I was getting desperate. I had run out of money, and there was no church in the whole city. I found myself wandering from place to place, looking for some work to tide me over for a few days. For a foreigner, there was no work in Turkey. This was doubly true since I was not a Muslim. Many of the Turks made racial jokes and insults, but I ignored it. Getting angry would get me nowhere. I just needed an odd job for the cash to survive as I waited for news of a visa.

I didn't know what to do, and I was feeling increasingly anxious, as the time on my visa grew short. It was beginning to look like I might end up back in Africa, facing destruction once again. As I wandered the city, I saw signs in English with directions to a military barracks. It was an American military barracks! I felt hope swell again in my heart. They would certainly have a chaplain there, and maybe I could get help with my visa!

I decided immediately to make a visit. I should have guessed how it might appear to the US military for a Sudanese man to come rushing up to the barracks. They immediately suspected that I was up to no good. I guess I can't blame them, since Sudan has been known for harboring terrorists. Still, I was surprised when they secured me and brought me in for questioning. They were pretty suspicious of my story of searching for a chaplain until my Bible fell out of my clothing.

"Hey, I guess this guy was telling the truth," one of the officers remarked as he thumbed through the worn pages of the New Testament. "He seems harmless enough."

"He can't stay here, though. We don't deal with asylum cases."

I was feeling discouraged as the soldiers discussed my fate. Finally, they decided to refer me to Father Nus, a French priest. I was grateful to have someone to turn to at last. Father Nus was very kind to me, and he went out of his way to make sure I didn't end up back in the Sudan. My passport was very nearly expired when he helped with arrangements to travel to France. He even gave me enough money for a one-way ticket to Paris! Once again, God provided for me in a miraculous way through the kindness of a stranger. Every time things were looking impossible for me, God delivered me from circumstances beyond my control. Even so, God's provision for me through the French priest took me by surprise. After all I had been through, it is a little embarrassing to admit that I had been living in anxiety and fear during my stay in Turkey. I should have been trusting in God all along! Even so, I was simply overwhelmed with gratitude and relief when I finally realized that I would finally set foot in a country where I would simply be free to be who I am: a Christian.

CHAPTER FIFTEEN
America

By the grace of God, I finally arrived safe and secure in the United States of America on August 28, 1988. It had been four years since I escaped from my native country of Sudan, yet I knew that my journey was just beginning. My travels now spanned four continents and three seas. I had passed the Great River, I had crossed a vast desert, and I had lived as a stranger among people who were strange to me. My journey had been fraught with uncertainty and peril; but God had kept me through it all, as though refining me by fire.

After my brief sojourn in Turkey, I spent time in Lyon, France. The French people were very kind to me and I was permitted to remain in their country. French was language number four for me, and I studied it with a vengeance as I worked dead-end jobs to get by. I soon realized that it would take several years of study to reach a level of fluency necessary for a college education within the French university system. Still, I kept trying to advance myself. Meanwhile, I discovered that truly godly men like Father Nus were not all that common in the "Christian" West. Although Europe in general and France in particular had much to offer, the post-Christian values of the French culture were quite a shock to my sensibilities. The moral codes of Judeo-Christian values were considered to be old-fashioned by the Europeans, and many European churches were lukewarm in their enthusiasm for the gospel. Still, I managed to find a church family in France.

After nearly two years in France, God finally opened the door for me to travel to the United States. The opportunity was like a dream come true for me. As my airplane arced into the sky, I felt like my life was about to start all over again.

I stepped out of a cab and into New York City at dawn, just as the golden rays of the sun were slowly spreading their light across the gleaming skyline. Glass, stone, and steel glowed with dazzling brightness before the residual dusk of the wakening sky. I stood awestruck, paralyzed by the sheer magnitude of the vision before me. Though the hour was early, I was already surrounded by a sea of strangers, and suddenly I felt as though I might drown in the crushing waves of rushed humanity all around me. Although I had lived in places like Paris, Cairo, Istanbul, and Ankara, nothing had prepared me for these first moments in America.

As I looked around to get my bearings, I noted that I was at the port authority. A sign near the street corner told me that I was standing near Forty-second Street. It didn't help much to know where I was, because I certainly didn't know where I was going. With only $100 in my possession, I did know that my options were limited. A sense of panic began to overtake me as I desperately tried to think of names or phone numbers of people I had met over the years who were Americans.

I must have looked as frightened and vulnerable as I felt, because as I crammed myself into a telephone booth to gather my thoughts, I was approached by a pair of unsavory characters hoping to take advantage of a foreigner.

"Speak-a you ENG-lish?" One man leered, his forced smile revealing his ill-kept teeth. "Gimme ten bucks and we will help you find someplace to stay."

The first man leaned forward aggressively, smiling and reaching for my backpack. "Here, I'll carry that pack for you, just gimme ten bucks."

The second man began pressing into me, trying to remove the backpack that held my few possessions. "Please, let me help you with that."

"No, thank you," I replied politely. I was unsure of how I ought to deal with these strangers who spoke like friends but felt like enemies. "I appreciate your offer, but I really don't need your help right now."

The two men refused to leave, and I didn't know how I could extricate myself from my uncomfortable situation. As the men continued to harass me, two patrolling policemen happened by. They seemed to know immediately what was going on, because they came over.

My tormenters beat a hasty retreat when they saw the cops headed our way.

"Hey buddy, this is New York City," one of the cops said. "Lesson number one is 'don't talk to strangers.'"

"Yeah, if anyone comes up to you and asks to take your luggage, don't give it to them, or you'll regret it." The second police officer paused, as if he wondered what advice he could give to someone like me—someone alone and scared in a strange country. He sighed. "If you need help, try to ask a police officer. Good luck, kid."

I thanked the policemen for their assistance and they went on their way. I was very desperate at this point, and I knew the One I needed to call on for help at this point was God. With my eyes open, I came before Him in silent prayer.

This is it, Lord. I don't know what to do. I'm stranded in New York City, and I don't have anywhere to go. Please help me now.

With a renewed sense of calm, I sorted through the contents of my wallet. As I smoothed out a wrinkled old piece of paper, my heart leaped with a sudden spark of hope. Crumpled and faded, but still legible, was the address and telephone number of my old friend Michael G. of Massachusetts. I hadn't seen Michael for nearly two years, when we had parted company back in Istanbul. Before he left, he had handed me the phone number of his folks back in the States. He told me that if I made it to America some day, to give him a ring. Well, I had made it to America, and now that phone number had resurfaced just at the time when I needed it most.

Thank you, Lord!

When I had spoken to him for the last time, Michael, the world traveler, had been headed for Japan. I had no idea whether or not my old friend was at home or abroad. Assuming he was in the US, would he be living with his parents again? Would he even recall our brief friendship?

I felt awkward and unsure of myself, but I really had no choice but to dial the number before me. *Please, God, let someone answer the phone* . . .

"Hello?" A voice I did not recognize picked up the line. "Who is this?" It was Eugene Jr., Michael's elder brother.

I decided to tell him my story. "You don't know me, but I am a friend of your brother, Michael," I began.

My words sounded a little odd, even to me. I wished that I could start over, but it was too late for that. I just kept on talking. "We met in Egypt in 1986, and he said to call him if I ever ended up in the States . . ." my voice trailed off as I considered what to say next. "I'm stranded in New York City!"

There was a pause on the other end of the line. This guy must think I'm a lunatic! I realized that Michael's brother had every reason to hang up on me. But he didn't.

"Uh . . . just a minute. My mom might be able to help you out."

A few seconds later, a new voice was on the line. "Hello? This is Kathleen, Michael's mother. How can I help you?"

I briefly explained my situation to her. I recounted my struggle to enter the US and my plans to head to DC to seek asylum. But what I really needed was a place to stay until I could decide what steps to take. I was in New York City and darkness was approaching fast.

There was another pause on the other end of the line as Kathleen digested the implications of my unusual and unexpected request. After consulting with her husband, she agreed to allow me to stay in their home.

"But we don't even know you," she added. "We can't be sure you are even telling us the truth. Call back in one hour. My son, Michael, is living in Phoenix now, and we will give him a call. If he can vouch for you, you are welcome in our home. Do you understand?"

I assured her that I did indeed understand, and I anxiously waited for an hour to pass before calling back. It was already getting late, and I was afraid to spend the night alone in the city with nowhere to go. I certainly had no desire to encounter more "strangers" like the ones I had met earlier that morning. I had a feeling that the strangers would become increasingly bold and threatening under cover of darkness. I called back in precisely one hour, and Kathleen G. answered the phone once again.

"William," she said, "we spoke to Michael, and he said that he was blessed and happy to hear that you finally made it safely to the US. You can stay with us for as long as you have a need to."

My relief and gratitude was so great that I could barely express it. I spoke with yet another boy, Patrick G., to figure out how I would get to Boston. As it turned out, I was near to the greyhound station. The one hundred dollars I had arrived with was enough to purchase a ticket on the next bus to Boston. Patrick agreed to pick me up at the bus station at 7 P.M. that evening.

"Once you get to the terminal, don't wander off. Just stay put, and I will be able to find you," he said.

I was more than happy to agree to his instructions, and I soon found myself aboard the bus bound for New England. I can still recall the wonder of that late afternoon trip. The bus wound its way through postcard perfect scenery and quintessentially American hamlets on the four-hour trip. I took it all in with relish. If God willed, America would be my new home.

I arrived at my final destination, Boston, promptly at seven. I had no idea what Patrick would look like, so I just sat down and waited. As it turned out, I could tell when I saw him that Patrick was Michael's brother. It was with relief that I found him to be genuinely glad to meet me. I was so warmly received by this family that I felt as though I was an old family friend instead of a foreigner and a perfect stranger. Over a hearty meal, they plied me with questions about my life back in Sudan, my family, and long journey to the States.

Soon the phone rang. It was Michael calling to welcome me! "Jesus is Lord, brother!"

"Amen to that," I replied.

"Where have you been for the past two years?"

I told him the whole story from where we had left off, and we reminisced about our days in Egypt and our journey to Turkey. It was then that we both realized that our friend, Steve, hadn't made it. We prayed for him then and asked God to protect him, wherever he might be. We gave thanks to God for bringing me safely to the United States. Then we turned our attention to practical matters.

"Look, William, I would love to get together with you sometime soon. But that won't happen for a while yet. I'm headed out again—this time to southern Africa. Do you have any type of visa or green card?"

I told him that I didn't. "OK, you will have to get some sort of permit before you can get a job. You can't just go and work somewhere without proper documentation."

"Yes, I know a little about how that works. I am hoping to get some paperwork when I apply for asylum. That is why I plan to head for Washington, DC, next."

Michael paused for a moment. "Hmmm . . . it won't be easy for you to get by before you get that taken care of. I'll tell you what; I'll wire you some money to help you until you can get on your feet."

Michael was true to his word and added kindness to kindness by assisting me financially. The family proved to be amiable hosts, giving me a quiet room with a bed on the third floor of their home. Eugene and Kathleen G. could relate to my story as an immigrant, because they were both immigrants themselves. They had been raised in Ireland before venturing to America in their youth. In America, they met, married, and raised six children before retiring and becoming happy grandparents. Of course, they loved to keep alive the memory of their old home in Ireland. I was inspired and encouraged by their story.

On Sunday, they invited me along to the local Catholic Church in town, where we had a wonderful time and I enjoyed the fellowship of brothers and sisters in Christ. Everyone was so warm and receptive that I felt right at home. During the two weeks that I spent with the family, I spent a lot of time talking with Patrick. Patrick and I had a lot of common goals and interests, and he was studying engineering at North Eastern University in Boston. I wanted to go to school so badly, so that I would be in a position to help my family and my country, but I didn't know where to start. I knew I had lost four years of schooling since leaving high school in 1984. I should have been a senior in college, if not for my need to flee the country. Patrick understood how I felt and was a big encouragement to me.

"American schools are no more difficult than any other schools," he reasoned. "Besides, foreign students always seem to do well if they study hard. You are fluent in French and English, and your science skills are strong, so you should do fine."

"How do I get into an American college?"

"Well, I know they have student visas for foreign students, but you would still need money for tuition, and you would need your high school records."

Unfortunately, those were three things I did not have. I was beginning to understand the obstacles I would face, but I was determined to remain undeterred. I knew I couldn't depend on the hospitality of this generous family indefinitely, yet I literally had no resources. Eugene Jr. and Patrick were resuming their studies as college was starting up again. I knew I needed God's help and direction. I prayed and cried out to God for an hour without stopping, and then I was quiet. I listened for God's plan as I searched my heart. Finally, I came to a decision.

My plan was simple. I purchased a round-trip ticket to Washington, DC as a sort of insurance policy. I felt that if a job opportunity did not present itself in DC, I could always return to New England to work while I waited for asylum to be approved. I said good-bye to my gracious hosts, and headed for the US capitol with nothing but a Bible and the clothes on my back. Little did I know that my life was about to take another unexpected turn.

While I was on the bus, I fell into a sound sleep. When I woke up, the bus was in the station. I was a bit groggy, but I disembarked and went to gather my wits about me and decide how I ought to apply for asylum. As it turned out, my journey had just ended abruptly in Newark, New Jersey. I just assumed that the bus had reached DC, when in fact it had only stopped briefly to board new passengers.

When I inquired at the ticket counter, I was shocked to discover that Washington was still 230 miles away and the bus was already long gone! I suppose I could have returned the following day to claim a seat on the next bus, but I didn't. I remembered the stories I had learned in school about the colonists in the New World. The pilgrims had landed at Plymouth Rock and then they settled nearby. I decided that I, like the pilgrims before me, would just settle where I landed. And I had just landed in Newark.

Of course, my decision was helped along a bit by the local police. It was illegal to stay in the bus station past midnight, so they suggested that I ought to move along. One of them mentioned that I might try to find the local YMCA if I needed a place to stay. I finally arrived at the Newark Y at around one in the morning. I was tired but hopeful.

At the desk, a security guard leaned back and eyed me suspiciously. "What do you want?"

"I need a place to stay, please, I have no where to go."

"Nope." The guard looked bored, but a hint of a smile played at the edge of his lips, as though he enjoyed the prospect of turning me away. "Got to fill in a form, and it'll take about a week for a room to open up for you. Go on, you can get a form tomorrow."

I edged toward a chair and tried to sit down.

"Go on, get out of here, I said." The guard was getting angry. "You can't loiter here in the lobby."

I persisted and continued to stand in the lobby. We continued to argue for some time, and we were still at it by 5 A.M., when a young guy came down the elevator. He overheard our argument and wandered over to check out the action.

"Hey, are you from Africa?"

"Yes, I need someplace to stay, just for the day."

He looked me over for a minute and then came up with a proposition. "Hey, I'm headed out for the day, and I need five bucks. If you give me five, you can stay in my room until I get back."

The guard nodded his assent, and the deal was made. I woke up at mid-morning and headed to Congressman Peter Rodino's office. I was able to speak with his secretary and explain my situation. Mr. Rodino's secretary was very kind to me. She wrote me a nice letter on behalf of the congressman, who was in DC at the time. With the benefit of her letter, I was entitled to get some help from Newark Christian charity organizations and churches. She specifically suggested that I should see Pastor Charles Brown and Bishop Lukas on Broad Street. She told me that they helped homeless people who needed shelter.

After I left the congressman's office, I headed to the office of the Immigration and Naturalization Service. I admitted that I was an unregistered alien, and I explained that the Government of Sudan was interested in ending my life. I was sure they believed my story, because they immediately sent me to the FBI office in Jersey City. They even put me on the Path Train for free. I was so excited that I was going to see the FBI. I didn't know what the FBI was, but I was still excited and happy. When I arrived at the FBI, two armed agents in civilian clothes came to greet me. I handed them the papers that the INS had provided for me and looked to them expectantly. I was sure that my asylum would be granted by these special government agents. I soon realized, however, that the FBI was not in the asylum business. In fact, I was led to a room to be interrogated.

They asked me many questions about the Government of Sudan and about spying and about communism. I answered everything to the best of my ability. Eventually, the agents were satisfied that I was not a dangerous spy, and they handed me a new set of papers and sent me on my way. By the time I got back to Newark, it was once again getting late in the day. I still was without legal papers to work in the US, and I was running out of money fast. I knew I didn't have enough money to stay at the YMCA, even if a room was available, so I took the advice given to me by the congressman's secretary and headed for Broad Street.

I found the Reverend Brown's office and gave him the note from Mr. Rodino's office. Reverend Brown was kind to me and gave me food and shelter for the night. I had no problem following the rules and going to church services as their shelter policy required. I soon discovered that many of the homeless people that Reverend Brown and Bishop Lukas helped were plagued by problems such as drugs, alcohol, violence, and prostitution. These men of God helped with the physical as well as the spiritual needs of all of these people without discrimination. The two preachers allowed me to stay at the shelter until I received asylum applications and a work permit from the INS, and then they approached me with an unusual offer. They knew that I was different from many of the young men at the shelter, and that I was a brother in Christ. Bishop Lukas pastored a church downtown that had once been a Jewish synagogue. The Jewish congregation had abandoned the building permanently after the riots of 1964. There was an empty room in the basement, and Bishop Lukas asked me if I would like to stay in the church rather than in the crowded homeless shelter.

I accepted immediately—I was thrilled with his kind offer. God must have a sense of humor, I thought. This old church still has a Star of David on it! God was not intending for me to forget my Hebrew roots as I settled in to my new Christian life in America. What a comfort He is to His people. God also must understand irony, because Reverend Brown soon approached me with an unlikely job offer.

"William, good news," he said to me. "I found a job for you." I assured him I was willing to take any job, any job at all.

"Listen, William, this is an election year in our country. The Vice President, George H. W. Bush, is running against the governor of Massachusetts, Michael Dukakis. They need people to run the 'Get out the Vote' campaign. The job only lasts one month, but you will have money until you can find a permanent job."

Reverend Brown took me to the campaign offices, and I was hired on the spot. The wage was $100 per week, which was a lot of money to me. My job was to take registration forms and approach people to sign up to vote.

For one month I pounded the pavement, asking strangers to sign up to vote. People scorned me, saying that I was obviously a foreigner who didn't realize that the government didn't care about their needs. I encouraged them not to take their freedom for granted. I told them that, in Sudan, we have no freedom at all and no right to vote for anyone. It was my great desire to be a citizen of America with the right to vote. Of course, as an unregistered alien, I couldn't vote; but ironically, I did convince some Americans to vote. I also had the opportunity to meet some political candidates, such as Donald Payne and Frank Lautenberg, who would later prove to be helpful in the advancement of my asylum case and educational needs.

Well, on November 7, 1988, Election Day came. Vice President Bush won handily, and my job was over. Armed with a new social security document and official working papers, I decided to network among my Christian friends. The Reverend Glen Hatfield was a brother who I connected with right away. He was the pastor of the First Baptist Peddie Memorial Church. His church was also downtown, located near the YMCA. He extended me an invitation to worship at his church and suggested that I might find work through the Catholic Relief Agency.

Things began to fall in place quickly for me. I got a job at Nurser Alloy Electrical Wire on the second shift, providing me with enough money to rent my own room at the YMCA. I thanked Reverend Brown and Bishop Lukas for their gracious provision for me and for the care I had received at the homeless shelter mission. They were so blessed to hear that I had found steady work and was now able to provide for myself.

I rented a single room at the YMCA and began to attend Peddie Memorial church. The YMCA was a convenient place to live because of its proximity to transportation, libraries, and government offices that I needed to visit. It was also affordable for me. Unfortunately, the YMCA had some problems that I was not aware of. I found out that the Y was known for all kinds of problems, including drug dealers, homosexuality, violence, and alcoholism. In fact, these problems were rampant at the Newark YMCA.

At first, I was terrified to live with the kind of people that I discovered were living all around me. I had never been around such people and I knew that I might be robbed, attacked, or even killed. But God spoke to my heart through His Word. "I can do all things through Christ, who strengthens me."[16]

I knew that God was with me and that He would keep me safe in His will. He taught me to love instead of fear my neighbors. As God emboldened me, I decided to become a part of the solution. I began to invite everyone I met at the YMCA to come to church and to seek God in his life. I shared my testimony with them. I challenged them to stay away from drugs and to keep sober. Some of the men I spoke with began to attend church and their lives were transformed.

Although God provided for me with a steady job and a place to live, I knew that I had to eventually get back to school if I had any hope of helping my family. One day I went to visit the campus of Essex County College with a friend from Nigeria who was a student there. He was very encouraging and sympathetic as I told him of my desire to attend college.

"Do you have a high school diploma?"

"Yes, I have one," I replied. "I sat for the London-based Ordinary Level General Certificate back in Juba, but when I fled the country, I did not stop to get a copy."

"Could you write for it?"

"Unfortunately, the high school I attended was Catholic, and all the non-Muslim schools were closed indefinitely due to war." I shuddered as I imagined what my old classrooms must look like now—empty or bombed-out shells. "Anyway, I know I can't go to college without a diploma!"

"That isn't always true, William," he said. "Have you ever heard of the GED?"

He explained to me that GED stands for "General Equivalent Diploma" and that it is given six times per year.

"If you're ready, you could sign up and take it tomorrow," he said. "If not, buy a study guide and take it the next time around."

My heart was revived by new hope after I learned of the GED. The very next day I purchased a study guide and began an intensive plan of study. I studied all day, worked the evening shift, and then studied all day on Saturdays. Sundays I worshipped at Peddie Memorial. Six weeks later, I sat for the GED and received a very high score. Reverend Hatfield was excited by the result and assured me that I would have full access to American colleges. I immediately applied to Essex County College for the spring semester, but there were challenges that weighed heavily on my mind. I did not have a student visa, so I could not qualify for any type of student loan. The only advantages I had were a student discount at the YMCA and a legal work permit. I had to continue to work full time, and I could only afford eight credits that first semester. I managed to take two more classes during summer session, giving me a total of thirteen credits with a 3.9 GPA. I knew that I needed to work full time, but I also wanted to attend school full time. I had to seek God's will once again.

God gave me the idea to quit my second shift job at Nurser Alloy and take a full time job as a night shift security officer. That would enable me to take a full-time schedule of classes while still working full time. The only problem with that arrangement was that there was no time for sleep. But I knew that God would sustain me, and indeed He did. The night watchman job was at a filthy garbage dump. My duties involved hourly patrols of the facilities and granting access to garbage truck drivers. I had a small office with a monitor screen and a coffeepot. The tiny space was quiet, and it was an ideal place for studying when I wasn't patrolling the grounds. My studies were helpful to keep me awake and alert on the job. Sometimes fellow students would show up at my little booth at the dump to ask for my help. I always was willing to help other students who needed assistance, and to be honest, I appreciated their company. Having a visitor at the job helped me to stay awake, which was not always easy with only three hours of sleep every twenty-four hours.

During the day, I learned to "power nap" between classes to keep my strength up. The brief naps kept my mind clear enough to absorb lectures about calculus, physics, chemistry, and engineering. Miraculously, I remained healthy and was able to maintain a 3.5 GPA with fifteen credits in my major of Computer Integrated Manufacturing Engineering that semester. With that hurdle under my belt, I applied for an academic scholarship, the Essex County College Presidential Scholarship. I won the scholarship, which paid full tuition for the next semester. In fact, I won this scholarship each semester for the two years I took to complete Essex College. I graduated with high honors and an associates degree in Computer Integrated Manufacturing Engineering. Thus the year of 1989 ended on a good note. I did well in college; I had a job, a church home at Peddie Memorial, and a room at the YMCA.

CHAPTER SIXTEEN

Higher Education

I graduated from Essex County College in the fall of 1990, and the following spring I was able to enroll as a junior at New Jersey Institute of Technology (NJIT). I signed up for a schedule to suit my engineering major, but I soon found out that I had unwittingly enrolled In "Human Relationships 101." Science and technology were so logical and easy for me to understand but understanding other people was not always so straightforward. I guess that I had been sheltered during my first two years in the United States, because I had surrounded myself with fellow Christians. The Americans I knew were people like the Reverend Hatfield and Michael G.'s family. These people treated me like family, encouraging me and caring for me freely. For me, there was always welcome. Perhaps that is why I was taken off guard by the depth of bitterness and racial division that I encountered on campus.

I moved out of the YMCA and into the NJIT dormitories, expecting to find an exciting academic environment with debates framed around great ideas and opposing worldviews. What I found was something a bit less lofty—racism. My roommate, Devon, had been deeply affected by racism throughout his life. There was anger and hurt just below the surface, always ready to spill over. His rage expressed itself outwardly in the form of hatred for white people in general and for our next door neighbors, in particular.

When I moved in, Devon and our neighbors in the dorm were already engaged in hostilities. I can't say who started it, but by then it didn't really matter. The Caucasian boys next door taunted Devon with offensive comments, and he responded in kind. The situation escalated daily, and every morning when I returned from my shift as a night watchman, I heard about the latest skirmish. For all of Devon's bluster, I could tell that he felt demoralized by the situation. His confidence in himself was shaken. I hoped that the student housing authorities would deal with the problem, but they really didn't seem to care. I guess they believed the old saying, "Sticks and stones may break my bones, but words will never hurt me." Well, words can hurt, and for people who don't have Jesus to turn to, the pain can turn into a deep well of bitterness.

One morning I returned from work to find Devon agitated and obviously angry. His expression was hard as he paced the floor of the small space that we shared.

"What's up, Devon?" I asked politely. To tell the truth, I had a pretty good idea of what his answer was going to be. I didn't really want my day to start out with more disturbing news, but I figured he needed to talk.

"Those white boys, that is what's up," Devon spat back, emphasizing his words with a punch of his fist in their general direction. "They said I would never get my degree. They said I was stupid, just like all the brothers." Devon took a deep breath, drawing air with a hiss through his clenched teeth. "They told me to give it up and learn to play basketball!"

As Devon's words hung in the air, I was stunned into silence. The insults were so outrageous and demeaning that I wasn't sure what to say. I did know that I needed to say something that would help my roommate feel better.

"Devon," I began, "you and I both know that you have what it takes to succeed. Those boys know it, too. They're just looking for trouble. They want you to feel angry, and they want you to react. Don't give them the satisfaction." I was trying to use reason to diffuse a volatile emotion, but it wasn't working too well. "Be the better man, and let those words pass. They don't even deserve your time."

I knew right away that my pep talk had fallen on deaf ears. I had spoken in platitudes, but he needed to hear something more practical. Devon had already dealt with more than he could take, and he was starting to lose control.

"What do you know, William? What do you really know about white oppression?" Devon turned to face me, his eyes dark with rage. He was tall and imposing, and he leaned closer to me as his voice rose in volume. "You're an African! You think you know it all, but you don't know *nothin'* about what it means to be oppressed!"

My roommate was breathing hard. I wanted to tell him to calm down, but I held my tongue.

"You have no idea what it is like to be hated for who you are! You have never been a slave in the white man's world."

I was unable to respond as Devon unleashed his verbal attack against me. I felt confused and even intimidated—there was no reason for him to accuse me! While it was true that I had not expe-rienced white-on-black racism during my life, I did know a thing or two about oppression. I doubted that Devon had ever been arrested, tortured, or forced to live in exile. I was pretty sure that his family was not starving in a refugee camp. He was probably unaware that actual chattel slavery was still a reality back in the Sudan. I just kept my mouth shut as Devon continued his tirade.

"You Africans think you are so superior, but you are just fools. You think you can be equal with whites with your college educa-tion and your shirt and tie. You are wrong! They will make you a slave again." Devon strode over to his side of the dorm room and pointed to a poster of his hero, Malcolm X. "Malcolm X under-stood," Devon continued. "The Nation of Islam understands. We don't need your white men. We need a revolution! That is what you can't understand."

Devon felt that I couldn't understand him because I was an African, raised where dark skin color was the norm. I had enjoyed status as a member of a racial majority. No one had ever looked at me and then looked away because I was black.

Similarly, I felt that Devon couldn't understand me because he was raised in freedom, far away from tribal warfare and religious persecution. He never had to run away from his own country. No-body had ever hunted him down because of his beliefs.

The oppression I had faced caused me to fear for my life. The oppression Devon had faced was very different—it caused him to question his identity. Our life experiences were very different, but in some ways they were the same. Both types of oppression struck at the core of who we were as individuals. The wounds, both physi-cal and emotional, could be very painful. But I knew that if Devon continued to seek vengeance it would only cause him more pain. How could I communicate to him that the best weapon to fight oppression is God's Word?

"Look, Devon, all that the Nation of Islam understands is hate. And hate breeds more hate. It numbs the pain for a while, like a drug—but in the end it destroys everyone. God is the one who understands. He knows what you are going through, and He can heal you. Jesus teaches us to love our enemies, even though we may have reasons to hate them. That brings healing to everybody. Take Dr. Martin Luther King, for example. He knew what racism was all about. In his day, it was a lot worse than it is now. He was able to overcome evil with good, like it says in the Bible."

"Yeah, right," Devon replied with a mirthless chuckle. "Just turn your sissy cheek. Dr. King was a coward."

"No way. What I'm talking about takes strength and courage. You have to trust in God to be able to love your enemies. It may be the hardest thing you'll ever do, but you won't ever regret it."

As I spoke to Devon, I was also speaking to myself. I had to depend on God daily to love my own enemies. But I knew that if I harbored hatred toward the jihadists, it would destroy my own spirit and ruin my Christian testimony.

"Devon, nobody can fulfill your God-given destiny in this world except for yourself. God made you in His image. You have a mantle awaiting you and nobody can wear it besides you. You can succeed—and you *will* succeed—if you study hard and stay focused. Don't let anger and revenge take that truth away from you."

Devon had every reason to feel angry, and I sensed that my words sounded empty to his ears. I just felt that he needed hope and confidence. Then I was reminded of James chapter two, verses 15 and 16: "If I see a man naked and hungry, and I say to him, 'be warmed and filled' and yet do not reach out to help him, what good is it?" How could I watch this freshman student struggle with calculus and physics and yet do nothing to help? I knew what I had to do.

"Devon," I ventured, "since I'm a junior, I have already taken all of your classes. I can help you work through the assignments. You will prove those boys are wrong about you when you get the grade. They'll have to eat their words."

I was faithful to my promise to Devon, even though it was hard for me. I was so tired after my night shift, and then I had to start the day with an overload of my own classes. But I understood that God was calling me to serve my roommate and to be a witness for Him in Devon's life.

God was faithful to me, as well. Through my involvement with Intervarsity Christian Fellowship, I developed a great network of supportive Christian friends. I met students from around the globe, representing many cultures and several nations. My friends from IVCF buoyed my spirit and helped me maintain perspective. What a contrast there was between the unity of believers and the divisions and racial tension that gripped the rest of the campus! Every morning when I returned from work, I spent an hour in Bible study and prayer back in the dorm room.

I invited Devon to study the Bible with me, and I was a little surprised when he agreed. It turned out that although Devon admired Malcolm X and the Nation of Islam, he was not a Muslim himself. He wasn't particularly religious at all, but he was willing to listen to what I had to say.

I shared verses of love from God's Word. I told my roommate that God loved him personally. I explained that we are to love God with all of our heart, mind, and strength—and love our neighbor as ourselves.

"Love your neighbor as yourself," I read aloud. "Did you know that God loves all of mankind?" I asked. "God does not care about your race, because He created all people in His own image. Our nation, our status, our race, our gender is meaningless to Him. We are all different, but we are one in Christ Jesus. Those students who live next door are not just 'white people,' they are God's creation, just like you and me. Jesus died for them and for us, too. He wants all of us to turn from our sins and be saved. In Christ, all men become brothers."

Devon glared at me. He hadn't seen much Christian brotherhood in American churches. "How can you be a Christian and love white people when you know that they used Christianity to justify slavery?"

"Evil men have used God to justify their own evil deeds since time began! Ever since Cain killed Abel, Satan has been at work spreading hate and division between brothers. Real Christians do not use their faith as an excuse to sin. When a Christian sins, he sins against a holy God. The Bible condemns oppression, cruelty, and hatred in the strongest terms. Read it for yourself and you'll find out."

Devon made no reply, giving me the opportunity to elaborate.

I flipped through the gospels, pointing out some of the statements that Jesus had made. "If you practice sin, you are a slave to sin. Hatred is bondage just as surely as chains. But Jesus is the Truth, and the Truth will set you free." Then I turned to Isaiah for a picture of the Suffering Servant. "Jesus Himself never tried to rule over anybody. He said that the greatest of His followers were those who served others, not enslaved them."

"OK, so those slave master Christians were hypocrites. Big deal. What do you expect from those people? Forget it. We don't need their religion anyway. Let the white folk have their religion; we have our own."

"If you think that Christianity is the white man's religion, you are very wrong." I was adamant about this particular point. Too many people wanted to portray Africa as a land of godless heathens with Islam as the only monotheistic tradition. Nothing could be further from the truth. The Hebrew traditions as well as the very earliest Christian traditions were cradled in Africa. "If you bothered to read your history, you would know that it was African missionaries who spread the gospel in Europe while white men were still pagans and barbarians. You might also find that the Irish made pilgrimages to Africa to learn how to be monks. Jesus wasn't exactly a Westerner, either. Aside from the fact that He owns the universe, He happened to choose to come to Earth as a Middle-eastern Jew. He spent His early years in Africa, where His people had been kept as slaves. The first churches outside of Jerusalem were in Asia Minor. Jesus died for the sins of the whole world. Christianity is a faith for all people of every race—it doesn't matter if you are black, white, yellow, or brown. Christianity is about God's Truth, no matter who you are."

Devon didn't reply. I couldn't help but wonder what he was thinking. There were deep wounds in Devon's heart, and I figured there was more to it than just a few racist remarks by the students next door. I didn't know what hate and rejection he had experienced, but I did know that more hate and rejection was not the answer. Only the love and forgiveness of Christ could give Devon peace of mind and a sense of personal worth. I prayed that he would find that peace some day.

One thing was certain and that was that Devon did not find peace that first semester at NJIT. His grades slipped as he became increasingly bitter and angry. One day I returned home to the dorm room to find that Devon was gone. He had overturned my bed and my books—the dorm room was a mess. He had written a vicious note and taped it to the door of our neighbors next door.

I felt hurt that he had taken out his rage on me, but more than that, I felt a deep sense of sadness for Devon. There was a human part of me that wanted to see Devon punished. But the Bible says to forgive. I couldn't pretend to teach forgiveness if I couldn't follow through with it myself. I knew that I needed to let it go. I could clean up my room, but would Devon be able to pick up the pieces of his life? I hoped so.

I didn't know whether Devon would be returning in the fall, but for the summer anyway, I was alone in my room. I decided to take summer classes, so that I could advance more quickly. It would be lonely on campus with so many of my friends leaving for summer vacation.

One day, when I was downstairs in the lobby, I met a Northern Sudanese student signing out for the summer. He introduced himself as Karim. I had heard about this student earlier in the spring, but I had hesitated to look him up because I had assumed he would be a Northern Muslim who would be hostile to me. For a whole semester I had kept my distance, but given the circumstance, I couldn't avoid speaking with him any longer. During the course of our conversation, it came up that he was a Sudanese Christian of Egyptian descent, not an Arab. I was embarrassed to realize that my own prejudice toward Northern Sudanese people had kept me from reaching out to him. He was only eighteen, and he was unaware of the depth and severity of the war, which was taking place mainly in the South.

I briefly described some of the problems that were occurring in the Sudan, and I suggested that we should get together after he returned from summer vacation. Even though we had only just met, we took a moment to pray for each other and for our families back home. As he turned to go, I told him that if for any reason he should decide not to return to the Sudan, he would be welcome to room with me for the summer. He thanked me and then left.

Two days later, I received a phone call at the dormitory. It was Karim, and his voice was trembling.

"William, I may take you up on your offer. I need a place to stay."

"Of course, Karim, you are welcome," I replied. "What happened?" It sounded like he had been crying.

"I can't go home. It is too dangerous for me. My father . . ." His voice broke. "My father was falsely accused of violating Islamic law. He didn't do anything! The Islamic regime is after him because he is not a Muslim."

"Is he safe?"

"I don't know. They confiscated his business and took all of our money. And that isn't the worst news."

"What else?" I didn't want to ask.

"My mother has a brain tumor. She has gone to Holland for treatment. I can't go home until further notice. I don't know when that will be."

"Don't worry, Karim," I said. "You can stay with me. We will trust God to carry your mom through her treatment and keep your dad safe."

Karim moved in with me right away, and we supported each other. Knowing Karim, a Northern Sudanese, helped to open my eyes to the persecution faced by Christians everywhere. It wasn't only the South Sudanese people who suffered. There were persecuted Christians in every country dominated by Islam.

We opened our dorm room for Inter Varsity small group Bible studies, which we led together. I continued to work full time and maintained a schedule of two classes. I also continued to participate in cross-country races. Karim found a summer job with one of the professors. We prayed every day for a miracle for Karim. I felt his burden and it became my own. Although we were constantly busy with work, studies, and Inter Varsity activities, I could tell that Karim was constantly thinking about his family, especially his mother.

In August, Karim got his miracle. His mother, Dr. Grace, arrived in the United States. The doctors in Holland were able to remove the growth in her brain, and she was regaining her vision! Originally, the surgeon had told Dr. Grace that she would lose her sight when the tumor was removed because of the precarious location of the mass. Miraculously, she was spared from that outcome. I was rejoicing with Karim, because I had begun to regard him as a younger brother during our brief time of living together. God was merciful to Grace and granted her healing and a reunion with her son. Even so, things were still going to be very difficult for his family. Grace was unable to return to the Sudan, and there was no longer any way for the family to earn a living due to the confiscation of their business and all of their foreign currency.

As it turned out, Dr. Grace was stranded at NJIT with nowhere to go. So, as Karim had become my brother, Grace became my mother. I offered her my room to sleep in since I was at work during the night shift. This arrangement worked out well for all of us. We got along very well together, like a real family. Grace's presence on campus seemed to strike a chord in the hearts of other foreign students who, for various reasons, were unable to return home. These students from places like China, Ghana, Ecuador, and Santa Lucia seemed to gain strength and comfort from Karim's mother. Our little family unit was a small reminder of the homes that they missed so much. More than that, it was an opportunity for us to minister to students from around the world with the gospel message. The love that we shared was tangible evidence of the faith that had brought us together.

Through the events of that summer, Karim and I grew and developed spiritually in ways that would stay with us for the rest of our lives. Through the hospitality of some local American Christian families, we learned a spirit of serving others and changing the society for Christ. Scott Davis, our Inter Varsity staff pastor, taught us leadership skills and responsibility. As co-leaders of a small group Bible study, we learned to reach across cultural divides to meet the needs of all different types of people. Although I was still very active in the Peddie Memorial Baptist Church, Karim and I decided to learn more about our fellow Christians by visiting several different churches in the area. God was hard at work preparing me for a role that I never dreamed I would play.

I had been praying for my Jewish people, and I began to wonder if there were Messianic Jews in America. God heard my prayers, and He was preparing my heart to return to the Messianic root of my faith. As it turned out, Karim was the one to visit a local Messianic congregation. He was excited about it and invited me to visit as well.

"William, you will never believe what I found!" I could tell by his expression that it was something good. "I found a church with people who are like you. They are Jews who follow Jesus!"

I was intrigued. "What sort of church is this?"

"It's called Beth Israel Messianic Center. I know you will really like the pastor there. Why don't we both go there on Friday for their Shabbat services?"

"Wow, I have been praying about this. But I can't go, because I work on Friday nights."

"How about Sunday?"

"I don't want to miss services at Peddie!"

I'm not sure why I made excuses, but eventually my excuses ran out. I went with Karim and his mother and visited Beth Israel. I was so excited to be with people who shared my heritage and traditions; it was almost overwhelming. Even though these Jews were not of African heritage, their welcome was just like family. For the remainder of my time at NJIT, I continued to build relationships with both Peddie Memorial Baptist and Beth Israel. I had a deep respect and affection for Reverend Hatfield of Peddie

Memorial, and his help and support was a real blessing to me. The Reverend Hatfield combined his concern for the physical needs of the poor with a genuine zeal for saving the lost. He reached out to students and helped mobilize a large group to attend a Billy Graham crusade held at the local stadium. So, although I felt that God was eventually going to lead me to service at Beth Israel, I knew that I had unfinished business at Peddie Memorial as long as I was going to be working with NJIT students.

The years I spent in college were incredibly full. I am still amazed that God preserved my health and gave me the ability to succeed with almost no sleep at all! I threw myself into my relationships with the same vigor that I threw myself into my studies, and I was blessed by both. During those vital, formative years, my professors gave me a wonderful college education. But my higher education came from the Lord.

Note: In this chapter, I use the word *race* to describe human diversity. This is simply a matter of convention, because it is a commonly used term. I believe that there is only one "race" and that is the human race. Skin color and cultural values are superficial differences. It is my firm opinion that if ethnic differences did not exist, people would find some other reason to hate one another!

CHAPTER SEVENTEEN

Operation Nehemiah

The summer of 1993 was a major turning point in my life. I had just graduated from NJIT, and my future was bright. There was one last retreat that I planned to attend with fellow students from Inter Varsity Christian Fellowship, only now as an alumnus. The IVCF students had become like a family to me, and I knew I would be missing them as we all went on our separate paths.

It was a great feeling to head to Camp Pinnacle, near Albany, New York. Spring was in full bloom and the optimism of the season seemed to fit my mood. I was ready for a time of spiritual renewal and direction, as I would soon be heading into a great new career. The theme of the section I had chosen to participate in at the retreat was "Christ and culture." This topic was of special interest to me, because I had experienced such vastly diverse cultures in my journey. Through each culture and each community, the Body of Christ was generally an example of a unifying spirit that was uniquely able to transcend ethnic barriers. Even so, I had also witnessed divisions that were all too similar to those found in the world of unbelievers. As a Sudanese national and a Messianic Jew, and now as an adopted American, I was already straddling some pretty divergent cultures. For that reason, I was more acutely aware of the challenges faced by the church today with respect to cultural diversity, racism, and ethnic strife. I wanted to be prepared to serve the community as a Christian leader as I entered the "real world" in my new culture. I wanted to understand how Christ and Christianity could interact with the culture and transform it for the glory of God.

Scott Davis, my roommate and college pastor, was leading the group meeting. I felt a heavy burden in my spirit as we discussed our responsibilities and roles as new graduates entering the workforce. I prayed earnestly throughout each session and continually grilled my teachers with questions. I just couldn't shake the feeling that God was trying to tell me something—but what?

After several rounds of pretty intense class work, the whole group got together for a special prayer meeting for the persecuted believers in the Sudan. Karim and Rami, brothers from Northern Sudan, and I had a special heart for this topic. We felt led to hold this special prayer session. I thought perhaps that the heaviness that I felt in my spirit was a prompting, an urging of the Holy Spirit to enter into prayer for my fellow Sudanese. Even so, after our time of heartfelt intercession, the burden persisted. I knew that God was at work. I really felt as though God was getting ready to do something big. I just didn't understand that God wanted to do something big *in my life.*

As the IVCF conference was drawing to a close, the staff called all of the Christ in Culture section students together for a special time of prayer. A number of the students in this section had received a call into full-time ministry. Some were planning to serve in the inner city; some were planning to serve around the world. The training they had received was sure to help them to adjust to their new lives in foreign lands or within an ethnic group that was different from their own. The staff called those particular students forward so that the rest of the students could pray over them and intercede for their calling. I drew close in order to pray for the students heading into ministry.

"William." I looked up and noticed that Scott was motioning to me. "Go and sit with the students in the circle."

"But I'm not going into the ministry," I whispered. "I'm an engineer."

"I think you have been called to serve," he insisted.

Some of the other students nearby heard our hushed exchange and began to encourage me. "Yes, William, go on!"

"We ought to pray for you, I feel it."

I didn't feel prepared. I didn't feel adequate. I felt awkward and unsure of myself. But still, there was a sense of rightness in my spirit as the sense of heaviness gave way to a sense of purpose.

God, is this what You have been trying to tell me?

I made my way into the circle and sat down with the other students who had been called to serve. As a multitude of hands stretched out over me, I felt God's power and confirmation that there was indeed a calling in my life. I still had no idea of what that calling might be.

We returned home from the retreat on May 22. Two days later, I received a visit from assistant pastor, Matt Simon, of the Beth Israel Messianic Congregation.

"William, how are you?"

"Great, Pastor Matt! What's new?"

"Well, I am coming to you with a special request, and I hope you can help."

I was mystified by Pastor Matt's words. What could I do to help him?

"Our district leader is retiring for the North Jersey area. We need someone to replace him, and we just felt that you would be the right person for the job."

"Me? I don't think I am really adequate for that. I . . . I don't know if I am the best person for a district leader position."

"Well, you just pray about it, then." Pastor Matt was very practical and matter-of-fact. "God will give you wisdom if you ask, and then you just let Rabbi Jonathan know what the decision will be."

He turned to go, leaving me with a flurry of doubts and questions. For the next two days, I was frequently on my knees in prayer. I just didn't understand what God was up to. The district in North Jersey that I was being asked to represent was full of rich people. These folks had good jobs, nice homes, and expensive cars. What did they need me for? I just didn't know what I could offer them. Besides, these people were so . . . well, they were different from me. How could I possibly relate to them? How would they react to me if I were to call on them? I didn't even have a car or a telephone line!

It was then that I recalled with sudden force and clarity all that I had learned just two days ago in the Christ and Culture session.

Was I so affected by cultural bias that I couldn't see the needs of these more affluent brothers and sisters?

Forgive me, Lord, I prayed, *for not seeing people as You see them.*

I had to admit that living in downtown Newark had colored my view of American culture. I had learned to associate spiritual needs, such as immorality, substance abuse, and criminal behavior, to poverty and lack of education. The real cause of spiritual need is simply the sinful nature of all human beings, whether they are rich or poor, educated or ignorant. Jesus Christ came to seek and to save that which was lost. He was seeking the suburbanites as well as the inner city folks. God had prepared my heart to work with the Beth Israel Messianic parishioners, even though they were culturally different from me. But would God prepare the hearts of the parishioners to accept me, a foreigner in their land? I felt sure that the people from North Jersey would have trouble getting past the fact that I was from downtown Newark—a place they associated with crime and poverty.

I told Rabbi Jonathan that I would accept the job if I could use the church telephone for my new duties. He agreed, and so I took on my new mission with whole-hearted enthusiasm. I was humbled to realize that I was in a position of ministry, and I wanted to do it all for Jesus and in His name. Being a minister isn't always easy. It was discouraging when some folks felt that they ought to receive the attention of the senior pastor instead of a district leader. At those times I was made to feel inadequate, like a nobody. But most people were very kind and accepting. I spent time visiting homes, praying with those who were sick, and counseling those who had problems in their lives. I also was able to coordinate arrangements for material needs such as transportation and job loss.

As I continued to serve the members of Beth Israel, I could feel myself being transformed into a servant of Christ. Even though my grandfather and my father had been spiritual leaders in their communities, I had never in my life felt any desire to follow in their footsteps. I was prepared to be a fine layman and church member but never a full-time minister. The future I had envisioned for myself involved material success. Pastors don't climb the corporate ladder. I believed that I could help my family most by earning money to support them. But God already had other plans in mind, and He was shaping me and molding me into the person that He wanted me to be.

So, while God was leading me deeper into ministry, I was still busy making other plans for my life. I was going full speed ahead with plans for my career. Success was so close I could almost taste it! God, of course, knew what was in my heart. He knew it would take some amazing "coincidences" to get my attention.

My cousin, the Reverend John, and his family were in town to visit with some friends from Grace Presbyterian Church in Montclair, New Jersey. I was glad to have a chance for some fellowship with him again, so I invited him to my church to hear a special speaker at my home church, Beth Israel. He was happy to accompany me. The speaker of the evening was Richard Wurmbrand, the founder of Voice of the Martyrs, a group dedicated to helping persecuted Christians around the world. He and his wife, Sabina, had come to my church to speak about Sudan! They came and spoke at services on Friday and Sunday morning.

That weekend, God used the Wurmbrands to prepare the hearts of the congregation to respond to the plight of the persecuted church in the Sudan. As John and I listened to Pastor Wurmbrand explain in detail the horrors of persecution in the southern regions of our homeland, our hearts were challenged and convicted. The seed that God had planted in my heart was beginning to take root and grow. It was quiet in the car as I drove John back to his friends' home in Montclair.

"John," I ventured, "I felt something tonight."

John nodded solemnly. "I felt it, too. God was really speaking to me back there."

"I have the feeling that God wants me to do something to help our people." I wasn't sure exactly where I was going with this, but I did have an idea for starters. "I think it might be a good idea to hold a prayer vigil in front of the United Nations building as a sort of protest against the treatment of the South Sudanese people. Maybe it would get people to at least become aware of the problem."

"I agree. Even I was shocked by what Pastor Wurmbrand said, and I've only been out of the country for three years. I don't think that most Americans have any idea about what is going on there."

"I'm sure that is true. I certainly haven't seen it on the evening news."

"William, I will pray about your prayer vigil idea. I will help you however I can. But I think you should know what God has laid on my heart."

"Go on."

"The reason I am here in New Jersey is to meet with some AIM officials. I wanted to discuss my decision to return to the Sudan to minister to my people there."

"That's a wonderful plan," I assured him. I knew that he had wanted to come to the United States to pursue his Masters of

Divinity, so it seemed only natural for him to return now that his studies were complete.

John's face looked pained. "It isn't that wonderful," he replied. "My whole community is gone. Every person is scattered in exile, and the church building is gone. What can I do?"

"Wow. There is so much trouble and so much has been destroyed." I thought for a moment. "But you can still serve your people. Why not go into the ministry in Uganda? You may even find many of your old congregants living together there."

"That might just work," John mused. "I just have to believe that God will provide a way for me to serve my people still, no matter what the circumstance."

"Amen to that!" I replied. Even so, the prospect seemed daunting. Humanly speaking, it hardly seemed possible. But I knew in my heart of hearts that God had put my cousin and me together at just the right time in both of our lives to hear Richard Wurmbrand's message. The pleas to help our brothers and sisters in Sudan seemed to be coming directly from the Holy Spirit, speaking to me and to John.

We could not say no. The following evening, I made arrangements to visit with the Wurmbrands at the home of some of their Romanian friends the next town on their itinerary, Cedar Grove, New Jersey. Richard had been extremely encouraging to me when I mentioned my vision to help the Sudanese people, and now I sought his advice. The Wurmbrands and their friends warmly welcomed me, as well as my friend Karim and several Inter Varsity students. Meeting with Richard and Sabina was like meeting with real saints of modern-day Christianity. They encouraged us to go forward with God to change the situation in the Sudan for all of the Christians there. We discussed several possible options, and Pastor Wurmbrand gave me thoughtful advice.

That evening, in June of 1993, I became sure of my calling. My vision to hold a prayer vigil at the UN was not simply an option; it was a must. I finally realized that if anything were to be done for my people, I would have to put my very life on the line. I decided to relinquish my worldly ambition and allow God to do His work through me. That night, I returned home to Newark a changed man.

The next few days brought a flurry of activity and phone calls as I sought help from friends and Sudanese nationals in exile. Within days, a meeting was arranged in New York City at the home of the Reverend Elioba Lado. A large group of exiled Christians from the South Sudan were mobilized to discuss the troubles of our people back home. I was energized by the belief that we would all be of one mind and one accord in our desire to help our brothers. But I was young and still a bit naïve when it came to the world of politics. I soon found out that my enthusiasm was not shared by all.

We began the meeting with the customary introductions and pleasantries all around. In attendance were Sabet, Simon, Santiago Yanga, Benedict Lagu, and several others, all exiles from the South of Sudan. I called the meeting to order with a time of prayer, and then I stood to address the group and explain my vision.

"Brothers," I began, "this meeting is the beginning of an effort to protect the future of our people and our country."

I could feel the weight of all eyes upon me as the group waited for me to explain what I was up to. I measured my words carefully, because I could sense that each man in the room was regarding each syllable with cautious scrutiny. There was a strange sense of unease in my heart as I tried to read each impassive face. Something important seemed to be missing from the group—I could feel it. That missing element was a spirit of unity among brothers.

I continued to press on, explaining my idea for a prayer vigil outside of the UN building. I reminded them of the pain that they themselves had managed to escape and urged them to do whatever was in their power to help others who remained behind in perilous circumstances.

"Finally, it seems obvious that something must be done soon," I concluded. "Who better to make the world aware of the suffering of our people than us? We were there; our families remain there. The voices of our people have been silenced. Who will speak for them? If we fail to take up this mantle, then who will do it for us? We need to take the first step and speak to the world for our people."

I had made my case for action, but the room was silent.

"What do you think?" I queried.

"You don't know what you are asking of us. We will be exposing our views in full view of the Sudanese officials at the UN building."

"That's right; we have to think of our safety first."

"I think we are perfectly safe to express our views in this country," I countered. "And I don't think our families back home will be in any more danger than they already are," I added grimly.

"How do you propose to finance such a thing? You can see for yourself that none of us here is a wealthy man."

"God will provide—Christians from this country will help us, I'm sure of it."

"Even if you do get the money for the permits, what use is it? We are just going to face ridicule by those who pass by. Nobody cares about us. It's no good to hold some prayer vigil, because it won't accomplish anything. Besides, William, you are too young. What do you know about life and politics?"

I was getting pretty exasperated, because it seemed like our discussion was going nowhere fast. It seemed to me that the older men were giving in to defeat and fear. If we didn't even believe that we could make a difference, then how could we expect the rest of the world to support our cause?

"I think William is right," said a voice from the back of the room. I turned and saw that it was Simon who spoke. "We have to start somewhere, and we have to do something. We owe our people that much. I think a march on the UN is a good idea, because it would be a way to gain some publicity for the plight of our people. Once we get some organization and some publicity, we will gain support. Who knows, maybe we can bring some political pressure to bear on Khartoum!"

"What do you say?" I looked around the room, stopping to catch the gaze of each person gathered. "Are you with me on this?"

There was a grudging approval on the part of the men in the room. They still had their doubts and it showed. It was clear to me that this project was going to have to be my baby. I was going to be doing most of the planning, fundraising, and implementation; but that was OK. At least a plan was in motion. I had a sense that God was really with me on this one, and I felt that there was going to be more to come in the future, if I kept my heart tuned to His will.

I drove back to Newark that night sobered but determined. I had a better picture of some of the obstacles that I was sure to face if I was going to continue on with the vision that God had given me. That evening, I stopped by the Beth Israel Messianic Center to speak to Rabbi Jonathan Cahn, Gary Saleman, and Matt Simon. I explained to them that I needed their support to mobilize a prayer vigil for Sudan. I briefly outlined the steps that would need to be taken to get the project off the ground.

God knew that I needed encouragement, and I had gone to the right place. The leadership of Beth Israel wasted no time in their wholehearted agreement to help. Soon momentum began to build. Looking back, I am still amazed at the way God orchestrated circumstances to make it possible for His will to be accomplished through me. I am even more amazed when I realize that He had to break my will to conform to His at almost every step. But of course, nothing is impossible with God! Because of the Christ in Culture retreat, I was prepared to minister among people who were not of my cultural background. Because of my willingness to work with the people of Beth Israel, I gained the trust and support of an entire congregation. Because of a visit from Pastor Wurmbrand, the hearts of that congregation were prepared to minister to Sudan, and I was given a vision. Because my cousin, John, happened to be in town, he also felt the vision. None of this was my own doing. Only God deals the cards like that.

I was blessed by the enthusiastic support of my church. Gary Selman, a pastor, and Paul Liben, a writer and historian, took the lead in helping me to get things done. Gary was also a radioman, one of two "Nice Jewish Boys" on a local station. He and Rabbi Jonathan broadcast a gospel program every Wednesday, and they brought me on the air several times to share my testimony. They also introduced me to Andy Anderson, a brother who broadcast the gospel from another local station. Paul Liben assisted me by writing professional articles for the print media and getting in touch with local news venues. The women of the congregation helped in so many practical ways. Jan Selman made a beautiful box to collect donations to offset expenses. Wonderful sisters designed and created banners and everything that was needed for the march at the UN.

The first seed money for the project was a small sum donated by a poor woman who lived on disability. Her generosity reminded me of the widow in the Bible who gave all that she had to the kingdom of God. I was simply overwhelmed by the love, the prayers, and the assistance given to me by the people of Beth Israel. Meanwhile, momentum was building among the Sudanese communities in New Jersey, New York, Ohio, and Washington DC. But the enemy was at work within the ranks.

Simon and I were in charge of weekly briefings to inform our Sudanese brothers of the progress of our project. Simon was much older than I was, and he knew everyone from the Sudanese community. Many of the men had been government officials back in the Sudan before they found themselves stranded in the United States. Simon was well aware of the political issues that were surfacing, and he was feeling the heat. One of the main tactics of the Khartoum regime has always been to divide the South based on tribal loyalties, and the repercussions of that tactic were being felt all the way across the Atlantic. Even though Simon and I were working together on the project, I felt that we did not have a spirit of unity between us. I could not help but wonder why.

The main political opposition to the Khartoum regime was the Sudanese People's Liberation Army, or SPLA, headed by Dr. John

Garang. But the Islamic regime in Khartoum was well aware of tribal differences within and successfully orchestrated a split in the SPLA. Two SPLA leaders, Dr. Riak Machar and Dr. Lam Akol, decided to form the South Sudan Independence Movement, or SSIM. Differences of opinion between these two factions tended to follow tribal lines. The SSIM maintained an office in Washington, DC, headed by a man named Moses Akol, from Simon's own tribe. Like it or not, the peaceful prayer vigil I had envisioned was rapidly becoming embroiled in politics. Simon was being pressured to turn the demonstration into a show of support for the SSIM.

I knew something was wrong between us, but I just couldn't put my finger on it. I didn't understand why Simon's focus for the rally seemed to be so different from my own. Finally, he opened up to me and explained what was bothering him.

"William," he said, "I have to tell you that I can't agree with your objectives for the rally at the UN."

I was dumbfounded. "Why not?" was all I managed in reply.

"Look. I agree with having a peaceful rally. But this isn't all about Christianity. There are other issues involved."

Slowly, I began to understand the tension that had been developing between us. I also began to see why my elders in the Sudanese community were initially so hesitant to go along with my proposal. Apparently, I had just opened up a Pandora's Box of conflicts that had been hidden just below the surface among my fellow exiles. Perhaps it was because of my own youth and naïveté that I hadn't recognized it before. I had to get to the bottom of this and fast!

"So Simon, what objectives did you have in mind?"

"This has to be about our political agenda. Nobody is going to respect us if we call ourselves the South Sudanese Christian Community in America. We need a broader tent."

I bristled. "What kind of tent do you propose?" I asked. "Isn't it good enough to stand up for people who are being slaughtered just because of their faith?"

"Hear me out, William," he countered. "We need to draft a letter to the UN Secretary General to represent our views."

"What views are those?"

"The views of the SSIM."

So, at last he had said it. Our motivations were entirely at odds. I wanted to develop grassroots support for the persecuted Sudanese church among the American believers and politicians. Simon wanted Boutros Boutros-Ghali and the international community at the UN to support a political faction. It seemed as though Satan had succeeded in driving a wedge between my own brother in Christ and me. Were we at an impasse? I was deeply discouraged.

That night, I returned to my apartment and began to pour my heart out before the Lord.

Lord, I prayed, *You called me to help Your children in Sudan. I know that with all of my heart. Why have You allowed political and ethnic differences to tear Your church apart? I know we are not fighting against the rulers in Khartoum, because they are men of flesh and blood. We are fighting against spiritual forces. Lord, You are greater than the powers that are working to divide Your church. You are greater than the spirit of evil that is pressing forward to kill Your children. I place this all in Your hands, because there is nothing I can do. I am powerless.*

What else could I say? My heart was broken for my people. I could see my father's face in my mind's eye. He was a precious, loving man who was murdered for his faith. I could picture my mother and sisters running for their lives, with eyes blinded by tears. How long could they survive the privations of the refugee camps? I no longer knew what I ought to pray, but I offered my weakness and my anguish up before my heavenly Father. Now was the time for the Spirit to pray in my stead, with groanings that only God would understand.

I fell into a troubled sleep, and when I awoke, the burden on my spirit was still heavy. I knew I had to talk to someone—someone who, like me, was neutral in matters of Sudanese politics.

I turned to my friends at Beth Israel for advice. They listened as I explained the situation that was developing. Pastor Gary Selman's face was grave as he nodded understanding.

"I'm not surprised," he said. "I was getting a sense that there was some division within the group."

Rabbi Jonathan agreed. "Believe me, William, this wouldn't be the first time these kinds of divisions caused problems in the church."

"But so much is at stake!" I protested. "Can't they see that? Can't they move beyond these petty differences for the sake of millions of dying people?"

"Maybe that is why God chose you to get this vision going," Jonathan mused. "Maybe you will be able to accomplish this, not despite your youth, but because of it."

"What do you mean?"

"Well, you didn't know what you were getting yourself into, for one thing. An older, more experienced man might not have even tried. Plus, you left Sudan when you were very young. You never had the opportunity to get involved in these issues, so you have an unbiased eye."

"That's right," Gary added. "The vision of this rally is being tested, but God will see to it that His will is done. You can count on that much. I will come with you to the next meeting. It might help to have a neutral party to moderate."

Gary was faithful to his promise, and soon we found ourselves at the last meeting before the scheduled march. The permits were in order and arrangements were made, but there was still a spirit of division to overcome. The atmosphere in the little apartment in the Bronx where we had all gathered together was so tense that I scarcely dared to breathe. On the very eve of the historic event of Sudanese exiles gathering together to support the cause of their people, there was a serious lack of solidarity. The same issues surfaced once again, only this time more loudly than before. Many felt threatened by the boldness of the statements I had proposed. Many felt that we would get no response from the UN if we called ourselves Christians, especially from the Islamic countries. They felt it would be more expedient to identify ourselves with a political faction. Still others felt that I was simply too young and unable to understand the subtleties of politics. After an extended discussion had failed to resolve our differences, it seemed as though all hope was gone.

It was then that Pastor Gary asked to speak to the group. He turned to the Bible and read from First Samuel the story of David's call from the house of Jesse. David was younger and smaller than all of his brothers, but God chose him to do His work. Everyone was surprised that God chose David.

"Do you see the parallel here?" Gary asked. "David was young and inexperienced, but he relied completely on God. Everyone was amazed at what God accomplished through him. I think you all will be amazed at what God wants to accomplish here. William is young and he is small of stature. He doesn't have political aspirations, and he isn't involved with any political faction. But it is not by might, power, or strength, but by My Spirit, says the Lord. Do you all really believe that with God all things are possible?" He looked around the room, a challenge in his gaze. "This is the work of God, so you have only two choices. You can get with the program or get out of the way, because God will prevail."

No one spoke. It was obvious that many resented Gary's stinging rebuke. I prayed that God would give me wisdom and words to say to fill the hostile silence. I was calm as I stood to address the group. "Listen, my fellow Sudanese, you seem to forget the reason why you are in exile. It is this very faith that you are now denying that caused you to face persecution and finally expulsion from your own country by the Islamic regime. Who has bewitched you? How can you start out in faith by the Spirit of God and then fall again into human works and bondage? I will not deny the name of Jesus, and I will not allow the church to fall into tribal differences and ethnic divisions. A house divided cannot stand."

Did I discern a softening of some of the hardened expressions around the room? It was difficult to tell. I knew I had to continue. I coveted the support of all of my brothers, no matter what their political persuasion. "We are fighting a spiritual battle, and we face a common enemy. We must unite. We all follow a living God and a Savior by whose name we are set free from the bondage of sin and disunity. There is no name whether in heaven or on earth by which we are saved except in the Name above all Names, Jesus Christ. I will not deny the name of Christ to appease some politicians at the UN. I do not fear men who can kill my body, but I fear God who has the power to cast my soul into hell."

I knew that this was going to be the final appeal. Either everyone would walk out, or we would all work together. I had to deliver an ultimatum. "This is my decision as the organizer of this rally. The original purpose of this demonstration stands. We go before the UN as Christians, and the power we wield is prayer. I challenge all of you to choose this day who you will serve, but as for me—I will serve the Lord. Whoever is not for us is against us and scatters us. You can choose to divide or unite. The choice is up to you. If you are with me, stand up."

For a moment, nobody moved. Then slowly, deliberately, an elderly gentleman rose to his feet. One by one, the men stood as the Spirit convicted them to rise. Before long, the whole group was standing. *Praise God!* I knew that I had just witnessed something miraculous.

Even as tears welled up in my eyes, I knew that the time for tears was past. After Nehemiah wept, mourned, fasted, and prayed, he knew that God was ready to move. And Nehemiah was there, ready to obey. A sense of calm and resolve spread over the group of men. They were ready to set aside their differences for the greater good. It was time to rebuild the walls.

> Then said I unto them, Ye see the distress that we are in, how Jerusalem lieth waste, and the gates thereof are burned with fire: come, and let us build up the wall of Jerusalem, that we be no

more a reproach. Then I told them of the hand of my God which was good upon me; as also the king's words that he had spoken unto me. And they said, Let us rise up and build. So they strengthened their hands for this good work.

—Nehemiah 2:17–18

Epilogue

On July 31, 1993, over 250 people converged at the United Nations for a peaceful prayer vigil. We had many speakers, including Manute Bol, Dr. Augustin Ladu, Simon, Gary Selman, Scott Davis, Rev. Glenn Hatfield, and myself. The Reverend John was also in attendance. The rally lasted for two hours. It was truly a breakthrough in that all of the Sudanese people worked together with all of their hearts. On this same day, a deadly earthquake rocked Khartoum. Was this quake a sign from God? Only He knows.

In the months following the rally, I worked full time toward the incorporation of this vision into a Christian organization. On October 15, 1993, Operation Nehemiah for South Sudan was established as a non-profit Christian entity. The vision statement was fourfold: Spiritual restoration of the Christian Church in the Sudan, education of the youth of Sudan, agriculture, and health care development. Paul Liben, Gary Selman, and I were the first board members. In December of 1993, Beth Israel Messianic Center contributed an office space to house the fledgling ministry. The board meetings gave rise to the *Nehemiah Trumpet Call*, a quarterly newsletter.

It was also at this time that my cousin, the Reverend John, was due to return to Africa. It was God's plan that he had witnessed the vision for Operation Nehemiah from the very beginning, because he was called to help. He became our first overseas field director with an office in Kampala, Uganda. In the fall of 1994, the Reverend Michael Longwa, my childhood friend and co- laborer in the Great Commission, became the overseas field director of Operation Nehemiah of Nairobi, Kenya. Over the next three to four years, Operation Nehemiah was involved in the shipping of over one million dollars worth of relief and development supplies to the South Sudan, and that was only the beginning.

Postscript

The Lord Almighty has heard our cries, bottled our tears, and answered our prayers! He has restored hope to our land and people. On May 26, 2004, the Sudan entered into a comprehensive peace agreement, ending one of the longest wars of religious persecution in world history. The church in the Sudan has endured fifty years of Islamic persecution and genocide. We have lost two million people and four million have been displaced. Even so, the body of Yeshua perseveres—though refined by fire. The Sudanese church is now poised to take on the challenge of rebuilding the nation.

Yes, the war is officially over in the South Sudan, although, unfortunately, violence continues to escalate in the western region of Darfur. *Now is the time, the opportunity we have prayed for . . . the door is open to restore the church to the Sudan.* We must pray that the Sudanese church returning from exile will grow in strength, unity, and spiritual focus. We must help them physically and disciple them spiritually.

In January 2004, almost six months ahead of the Sudan peace agreement, Operation Nehemiah Missions officially moved its permanent base out of the Ugandan refugee camps and into Corom, New Sudan. This is where all of our missions work will now be conducted. We have dedicated this village to God to address the needs of the returning exiles. While we were there, we saw and experienced demonic oppression, gloom, destitution, and depression infecting the land and her people. We need your help more than ever to rebuild a broken culture.

In 1972, there was a peace accord, but eleven years later it was followed by renewed oppression and genocide. Please help us build a strong and united biblically based Christian community in the South Sudan and throughout the entire country during this window of opportunity.

Endnotes

[1] Matthew 25:42

[2] Hebrews 10:30

[3] Romans 3:10

[4] Matthew 5:44

[5] Matthew 19:26

[6] Nehemiah 1:4

[7] 2 Corinthians 4:9

[8] Psalm 8:4

[9] Ephesians 6:10-13

[10] Matthew 6:33

[11] John 14:6

[12] Hebrews 13:5

[13] Matthew 5:48

[14] John 17:3

[15] 1 Thessalonians 5:17

[16] James 2:15-16

APPENDIX ONE

Church and Evangelistic Missions—Since 1993

Services at Beth Israel on the Nile are held in a tent

Vision: to rebuild the spiritual lives of displaced Christians in South Sudan and Uganda. The goal of this mission is to restore solid biblical teaching through the development of indigenous pastoral leadership. Operation Nehemiah has established the following programs:

- Pastoral leadership seminar—raising up pastors to teach and disciple
- Establishment of a local church led by a local pastor—the Beth Israel Messianic Congregation on the Nile, in Kampala, Uganda was founded in 2000
- Bible distribution in tribal languages
- Crusade and evangelistic outreaches in the refugee camps
- Mobile radio to spread the gospel in native languages of the people

Education—Since 1993

Dr. Godwin teaches health and medicine in Nimule

Vision: to rebuild the future of the youth of South Sudan. Displaced children lack even the most basic educational opportunities. Uneducated children will propagate the cycle of poverty and lack of leadership in the Sudan. In order to produce the future pastors, teachers, and leaders of our community, we cannot neglect our most valuable asset, our children. This is true in any society, but especially in a region that must be rebuilt from the ground up. Operation Nehemiah has responded by establishing the following programs:

- Sponsorship of students from elementary school through advanced studies
- University scholarships for qualified students through the Internet Café project
- Establishment of the Nehemiah Polytechnic Institute

Nehemiah Polytechnic Institute—Since 2003

Operation Nehemiah Construction Department builds the
NPI from the ground up.

Vision: to rebuild the skills of the displaced community. Not every student will go on to a university; and there are many trades that are necessary to rebuild the South Sudan. The NPI was founded to address this issue. It is located in Adjumani and was founded in 2003 by the Wisconsin, USA ON Construction team. NPI programs include:

- Carpentry
- Masonry
- Auto mechanics
- Tailoring
- Engineering/drafting
- Plumbing
- Electrical work
- Healthcare
- Computer technology

Nehemiah Internet Café—Since 2003

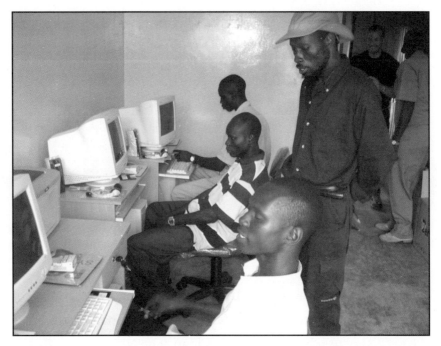

William Levi looks on as students and faculty try out the new computers.

Vision: to rebuild the financial independence of the Operation Nehemiah scholarship fund. It is becoming increasingly difficult to raise funds for education, but students still need to attend universities. The goal of Operation Nehemiah is to found a self-sustaining source of income to fund the university tuition for deserving students. The Nehemiah Internet Café was established in Kampala, Uganda in 2003. All profits will go to the educational needs of Sudanese young people.

Microeconomic Business Investment— Since 1999

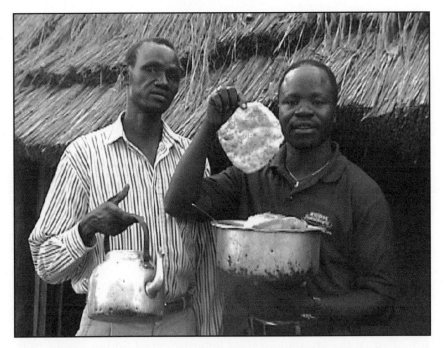

Rumeo Mude and Rev. Michael Longwa enjoy the success of a
new bakery business.

Vision: to rebuild the self-worth of men and families in the South
Sudan through financial independence. Families in refugee situations find themselves demoralized, and they are without the means
to support themselves. The goal of the microeconomic business
investment program is to provide families with the capital they
need to become financially independent. A loan of three hundred
US dollars is given to families who have a business proposal. They
are expected to repay the loan interest-free in one year. Families
who succeed in business are then empowered to support the work
of the church through their tithe.

Agriculture—Since 1993

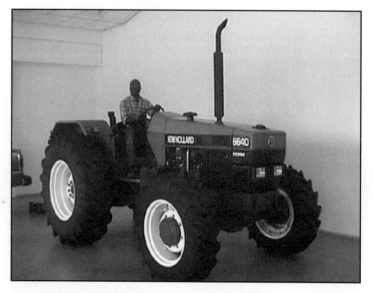

Rev. Michael Longwa tries the brand new tractor for Kiriadongo.

Vision: to rebuild the food supply infrastructure of the community. Part of the strategy of the Government of Sudan has been to subjugate the people through artificially induced famine and starvation. Food has been brought in from foreign aid organizations, but this does not solve the underlying problem. The displaced people have not had the stability or the resources necessary to produce food for themselves. That will change with Operation Nehemiah's agriculture initiative. To date, the following programs have been instituted:

- Purchase of a tractor for Kiriadongo refugee camp
- Distribution of hoes, seeds, and machetes
- Plant rotation education
- Purchase of oxen for plowing (in progress)
- Poultry start-up supplies

WATER

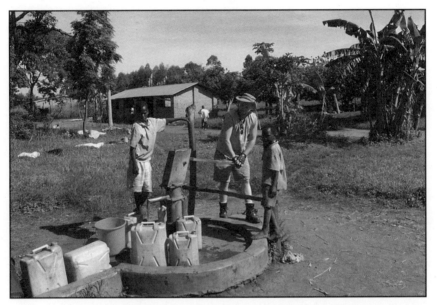

Brian Gantt pumps water from a new well in Kiriodonga

Vision: to rebuild the infrastructure of the South Sudan community and provide better sanitation. Waterborne diseases have exacted a tragic toll on the refugee people, especially the children. Most camps are not located near rivers, so even unsanitary water has been hard to come by. Operation Nehemiah has been working hard to drill wells and install pumps in the refugee camps.

CONSTRUCTION DEPARTMENT

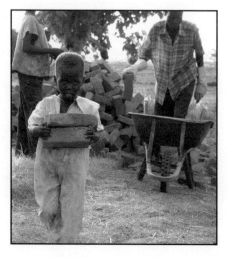

A little child helps to rebuild his future during construction of the NPI.

Vision: to rebuild the walls of the schools, churches, and homes. Just as in the days of Nehemiah, the infrastructure of our communities has been destroyed. We must literally rebuild from the ground up. That takes supplies and skilled labor. A group of skilled men from the United States has volunteered not only their money but their time and sweat as well. But these men want to empower their Sudanese brothers to take up this work on their own. To address this issue, Operation Nehemiah has begun the following projects:

- Nehemiah Polytechnic Institute, training hands for the work of rebuilding
- Building a pastoral library in Nimule
- Poised for building a compound in Nimule in anticipation of peace agreement

For more photos, please see the Operation Nehemiah web site.

The Politics of Jihad in the Sudan and Hope for Future Peace

T here has not been much coverage of the situation in the Sudan by the traditional media. Even those who are aware of the conflict often do not understand the political root of the problem. Westerners are unfamiliar with the theocratic style of government and the complex issues that result from the combination of religious and political powers. The current civil war in the Sudan is a volatile mixture of greed, political ambition, and Islamic fundamentalism. The goal of the Government of Sudan is simply to possess all of the resources of the country and to cause all the people of the country to submit to their radical style of Islam. The perpetrators of the human rights abuses and genocide that are being inflicted toward these ends feel that their actions are completely justified. Indeed, they deeply believe that Allah sanctions their actions. Of course, the lust for a wealth of oil and personal power only adds fuel to the flames. Members of the most radical group, known as the National Islamic Front (NIF), are akin to the Mahdists of the 1800s in their philosophy. They, like the now infamous Taliban of Afghanistan, follow the literal interpretation of the Koran and believe in the spread of Islam by the sword. They view the Southerners as ignorant infidel savages; and as such, truly deserving of forced conversion or death.

There are many groups of disaffected Sudanese Muslims who, for various reasons, do not share these beliefs. Some feel that their ethnic group has been wrongfully denied access to political power. Some understand that radicalism excludes Sudan from the global economy. Some are simply not zealous for the ideas of jihad and Koranic theocracy. The Muslims of the Nuba Mountains, the Darfur, the Southern Blue Nile, and Eastern Sudanese Muslims are examples of these moderate Muslim groups who are regarded as traitors and are treated with disdain by the Khartoum regime. Recently, these Muslims and others have rebelled against the oppressive and discriminatory regime of Khartoum. Some groups have joined the Christians in opposition to the Arab regime. The GOS has responded to these African Muslims by burning their mosques and treating them as infidels. So, even for a Muslim it is a difficult thing to disagree with the fundamentalist ruling elite.

At least the jihadists who kill genuinely believe they are doing the right thing; sadly, the Canadian and Asian oil interests who are aiding and abetting the genocide have no such excuse. They simply value their economic interests more highly than the lives of millions of human beings.

The Africans who are fighting back are using guerilla tactics of necessity. They are poor, dispirited, and fragmented by tribal differences. However, in the last several years, the Sudanese People Liberation Army, under the command of Dr. John Garang, has made a remarkable effort in reuniting most of the factions. They have set up civil administration in the areas under their control through out the South Sudan and other marginalized regions in the north.

The millions of people displaced into refugee camps are starving and dying every day. Orphaned children who have lost their past are now destined to lose their future as well. There is no education, no food, and no health care. That is the consequence of this jihad.

THE NATURE OF JIHAD

Jihad as a political system has often been used for ethnic cleansing purposes. The tactics are similar to those seen during the imposition of any type of totalitarian government, be it secular or theocratic. With the murder of men, the raping of women, burning of churches, synagogues, and even mosques, and brainwashing of the children, they can succeed in eradicating a culture and a generation of people. The following generations have no memories of their past and know only the dominant form of Islam. According to the research of Dr. Robert Murray of the True Seekers, the following methods of jihad are commonly employed.

The Jihad of the Sword

In one version of the Hadith section of the Sunnah, chapter nineteen, it speaks of those converted to Islam by the sword (vol. 1, no. 27). Mohammed said, "I have been ordered to fight against people until none has the right to be worshipped but Allah. And that Mohammed is Allah's prophet and offer prayers and give obligatory charity, so if they perform all that, then they can save their lives and property" (vol. 1, no. 24). The Hadith records how Mecca was conquered by force (vol. 1, no. 104). In volume 3, number 495, we read, "Allah made the prophet wealthy through conquest." When a Muslim murders someone through jihad, he has the right to take the man's property, wife, and children. The prophet said, "Whoever killed an enemy and has proof of that, will possess his spoil" (vol. 4, no. 370). These words of the Islamic scriptures provide the driving force for fundamentalist Muslim violence in Sudan, Egypt, Israel, Lebanon, Iran, Iraq, Libya, Algeria, and much of Africa today.

The Jihad of Financial Reward

The tactic of bribery begun by the Islamic invaders of old is still in use today. A free university education, a free Muslim wife, and a free home can be offered to any Jew or Christian who will convert to Islam. When I was in Egypt, a wealthy Muslim man offered me his daughter, a car, and a home, if I would convert. I turned him down. A bounty of a thousand dollars has been offered to any Southern Sudanese man who will renounce Christianity and convert to Islam. In Juba, the Islamic relief hospital will care for a sick child only if the parents embrace Islam.

The Jihad of Taxation

The ancient practice of "*dhimmi*" is alive and well. Muslims have always boasted of their "tolerance" of Jews and Christians; but this benevolent protection has always come at a price. To enjoy freedom of conscience, non-Muslims are required to pay *al-jizya* (vol. 4 chap. 21:51–252). This tax is a heavy financial burden, and those who can't pay are often killed. The *dhimmi*, or protected religious minorities, are not permitted to hold positions of rank and are only permitted to take jobs that result in a lower socioeconomic status. When I was in Cairo, I spoke with a Coptic priest, whose name I won't disclose. He told me that his great-grandparents had the money to preserve their faith. Those who did not have money were forced to renounce Christianity or be put to death. Some fled and left their land and belongings behind. This practice is being enacted in Sudan. Churches and schools are brought to their knees by the punitive religious taxes. If unable to pay, the institution must close down. The Islamic authorities then confiscate the closed buildings. This law also makes it impossible to erect new churches and schools.

The Jihad of Fear

The death penalty is applied to any "apostate" Muslim who embraces another faith such as Christianity. There are countless Christians in the Sudan and Egypt who are being tortured even now. Their only crime was converting to Christianity. The jihad of fear is also being waged in the arena of world politics. Even after September 11, 2001, nations fear to speak against Islamic imperialism and aggression. Human rights violations are overlooked for fear of retaliation. An example of this tactic can be seen in the treatment of author Salman Rushdie, whose book, *The Satanic Verses*, was considered to be anti-Islam. He was forced to live in hiding after a *fatwa* was issued on his life.

The Jihad of Slavery

The only place in the world today where African blacks are being bought and sold as chattel slavery is in the Arab Islamic world. South Sudan and Mauritania are the most noted examples, but this is occurring in many other countries as well. In a shocking display of hypocrisy, the African-American leadership of the Nation of Islam has denied the existence of this atrocity.

The Jihad of the Courts

Non-Muslims are denied equal protection under the law. Their testimony in court is not valid against a Muslim (vol. 3, chap. 31, pp. 525–526) This even applies to murder: "No Muslim shall be killed for killing an infidel" (vol. 4, no. 283; vol. 9, no. 50).

I am very aware that it is not politically correct to expose examples of Islamic atrocities. However, it is the truth, and I have experienced it firsthand. *On the other hand, it is impossible to generalize the beliefs of all Muslims.* The majority of those who consider themselves Muslims only want to live their lives and raise their families in peace. Even so, the beliefs of the violent extremists are taken directly from their holy scriptures, the Koran and Sunnah.

It is difficult to determine what makes a moderate Muslim become an extremist. We know from history that Mohammed himself made such a switch in his effort to conquer Mecca. When he was militarily weak, he behaved as a moderate; but after he gained military strength, he behaved as an extremist.

These days, it seems as though a pious devotion to the most strictly literal interpretation of the Koran leads to jihad. According to the Associated Press, al Qaida leader, Osama bin Laden, explained his beliefs in a tape aired by al-jazeera in October of 2003. Bin Laden said that there have been voices calling for "peaceful solutions and democracy" in places like Iraq, Palestine, Egypt, Jordan, and Yemen. "This is illegal and against God's book," he said, referring to the teachings of the Koran.

What would make a man like bin Laden claim that peaceful solutions and democracy are wrong? The Koran is crystal clear in its call for Muslims to go to war to fight "oppression" in the "way of Allah." But what is oppression? For a Muslim who yearns for the full flower of Islam to be expressed in every aspect of life, all secular democratic governments are oppressive. The Koran is also clear in its prohibition against killing "the innocent." But who is innocent? Those who believe in and support "oppressive" western style democracy can no longer be considered "innocent."

Once a fundamentalist Islamic regime gains power, what happens to non-Muslims? The Koran repeatedly contradicts itself with regards to the place of the unbeliever. At one point, the Koran states: "say to those who disbelieve: you shall be vanquished and driven together to hell" (Surah 3:12); and at another place it insists that "there is no compulsion in religion" (Surah 10:99). Which is it? To find practical answers, one must look to the Sunnah, a dauntingly massive compilation of rules for living from the life of Mohammed. The Hadith of the Sunnah contains a disturbing list of rules for the equitable distribution of booty taken from slain "unbelievers." It even describes the removal of personal effects from a dead "infidel's" body. This information is not secret: it is posted in English on mainstream American Islamic web sites.

Some pundits claim that a fundamentalist-style adherence to any religion will result in violence and oppression. I humbly argue that this is not the case. The teachings of Jesus Christ, who stated, "My kingdom is not of this world" (John 18:36), are thoroughly anti-theocratic. A fundamentalist Christian is commanded by God to love his enemies and pray for those who persecute him (Matthew 5:43–44). Violence, revenge, and hatred are utterly foreign to Christian fundamentalism. So, I can only conclude that it is not the fundamentalists, but rather the fundamentals of doctrine that are inherently good or evil. In this vein, I might suggest that if a doctrine leads to genocide and terror, it may be time to re-think that doctrine.

The Hope for Peace

Jesus says, "Peace I leave with you, my peace I give unto you: not as the world giveth, give I unto you. Let not your heart be troubled, neither let it be afraid" (John 14:27 KJV).

After many years of war, there is finally some progress being made toward a peace agreement. Through prayers from all over the world and through intervention from the international community, a framework is being constructed to bring a permanent resolution to this conflict.

Negotiations have been conducted in Naivasha, Kenya with representatives of both the Government of the Sudan (GOS) and the Sudan People's Liberation Movement/Army (SPLA). In September of 2003, an agreement was reached regarding security arrangements for an "interim period," during which a final peace agreement will be negotiated.

There are still many complex issues to be worked out, but this is a step in the right direction. However, as Christians, we believe that true peace comes only through Jesus Christ. Our hope and prayer is that in the post-war era of New Sudan, Christians will remain faithful and Muslims and animists of the Sudan will be free to come to Christ if they choose. This coming era of peace will give the church in the Sudan expanded opportunities to share the gospel without threat of the sword.

There is no evidence at this time that the Khartoum elite has changed their philosophy of government, and when pressure from the western world eases off, the agreements may once again be threatened. When dealing with "infidels," such agreements are considered non-binding. The oil reserves located in the southern territory complicate the peace process even further.

After hundreds of years of conflict, there is reason for concern. It makes one wonder if Christians, Jews, and Muslims can ever live side by side in peace in this war-weary nation. The deep-rooted historical conflicts between the Judeo-Christian world and the Arab Muslim world, which persist in the Middle East and North Africa, need more than a political or economic solution. It is an age-old conflict between the children of Isaac and the children of Ishmael (Genesis 16). Until God works out a spiritual solution, what can be done? Some groups favor a separate, independent nation in the South Sudan. A sovereign nation of South Sudan would provide a permanent solution to this particular civil war. However, even an independent South Sudan will prosper only as long as they follow God's laws—not as a government imposed theocracy, but as a living law of love in each heart.

The Muslims of the Nuba Mountain region are also considering an escape from the Khartoum regime. They could opt to join the South for a secularly governed state with religious freedom and autonomy, or they could form their own independent country without the Shari'a and without the constant discrimination that they currently face from their Khartoum brethren. If their dream to join the South becomes possible through the current peace arrangement, we welcome them to live beside us; and we will pray that they too find true peace and freedom.

Even if the peace agreement works out in the most favorable possible way, there will still be tremendous obstacles to overcome. Two generations of Southerners have grown up without any education. They have learned to depend on handouts in the refugee camps. Many have lost the skills and traditions of their families and have not had the benefit of their own religious leaders. Tribal conflicts and immorality are on the rise among people forced to live under unnatural conditions. Infrastructure does not exist. Roads, schools, wells, hospitals and the like have all been destroyed. An entire culture must be rebuilt.

If Christians do not step in to help their brothers in this time of need, many will lose their Christian heritage and faith. The jihad will have achieved its purpose.

If Southern Sudan cannot rebuild, the door will open for radical Islam to gain more control in the southern portion of the entire continent of Africa. If this happens, we will surely see more persecution and violence of the many millions of Christians throughout sub-Saharan Africa. If the Sudan can rebuild, we may see an example of a stable secular government with religious freedom for all that would be a model for other African nations. Let us pray for peace and freedom to rule the hearts and minds of the Sudanese; and let us help Sudan rebuild.

To the Sudanese people, I would like to add some advice for a new nation. My life here in democratic America has taught me great lessons about freedom. I love this country; it is beautiful and industrious. But it is also miserable in many ways. There is crime and violence and immorality everywhere. That is the result of freedom without the restraint of moral conscience. The misery here in America is largely due to the fact that this country has strayed far from its biblical roots. I don't think it will be healthy to copy everything from western democracy, any more than it would be healthy to resort to tribalism or communism. As God is systematically eliminated from public life and the rule of law, the republic degenerates into a baser form of democracy and finally into tyranny where man ultimately will play God.

What can a New Sudan do to avoid the pitfalls experienced by the United States? You would do well to learn from her mistakes, if you can, while emulating her triumphs. While I do not advocate any type of theocracy, I would advise a new nation to acknowledge God as the founding fathers of the US did so long ago. Safeguard the rights of citizens to reverence Him in all aspects of their lives, public and private. Support the institution of the family and encourage morality, spiritual growth, and personal responsibility. Respect life in all of its many forms. It is, after all, the character of the people as a whole that shapes the way of a nation. May God bless the New Sudan.

What Can I Do to Help?

All proceeds from the sale of this book will go to Operation Nehemiah to rebuild the South Sudan and to build up the Body of Christ as we continue to work in the Great Commission. You can help by introducing this book to your families, friends, churches, local libraries, bookstores, and radio stations. We believe that if Christians were aware of the depth of suffering in the Sudan, that they would be moved to help. Mr. Levi is available for conferences and speaking engagements. He would be happy to arrange a presentation for your local church or radio station.

You can help by keeping informed and making your opinions known to policy makers.

You can help by entering into heartfelt, earnest prayer for your persecuted brothers and sisters in the Sudan.

You can help with tax-exempt financial* gifts.

Contact us for more information:

---

*We are happy to disclose financial records for your inspection.

Operation Nehemiah Missions International, Inc.
P.O. Box 2
Cheshire, MA 01225
Web site: *www.operationsnehemiah.org*
Email: *levifamily@adelphia.net*
Phone: 1-800-728-3783 or 413-743-8008

Meet our Staff Members

William Levi is the founder and president of Operation Nehemiah. He and his wife, Hannah, are involved in the ministry full-time, in charge of administration and planning. William is available for speaking engagements and interviews in churches, schools, radio, and television across the United States. The Levis live in Massachusetts with daughter, Abijah, and son, Nechemyah.

The **Reverend Michael Longwa** has been the senior field director of Operation Nehemiah since 1994. Michael and his wife, Palma, are on staff full time, with an office in Kampala, Uganda. Reverend Longwa pastors the Beth Israel Messianic Congregation on the Nile. This church was established through Operation Nehemiah as a ministry to the spiritual needs of the Sudanese refugees living in Uganda. They receive short-term missionaries from the USA and around the world. They are also in charge of gathering information concerning the needs of the refugee population in terms of health, education, agriculture, and church outreach.

Robert Kirkman is Operation Nehemiah Missions' Director of Medical Care and Project Development. He and his wife, Ruth, are part-time volunteer staff who have a heart-felt burden for the plight of the suffering Christians in the Sudan. Robert has visited the region and was challenged by the needs of the refugee children who yearn for an education. His goal is to see that every child under the education project receives sponsorship. The Kirkmans live in Massachusetts with their six children.

The **Reverend David Liebherr** of the Church of Acts in Waukesha, Wisconsin is the stateside director of Operation Nehemiah's construction department. He works with **David Lipinski** to help train displaced refugees in much needed construction skills.

Reverend Michael Gantt is the pastor of Agape Fellowship and president of Friends of Sudan, a ministry that is dedicated to help alleviate the plight of the suffering church in the Sudan. Rev. and Mrs. Barbara Gantt and their children reside in Brattleboro, VT. Pastor Gantt is also on the board of directors of Operation Nehemiah Missions.

Reverend David Abirigo is the Operation Nehemiah field director for construction and for the Nehemiah Polytechnic Institute based in the Adjumani refugee camps. He and his wife and six children live in a refugee camp in Northern Uganda.

Dr. Minda Godwin is Operation Nehemiah Missions field director for health and the mobile clinic. He resides in Kampala, Uganda.

The **Reverend John** is the director of the Nehemiah Internet Café and senior advisor for Operation Nehemiah. He and his wife, Susan, and four children live in Kampala, Uganda.

Linous Anduga and **Isaac Idra** are directors for education leadership. They and their families reside in Adjumani refugee camps in Uganda.

Dr. Stephen Chudkowski is director for pastoral leadership. He lives in New Jersey with his wife and two children.

Gordon Clark is director of agriculture development. He and his wife live in Massachusetts.

APPENDIX FIVE

Sudan Map

To order additional copies of

the Bible or the Axe

Have your credit card ready and call

Toll free: (877) 421-READ (7323)

or send $19.95* each plus $5.95 S&H** to

WinePress Publishing
PO Box 428
Enumclaw, WA 98022

or order online at: www.winepressbooks.com

*WA residents, add 8.4% sales tax

**add $1.50 S&H for each additional book ordered